THE ULYSSES CONTRACT

HOW TO NEVER WORRY ABOUT THE SHARE MARKET AGAIN

Michael Kemp

MACMILLAN

About the author

Dr Michael Kemp completed an MBA from Monash University before embarking on a stellar career in corporate finance during the mid-1980s bull market, then switching to a career as a pre-eminent periodontist running a successful practice in Brighton, Victoria, for almost 20 years.

Throughout both these careers, Michael maintained a fascination for the share market. As well as managing his own portfolio, he's spent a lifetime reading and researching to find out what works and what doesn't, and what it takes to be a successful investor. He shared some of this thinking in his first book, *Creating Real Wealth* (2010); this was followed by *Uncommon Sense* (2015). By this time, Michael's work had attracted attention in the US, with Robert P Miles, author of *The Warren Buffett CEO*, inviting Michael in 2015 to address fund managers and investors from around the world at the annual Value Investor conference, which precedes the Berkshire Hathaway AGM in Omaha, Nebraska.

From 2011 to 2020, Michael Kemp was the chief investment analyst for Scott Pape's *Barefoot Blueprint* newsletter.

Today Michael spends his time with family and friends, travelling, investing on his personal account, and writing articles and recording podcasts for a business consultancy firm.

To Michael, finance has always been a passion, never a job.

About the author

[illegible]

For my grandchildren, great-grandchildren and great-great-grandchildren.

In finance, like in life, the more things change the more they stay the same.

First published in 2023 by Major Street Publishing Pty Ltd

First published in India 2023 by Macmillan
an imprint of Pan Macmillan Publishing India Private Limited
707 Kailash Building
26 K. G. Marg, New Delhi 110001
www.panmacmillan.co.in

Pan Macmillan, The Smithson, 6 Briset Street, Farringdon, London EC1M 5NR
Associated companies throughout the world
www.panmacmillan.com

ISBN 978-81-96365-31-8

1 3 5 7 9 8 6 4 2

Internal design by Production Works
Printed in India by Gopsons Papers Pvt. Ltd., Noida

Contents

Foreword by Scott Pape

You've lucked onto something very special by picking up this book.

You don't know it yet, but it's going to totally change the way you think about the share market.

Yet I'm getting ahead of myself.

If you're reading this right now, I can guess a few things about you:

You've probably been investing for a while, maybe a long while.

You've got the basics under your belt. And you've been around the block too many times to get greased by gurus' get-rich-quick claims. But there's one fear that's always, somewhere, at the back of your mind…

The 'big one'.

A catastrophic collapse that smashes shares down by over 50 percent (GFC 2007–2009), almost 70 percent (Japan in the 1990s), or almost 90 percent (the Great Depression in the USA).

Most investors perpetually live with this fear (after all, most economists have predicted nine of the last three recessions!).

But not all of them.

Every now and again you come across an investor who has something most investors don't have:

Confidence. A deep, unshakeable confidence, no matter what happens.

Let me tell you about one:

Mike Kemp.

Mike has seen it all.

He was standing on the floor of the stock exchange on the day of the 1987 crash. He's been through the Dot.com bubble, the GFC, and every downturn and panic. And through it all… he's kept right on investing.

That's why he's a very wealthy man.

And that's why this book doesn't need to sell you anything.

Mike's passion is simply to share with you what he's devoted a lifetime to learning.

And he sums it all up in one simple idea:

A Ulysses contract.

That's what the book you're holding is all about.

Mike sent me this book in manuscript form to review.

However, after reading the manuscript cover to cover, I circled back to Mike with only *one* edit.

'This book needs a subhead', I told him. 'Something like "How to never worry about the share market again". Because that is exactly what this book delivers.'

So, you are holding in your hands something very valuable.

If you follow the (admittedly unconventional) steps in this book, you will save yourself tens, if not hundreds, of thousands of dollars in costly fees, *and* you'll earn higher returns because of it. Yet, more importantly, you'll free yourself up from the stress and strain of constantly worrying about share price drops. And the time you have left is your most precious gift, your most valuable asset.

This book will show you how to never worry about the share market again.

Scott Pape
Pape Family Farm
December 2022

Preface

This is my third book, but I only recently worked out why I write the things. For me, writing is a form of self-expression – like when a musician senses a new tune welling up inside and they look for a piano or a guitar in order to express it. But I'm a musical klutz, so I tap away at a computer keyboard instead.

Each of my books has reflected a new stage of my still-unfolding life. Take, for example, my first book: *Creating Real Wealth: The Four Dimensions of Wealth Creation*. It was born from my attempts to resolve an inner conflict between my career and my happiness.

My job was like a bad marriage. While I felt a sense of commitment towards it, it wasn't bringing me the joy that I demanded. I was a practising periodontist (a specialist arm of dentistry), but I had long been in an 'extramarital affair' with investing and the financial markets. I wasn't reading medical or dental journals in my spare time; instead, I was devouring books on financial history and stock valuation. (I had worked in the financial markets as a younger man, and I'd also studied for a couple of tertiary qualifications in finance when I was in my 20s.)

Researching and writing the book was a good move, because it proved to be a catalyst for change both at a professional and a personal level. It resulted in me leaving periodontics and working for nine years as a financial analyst and writer with Scott Pape (aka 'the Barefoot Investor'). I thoroughly enjoyed it. What's more, the career switch delivered the added benefit of fewer work hours and more time to spend with friends and family.

Then came my second book: *Uncommon Sense: Investment Wisdom Since the Stock Market's Dawn*. That book opened more doors, and it elicited an invitation to present at the annual Value Investor Conference in Omaha, Nebraska, USA. The conference is held each year over the days leading up to the Berkshire Hathaway Annual General Meeting.

It was but one of five trips that I made to Omaha. I went there primarily to hear Warren Buffett and Charlie Munger speak at the AGM. The trips were a lot of fun. My visits to Omaha also delivered me the opportunity to meet with a number of the CEOs of Berkshire Hathaway's subsidiaries and hear them talk about their companies. It allowed me to gain precious insight into the modus operandi of investment great Warren Buffett.

As my investment knowledge grew, I was happy – well, sort of. I still needed an answer to a gnawing question. What I didn't know for sure was whether my above-average investment returns were the result of skill and hard work or simply plain, dumb luck.

So, I started exploring the research. The more I looked, the more sceptical I became regarding my investing ability. I became obsessed with the whole question of skill versus luck. What I discovered during that search spawned this book: book number three.

I have come to realise that genuine market-crushing investing skill is rare – so rare, in fact, that you are unlikely to ever develop it yourself or even to meet anyone who has. I have also come to realise that successful investing is more reliant on personal qualities than it is on intellectual ones, and at the top of the list are discipline, consistency and patience.

In this book, I will show you how to put in place an investment plan that embodies these personal qualities, even if you don't feel that you currently possess them. I will show you how remarkably easy it can be for anyone to develop into a successful investor – not necessarily an outperformer but certainly a genuine success.

Yes, that can include you.

That's why I wrote this book.

Introduction

This book is about investing. There are plenty of things that you can 'invest' in, so I could have written about real estate, fixed-interest securities, fine wine, vintage motor cars or cryptocurrencies. But this book is about none of those things. It's solely about investing in the stock market.

The first stock market (as we understand stock markets to operate today) kicked off in 1602. It started for one simple reason: to provide a large and flexible source of funding for commercial enterprise. Stock markets work on the principle that a person or group of people develop a business or a business idea, then others help bankroll it through a stock market offering of shares in the enterprise. If the business flourishes, then those who bought shares share in the profits. If the business goes sour, then investors lose some or all of their money. Stock markets also provide a secondary marketplace where investors can sell or buy existing shares with other investors.

There it is: Stock Market 101.

It sounds simple enough, but investing is like an onion: you peel off one layer, only to discover another layer underneath. And yet another, and another. For that reason, it can appear to be complex to inexperienced investors. But here's the great thing: you don't have to peel away many layers in order to become a competent investor. What you do need to understand, however, is where your investing limitations lie and, then, how to work within them. My aim in this book is to help you to develop a clear understanding of what your limitations are likely to be.

The book is divided into four parts:

1. **Siren Songs:** Part I alerts you to the investment traps out there. I don't want you falling into any of them.
2. **Gaining an Edge:** Part II explores how a successful minority has been able to generate market-beating returns through the application of skill. My aim is not necessarily to encourage you to emulate the market greats; rather, it's to demonstrate the onerous and near-impossible task of doing so.
3. **The Mast:** Certainty and truisms are rare in the investment world. Once identified, you need to embrace them. Part III helps you to identify them.
4. **The Ulysses Contract:** Part IV delivers a watertight plan for you to pursue your own form of investment success and financial freedom.

When I speak of financial freedom, I don't mean a Monte Carlo, Learjet, 100-foot-private-yacht type of financial freedom. I mean the ability to live a meaningful life as one chooses: to be able to spend time with friends and family; to help your children achieve their life goals; to dispense with the need to service a crippling mountain of debt or suffer a job that you can barely tolerate.

In a nutshell, I'm talking about the three 'Fs': family, friends, freedom! These represent the important stuff in life.

Financial freedom has always appealed to me. In my youth I used to watch the 1960s TV show *The Saint* (and, to be quite honest, I still watch it now). It used to intrigue me how the main character, Simon Templar (played by Roger Moore), never went to work; instead, he drove around the countryside in his little white sports car saving fair maidens in distress. That's what I call financial freedom!

Well, just like him, I'm now spending my time doing as I please – not saving fair maidens, but in my own way. I can think of nothing I'd rather be doing than exactly what I'm doing right now as I write this: sitting at my keyboard, typing out my thoughts while gazing across the broad expanse of blue ocean in front of me. This afternoon I'll take the dog for a walk on the beach below our house, or maybe I'll go paddleboarding from the pier to the surf lifesaving club (depending on the breeze). Then I'll check in with my two children (they are adults now). Before dinner, I'll sit and chat with my wife on the sundeck. Next Friday I'll spend several hours working with my daughter (as I do on many Fridays), then later that day is snooker night with a group of my buddies. I'll spend the weekend watching the footy with my son and playing fetch with the dog.

Bliss.

Unlike for Simon Templar, financial independence didn't come gift-wrapped. I had to earn it. That's what this book is essentially about: how you can gain your own slice of financial freedom.

Happy reading.

PART I

SIREN SONGS

Chapter 1

One Now or Two Later?

'Before we set our hearts too much upon anything, let us examine how happy those are who already possess it.'

– François VI, Duc de La Rochefoucauld

In 1972 a US research team carried out a psychology experiment that shed new light on human development. In the study, led by Stanford University psychologist Walter Mischel, children aged between three and five were given either a marshmallow or a pretzel (their choice) and promised a second if they could refrain from eating the first for a period of 15 minutes. In each case the adult researcher was absent from the room while the child contemplated the two options.

The study was titled 'Cognitive and attentional mechanisms in delay of gratification', but, as far as the children were concerned, a more appropriate title would have been '15 minutes of torment': during the 15-minute period that the children were left alone to contemplate their choice, the first tempting treat was left sitting on the table in front of them.

The study is best known for its conclusion. The children who were able to refrain from eating the first treat (and so receive a second) tended to have better life outcomes later on: enhanced academic results, lower body mass index (BMI) and success in other life and career measures. It seemed that an enhanced capacity to delay gratification delivered larger rewards in life.

However, it's important to note that subsequent studies, by other researchers employing similar experimental protocols, failed to confirm Mischel's initial findings. So, why am I telling you about Mischel's study at all? Because I find a lesser-known but peer-study confirmed outcome of Mischel's research far more interesting.

Mischel actually conducted three separate studies. The famous 'marshmallow study' was the second in the series, but in an earlier 1970 study he and fellow researchers had hypothesised that having the treats in plain sight would enhance the children's capacity to delay consumption. In other words, the researchers believed that with the prize right in front of them, children would be better able to hang on for the full 15 minutes in order to qualify for their second treat. But the researchers observed the opposite: they found that the children who could successfully divert their attention away from thinking about the additional reward – by covering their eyes, singing, playing or, in the case of one child, falling asleep – were more likely to resist. It was removing the prize from consciousness, rather than thrusting it into full view, that worked best.

The researchers concluded that delayed gratification depended more on cognitive avoidance or suppression than it did on physical avoidance. The fact is that our imagination can be a very powerful motivator, both in a good way and in a bad way.

Sound investors appreciate how powerful our minds are. Perceptions often trump realities. It is our imaginations that often guide investment decisions.

The Greeks knew all this stuff!

OK, let me now swing from marshmallows, pretzels and child psychology to Greek mythology. (You can't say that we won't be covering all bases in this book!)

More than 2000 years ago, a Greek philosopher called Plato trod the narrow, dusty streets of Athens. They tell me that he was a bloke worth listening to when he stopped for a yarn. He ran a university called 'The Academy' where young Athenian males engaged in academic discussions about important issues of the age. They studied literature and covered a diverse range of disciplines, including philosophy, politics and mathematics.

Plato's legacy lives on in the form of his writings, which have been captured for eternity. In his book *Republic*, Plato tells the story of a man called Leontius, who was walking along next to the wall of his city and encountered a pile of corpses. He experienced conflicting emotions: while he possessed a desire to look at the bodies, he was also disgusted by this desire. Plato was making the point that within us there are multiple 'people' pulling us in different directions. These opposing views create internal conflict, despite the fact that they are held by the same person and in relation to the same set of circumstances.

Wind the clock two millennia forward and we still experience these internal frictions today. Times have changed, but human emotions remain the same. Let me provide a couple of simple examples that you might be able to relate to. When we wake on a cold, winter morning, we know that we need to get out of bed, but we want to stay under the warmth of the covers. Health choices provide another example: we know that going to the gym is good for us, but it's far easier to stay on the couch and watch Netflix. Self-induced internal conflict!

In another of Plato's books, *Phaedrus*, he likens a human to a chariot being pulled by two horses: one is a noble horse, the other a wild horse. The wild horse is difficult to control. Its actions are driven by desire rather than reason. Left to run uncontrolled, the wild horse will lead us to undesirable outcomes. Plato tells us that in order to achieve happiness, we need to control the horse of desire; in other words, we need to rein in our unproductive passions. Plato's analogy acknowledges that humans are driven in part – a large part – by the same forces that drive all other members of the animal kingdom.

This leads me to another tale from antiquity that addresses this whole marshmallow, getting-out-of-bed, going-to-the-gym issue. Even though this tale dates back over 3000 years, there's a fair chance you will have already heard it. The tale is about a guy called Odysseus, also known by the Latin variant Ulysses.

Ulysses was a legendary Greek king whose story is told in an ancient poem called *The Odyssey*. The part of the story that most people remember is when Ulysses is about to sail his boat past an island that's inhabited by sirens. The bewitching sounds of the sirens compelled sailors to steer their boats onto the rocks that surrounded the island and to their ultimate death. So, in order to avoid near-certain destruction, Ulysses told his men to put wax in their ears so they couldn't hear the sirens as they sailed past. But Ulysses wanted to hear the sirens, so he told his men to tie him firmly to the ship's mast (minus the wax in his ears). Being securely bound meant that the struggling Ulysses couldn't succumb to the sirens' seductive sounds and steer the boat onto the rocks.

Ulysses has become such a famous dude that today there's even a contract named in his honour. It's called a 'Ulysses contract'. Let me explain the link.

The Ulysses contract

Yes, *The Ulysses Contract* is the title of this book, so allow me a brief diversion to explain how I came up with the title. After all, it's kind of a weird title for a book about finance, isn't it? You'd perhaps expect a title like that to be on the cover of a book about Greek law!

Let me explain by starting with a definition: a Ulysses contract is a freely made decision that is designed and intended to bind oneself to a specific action in the future. Put another way, it's basically a promise you make now that will stop you doing something stupid later on (in fear that you might not be thinking too straight at the time). That's the link with Ulysses: he had his men tie him to the mast to prevent him from doing something stupid later on.

On a far, far lesser scale, it's like when you're on a diet and you know there's a delicious chocolate cake in the fridge. You know deep down that you shouldn't eat the cake. You're on a diet, right? But there's a problem: you crave a piece. And knowing that it's sitting in the fridge is going to drive you crazy all day. (There's Plato's wild horse of desire kicking in again.) So, how can you resolve the inner conflict? You could throw the cake away. But that would be such a waste.

That's where a Ulysses contract comes in. It's like an advance directive – a practical form of self-discipline, a promise to oneself. You are protecting yourself from your own worst enemy: yourself.

I often made contracts like this with myself when I was a kid. (To be honest, I still do.) On arriving home from school, I used to say something like, 'I promise that I won't watch TV until I've done two hours of study'. So, instead of kicking back in front of the TV and watching *Batman* or *Get Smart*, I committed to a hardcore, TV-show-denying Ulysses contract! I'd then study with a clear conscience and bold conviction for the next two hours. After all, you can't break a promise, can you? Well, I can't, anyway.

There are two payoffs that will come if you are able to successfully commit to a Ulysses contract. First, you will be happier because you've resolved the immediate inner conflict. Second, by denying yourself a lesser reward now, you will receive a bigger reward later on – like the children who received a second marshmallow by refraining from eating the first, or like passing an important exam by committing to study rather than watching TV.

But this is a book about finance – not chariots, horses, marshmallows, TV shows or sailing boats on the Aegean Sea. So, let's get back to finance, because all of this stuff can be applied directly to favourable financial outcomes.

A financial Ulysses contract

Money is to be spent. After all, that is its purpose, isn't it? But, equally, it's a folly to believe that using it to buy things we don't really need will deliver us happiness. Yet people screw this one up all the time and continue to do so over time.

But don't just take my word on this one. Two and a half centuries ago, US Founding Father Benjamin Franklin expressed well the folly of trying to achieve happiness solely through money:

> 'Money never made a man happy yet, nor will it. There is nothing in its nature to produce happiness. The more a man has, the more he wants. Instead of its filling a vacuum, it makes one.'

Let's add to that the words of 19th-century US philosopher Henry David Thoreau: 'That man is richest whose pleasures are the cheapest.'

Despite the sense of these wise men's words, it's not how most of us behave, is it? Most people in our society spend excessively. And, rather than delivering happiness (as is expected), spending ultimately delivers the opposite result.

This can largely be rectified by committing to a financial Ulysses contract, a commitment that protects us from our innate urge to spend unnecessarily. As I will discuss later, regular saving, linked to an investment plan, is far more likely to deliver happiness than unbridled consumption will.

Ulysses's job was relatively easy compared to the challenges and temptations that you will face as an investor. If his men hadn't bound him to the mast then he, his boat and his crew would have been destroyed. That's quite a motivator for action! But the seductive siren songs that you will face as a saver and investor will be more subtle, more persistent and, ironically, just as difficult to resist.

Let's look at the factors working against our capacity to save. They hit at two levels: hedonism and our desire for acceptance.

Level 1: the hedonic treadmill

Let me ask you a question: have you ever experienced a gnawing feeling that you need more than what you already have?

Just kidding. You've experienced it heaps, right? And it doesn't matter that you already have plenty of stuff. You just need that something extra in order to achieve happiness. It usually starts with the words, 'Life will be better when I get…' (you fill in the space). You also kid yourself that, once that something extra is obtained, your desire will be satisfied and the craving will go away.

So, you buy the thing. It could be a nice wristwatch, a beautiful piece of jewellery, a new car, a boat, or a bigger, newer house. The problem is that, once the thing is obtained, the gnawing feeling invariably returns. You replace the previous object of desire with a new one. Rinse, repeat; rinse, repeat; rinse, repeat. It's a perpetual state of wanting more.

Let's look at a specific example: cars. Lots of people buy cars purely for utilitarian reasons. After all, you need one to get the kids to and from school, don't you? But for many people, a car purchase takes on an entirely different dimension. Rather than being a utilitarian requirement, car purchases are often based on such things as:

- performance (it has to be fast off the lights, right?)
- prestige (people have to be impressed by how much your new set of wheels cost you, right?)
- image (a Tesla is cool, but a second-hand Hyundai? Let's take the backstreets!).

This is how it works: your current car is fine until you spot the new model. You reckon that the new model looks great. So, you start looking out for them on the road. You pose self-directed questions such as, 'What colour do I prefer? What style of wheels look the best?' You start reading the car reviews about that particular model; you accept the favourable reviews and dispense with the bad ones (hell, that guy has no idea what he's talking about, anyway). And, by employing that powerful tool called your imagination, you now visualise yourself behind the wheel. Before you know it, you're down at the local dealership pressing the flesh with a new-car salesperson.

But here's the problem: after a brief dopamine hit, the new car becomes the old car. Once again, it's nothing more than a way of getting from A to B. Rarely washed. Food and dog hair mashed into the carpet. Two years later you spot the new model, and so you go through the whole process again…

Psychologists call it the 'hedonic treadmill'. The 'treadmill' bit refers to the fact that this futile activity gets you nowhere. As I said, it's not limited to cars: it applies equally to clothes, houses and all manner of trinkets. Much of this stuff ends up forgotten in self-storage facilities or dumped into landfill.

These inner pangs of desire to own what we don't yet have are not a new phenomenon. Nineteenth-century French political philosopher and sociologist Alexis de Tocqueville travelled to the USA in 1831 with the aim of studying what he called 'the future shape and temperament of the world'. He found that, unlike in Europe – where people were more accepting of their place in society – Americans were unhindered in their pursuit of the American (materialistic) Dream. What struck de Tocqueville was that, despite Americans enjoying a higher standard of living than those in his native France, they were more dissatisfied with their lot in life and wanted more.

The dissatisfaction experienced today is even greater than when de Tocqueville made that observation, and that's despite the massive advances in the standard of living in Western societies since then. We can only assume, then, that the problem lies not in an absolute level of affluence; rather, it's due to a dissatisfaction with the current one, whatever that might be at the time.

The famous 19th-century economist and philosopher John Stuart Mill expressed it succinctly: 'Men do not desire to be rich, but to be richer than other men.' No doubt Mill was well versed with the writings of 18th-century Genevan philosopher Jean-Jacques Rousseau, who wrote, 'Wealth isn't an absolute, it's relative to desire. Every time we seek something that we can't afford, we can be counted as poor.' Every time we are satisfied with what we have we may be counted as rich.

Interestingly, one of the most stark and powerful descriptions of this behaviour can be found in the journal of the great 18th century English maritime explorer Captain James Cook. Cook sailed to Australia when the continent was solely inhabited by one of the world's oldest societies: Indigenous Australians had lived a hunter-gather existence for tens of thousands of years. They knew nothing of European society or its excesses before Cook arrived. Following some early interactions with the Indigenous Australians, Cook wrote in his diary:

> '... but in reality they are far happier than we Europeans; being wholy unacquainted not only with the superfluous but the necessary conveniences so much sought after in Europe, they are happy in not knowing the use of them. They live in Tranquillity which is not disturb'd by the Inequality of Condition.'

The Indigenous Australians weren't dissatisfied (like the Europeans were) because material inequality simply didn't exist.

John Stuart Mill applied this thinking for his own benefit. When he experienced a material desire, he would actively push it from his mind. He knew that a capacity to banish the desire would be more effective in achieving a sense of inner wellbeing than attempting to satisfy the desire through obtaining the material item.

Henry David Thoreau undertook similar but more dramatic behaviour: he removed himself from society altogether and lived alone for more than two years in a simple timber cabin that he built in woodlands near Concord, Massachusetts. Devoid of any symbols of materialism, Thoreau discovered an inner peace that is denied to most of us today in modern society. (I experienced this in my own way when I was younger. My family used to own a log cabin buried deep within the forest. I loved being there, shut off from the rest of the world. The concept of materialism evaporated.)

So, despite the obvious logic of all of this, why do we continue to feel such an unrelenting urge to buy more shiny stuff? It's because the behaviour is innate. We are born with it and it rarely leaves us. Obtaining the object of desire doesn't remove it. It's an unrelenting inner siren.

So, if it's innate, then why did the Indigenous Australians appear (to James Cook) to be more content than those people back in his homeland, England? Shouldn't they have been experiencing it as well? Well, in ancient societies this innate behaviour was applied for an entirely different purpose, a life-preserving purpose. Desire wasn't directed towards superfluous materialism; rather, it was applied to basic needs.

If you go back far enough in time in any society, scarcity was the norm. This meant that people died if they didn't sense the constant need for more. Each one of us owes our very existence to ancestors who once fought for their fill while weaker beings perished around them. Can you imagine the outcome for your distant ancestor Carl the Caveman if, after taking his fill of barbequed wildebeest, he simply lay down on the floor of his cave and took it easy for a few days? No, food was scarce and difficult to obtain, so Carl had to sharpen his spear and plan his next hunt.

In the face of scarcity, perpetual desire is essential to maintain life. More food. More water. More shelter. More warmth. Survival was (and continues to be) necessary in order for us to pass on our genes. But in today's developed societies, that gnawing feeling is no longer about meat, berries, water or shelter. It's now directed towards new cars, bigger TVs and overseas holidays.

Level 2: the desire for acceptance

The roots of our desire for acceptance extend way back. People desire to be part of the group. People crave acceptance. We are tribal. Again, it's how our distant ancestors survived and flourished. To be accepted has always been a passport to the warmth, safety and security of the tribal community.

Loners, and those who are different to the pack, are ostracised. They are bullied, picked on and left out of the group. I'm not saying that this sort of bullying behaviour is acceptable; I'm simply saying that it has roots that go way back.

Using the car analogy again, some believe that driving around in a new Ferrari or Porsche will engender acceptance from others. Even the briefest expression of admiration for their set of wheels from a passing stranger is enough to satisfy the owner of such cars. But it isn't really true acceptance, is it? After all, the admirer is commenting about the car, not the driver! More likely they are imagining themselves to be in the flash car; the car's owner is rarely in the picture.

I don't want to explore this one in too much depth, other than to say that buying any object in an effort to gain acceptance from others is an exercise in futility. Genuine acceptance is more about how others perceive our personal qualities, such as compassion, empathy, generosity, appreciation, warmth and humility – none of which have a price tag attached to them.

I also hope that, by encouraging you to reduce consumption, I can help you to save and invest more. That's important, because saving and investing will ultimately deliver far more favourable outcomes than uncontrolled spending and consumption. Saving and investing leads to the development of a pool of investment capital, which, once established, can deliver an ongoing stream of passive investment income. This can then free up time for you to pursue far more important things in life than a perceived need to work and accumulate objects, such as spending time with family and friends and engaging in life's (non-material) passions.

So, let's get started. Bind yourself to the mast – we are setting sail. We have a long journey ahead of us and I need to alert you to the many dangerous sirens that lie ahead, sirens that you will need to avoid if you hope to achieve investment success.

Chapter 2

Believing What Isn't So

'It ain't what you don't know that gets you into trouble.

It's what you know for sure that just ain't so.'

– Attributed to many

On 19 April 1995 a gun-wielding bank robber boldly entered two separate Pittsburgh banks and demanded cash. Security cameras were rolling and clear images of the robber's face were recorded – he had brazenly entered both banks without any form of face covering. The footage was shown on the nightly news and McArthur Wheeler was arrested at his home a short time later.

Amazingly, he was shocked that he had been easily identified. At the time of his arrest the incredulous Wheeler bemoaned, 'But I wore the juice'.

You see, before Wheeler had entered the banks, he'd rubbed lemon juice on his face in order to render it invisible. He had heard that lemon juice could be used as a form of invisible ink, so he truly believed that no one would be able to see him.

There are a great many lemon juice 'investors' out there. They believe that they possess what it takes to succeed. In fact, all that most possess is a worthless collection of concepts, ideals and rituals. Their valued investing tools are little more than proverbial lemon juice.

Know thyself

My aim in this chapter, and the ten chapters that follow, is to describe some of the most powerful and seductive siren songs that you will be exposed to as an investor. Far from enhancing your chances of investment success, they are more likely to send you onto the rocks of financial underperformance. They come in the form of financial fictions that are peddled as financial truths.

Let's kick off with the first siren song.

Researchers tell us that, when it comes to recognising our deficiencies, we are, well… deficient. This even has a name: the Dunning-Kruger effect.

Of course, some of our inabilities are painfully obvious even to ourselves. For example, you know you aren't a strong athlete when you can't run a mile inside of ten minutes, or that you suck as a pianist when you can't play a single note. But what about when things aren't quite so obvious? What about how you perform at your job, or how well you drive a car?

Or, in the case of many of you, your ability as an investor?

In a study published in the *Journal of Business Venturing*, 2994 businesspeople were asked about their chance of success in a new business venture. Of those surveyed, 70 percent felt that they had a good chance of success. Of this group, only 39 percent felt that others undertaking a similar business to theirs would be as likely to succeed. These are astounding conclusions given that respondents were judging their own business acumen against that of perfect strangers!

There's a likely reason the Dunning-Kruger effect exists: if we had a realistic handle on all of our deficiencies, then we'd be beaten before we tried to do anything at all. It would stifle ambition and effort. Clearly, optimism – enhanced with a good dose of self-delusion – is what makes the world go round.

But the financial markets don't tolerate self-delusion. The self-deluded are less likely to end up with big investment portfolios than they are to lose money.

So, if you want to become a good investor, it's essential that you try, as best you can, to get a realistic handle on your strengths and weaknesses. As George Goodman said of the stock market in his book *The Money Game*, 'If you don't know who you are, this is an expensive place to find out.'

Why are financial markets a breeding ground for self-delusion?

I struggle to think of any activity where the Dunning-Kruger effect is more prevalent than investing.

I'm sure that I've suffered from it myself. It's a trap. But humility is a far safer platform to work from than arrogance when it comes to investing. It's this which led former chairman of the Australian Securities and Investments Commission (ASIC) Alan Cameron to define a sophisticated investor as someone who has lost money.

Incredibly, many investing novices believe that they're good investors. I put this to the test several years ago during a presentation that I was delivering to about 50 inexperienced investors. I asked who in the audience knew what the All Ordinaries index was. Nearly everyone confidently shot their hand into the air. I then posed a second question. I asked who would be prepared to stand up and explain to the group how the index was constructed – in other words, how many stocks it included and the weighting criterion for the individual stocks in the index.

Faced with the threat of their limited knowledge being exposed, all but a few quickly lowered their hand. I explored the reasons behind their retractions. Nearly all had heard of the index – but that's all.

What people were doing here was confusing familiarity with knowledge. They aren't the same thing.

One of the biggest mistakes that inexperienced (and many experienced) investors make is believing that their knowledge is complete. No one's investment knowledge is ever complete.

In his insightful book *Thinking, Fast and Slow*, Nobel Prize–winning behavioural psychologist Daniel Kahneman refers to this phenomenon as WYSIATI – what you see is all there is. WYSIATI refers to our unerring capacity to hold strong views despite being armed with limited facts.

None of us is immune from doing this. It's the root of many arguments. Consider when a person is passionately espousing their views on a subject that they know little about (a common occurrence, I'm afraid). Then, a second person accuses the first person of being wrong. The sad thing is that, often, both are equally ignorant; so, both might be wrong, or one might be right but for all the wrong reasons! Without the complete set of facts, neither is justified in holding their view so strongly.

WYSIATI applies to all aspects of our lives. However, since this is a book about finance, I will address it primarily from a financial perspective.

In the world of finance certainty is a rare commodity. Investing is necessarily all about the future, and the future is largely indeterminable. But people can't stand a void of knowledge, so investors fill this void with fabricated facts.

It's why we see 25-year-olds arguing with passionate conviction in favour of a stock – not because they've undertaken any form of sound analysis but simply because the price of that stock has been rising, or it belongs to an asset class that is the latest thing to own.

It's why we might hear someone arguing adamantly against any of the benefits of share ownership just because they lost money years ago on a single stock.

It's why we see anointed finance 'experts' talking nonsense on TV – not because they are in possession of the facts but because they are basking in the attention that TV has delivered them.

Now, I'm not claiming any immunity to WYSIATI myself, but it does help if you are aware of its capacity to erode sound decision-making. Truly skilled investors are more aware of this problem than most. They know that we live in an uncertain world; therefore, they focus on what is knowable and place far less reliance on what is not. They explore views that oppose theirs. They accept that, despite their skill, their knowledge has its limits. They understand that investing is, at its very best, a very hazy look into the future, and they appreciate that, with all the effort in the world, there can only ever be a degree of 'knowing'. Because of this, they appreciate that they will still get things wrong.

It's this brutal reality that prompted Charlie Munger, the vice-chairman of US company Berkshire Hathaway (and someone who knows far more about investing than most), to state, 'Acknowledging what you don't know is the dawning of wisdom'. Adding power to this profound statement is the fact that, as these words are being written, Munger is 98 years old – he is still learning about investing, something that he's been actively doing for more than six decades now!

How large is the universe of investment knowledge?

When I kicked off my career in finance several decades ago, I believed that I could make sense of the stock market by applying my abbreviated knowledge of mathematics, accountancy and economics.

How wrong I was.

I soon appreciated that there was a gaping hole in my knowledge: my limited appreciation of human behaviour. Markets are moved by how people are thinking and their actions as a result of that thinking.

But that's just the start of it. Financial markets are multilayered and complex. So, any attempt to get a handle on how they work requires a multidisciplinary approach. A knowledge of history helps enormously because it showcases how people have behaved in the past, and are likely to behave again given a similar set of circumstances.

All of us have gaping holes in our knowledge. For example, I question whether you should be heavily invested in a biotech company if you know nothing about microbiology, biochemistry or cell biology. And how can you reasonably invest in a mining company if you don't know the difference between electrorefining and bioleaching? And how can you confidently invest in any company if you can't read and understand a balance sheet or a profit and loss statement?

Well, the sad truth is that we all can invest in any listed company we choose to. Simply open up a broker's account and away you go. Hey, look guys, I'm investing!

Familiarity, rather than genuine understanding, is a trap of self-delusion that's all too easy to fall into.

There's lots of crazy stuff going on out there

As I write this, I'm confined to my home study during Melbourne's sixth COVID-19 lockdown. Despite the obvious gravity of the pandemic and its negative impact on businesses around the globe, stock markets are soaring (in the wake of an initial collapse), the stock prices of many loss-making companies have become the plaything of time-enriched millennials and, buoyed by the climbing price of Bitcoin, countless new (and worthless) copycat cryptocurrencies are being launched every day. The prices of many assets (I use the word 'asset' loosely here) are defying economic reality.

Now, it's not up to me to cast aspersions about how others might be behaving. But I'm going to cast them anyway.

Today too many 'investors' are sourcing their investment 'education' from social media. Anonymous posts on Twitter seem to pass as investment advice these days. There are plenty of benefits that come from the ongoing digitalisation of our world, but gaining a financial education from a smartphone isn't one of them. Digital platforms have, unfortunately, provided a voice to the unenlightened, who are using this voice to guide the blindly unaware.

I was listening to a podcast the other day in which a young market professional was describing social media as a major influencer of the market prices of financial assets. He's both right and wrong: it might influence prices in the short term but, over the long term, the brutal force of economic reality does eventually bite.

Investors are better guided not by social media posts but by applying the Socratic method. Investor and author Benjamin Graham delivered a nod to the ancient Greek philosopher Socrates in his book *The Intelligent Investor* when he wrote, 'The stock investor is neither right or wrong because others agreed or disagreed with him; he is right because his facts and analysis are right'.

The problem, of course, is that working stuff out for yourself takes effort. Why bother undertaking all that hard work when social media delivers the answer right there in the palm of your hand? To that I would say one of the most dangerous things you can do is to rely on investment advice from strangers.

Canadian-American economist John Kenneth Galbraith died before smartphones were invented, but the following quote seems prophetic in describing how the hand-held device is being misused today:

> 'Between human beings there is a type of intercourse which proceeds not from knowledge, or even from lack of knowledge… but from a failure to know what isn't known.'

There is no way of escaping it: you must learn for yourself what is fact and what is fiction, what is known and what can never be known. Only then can you stop yourself from falling prey to believing what isn't so.

Chapter 3

The Siren of Bias

'The investor's chief problem – and even his worst enemy – is likely to be himself.'

– Benjamin Graham

Behavioural psychologists have long identified a substantial list of faults in the way we process information. When investing, we misprice, misconstrue and misinterpret to the detriment of our bank balance.

Here is but a bite-sized taste of our investing frailties as identified by psychologists:

- anchoring
- availability heuristic
- endowment effect
- fear
- gambler's fallacy
- greed
- groupthink
- hindsight bias
- hope
- illusion of control

- impatience
- improper framing
- irrational escalation of commitment
- overconfidence
- regret.

As lengthy as the list might seem, it is far from complete.

All of these behavioural deficiencies are swirling around in our heads without us even being aware of them. When it comes to making investment decisions, they create a subconscious cocktail of confusion. And it's our lack of awareness of these frailties that makes them so dangerous!

I see little point in exploring them all here. It's a huge topic and there have been plenty of great books that have already been written on them. But I do want to expand on one of them in this chapter: the siren song of bias.

As with other innate behaviours, we can link our behavioural bias to human natural selection and survival. Bias enabled our ancient forebears to make fast decisions. Quick thinking was essential in the face of danger. Those who were incapable of reacting quickly could die. Consider the actions of our forest-dwelling forebears when they heard a twig crack in the darkness. They didn't have the luxury of time to consider all the possible causes of the sound. If the tribe sat around the campfire brainstorming the issue, they could well have become dinner for some wild beast.

This need to come to conclusions quickly is still with us today. We have to make many, many decisions every day. We don't have the time to research and weigh up the pros and cons of every possible outcome before we act.

The downside to bias is that it can lead to us making some pretty poor choices, particularly when it comes to investing. But here's the thing about bias: people don't appreciate how biased they actually are. Sound investors acknowledge that *everyone* is biased – and they know that includes them.

Nobel laureate Herbert Simon spent four decades studying our capacity to process information. He found that we react to only a fraction of the information available to us. This means that, when we make important decisions, we make up our minds far too quickly and usually with insufficient information.

In order to demonstrate how powerful and pervasive bias can be, let me share a story about how the self-interest of a few, and the bias of a multitude, swayed the thinking of a nation. This story is not about investing, but that doesn't matter because it highlights the extent of cognitive distortion that the human brain is capable of. Remember, this is the same brain that we bring to the investment arena. When investing, we are equally as biased in our decision-making – perhaps more so!

This is a story about a mother and her baby.

The baby taken by a dingo

It was mid-August 1980. Seventh-day Adventist pastor Michael Chamberlain was driving his bright yellow Holden Torana into what was to become the most infamous camping ground in Australia's history.

The region was dominated by the sandstone monolith Ayers Rock (now commonly known as Uluru), which towered 348 metres above the arid and otherwise flat landscape. The massive red rock was impressive but Pastor Chamberlain didn't have time to admire its grandeur. He was focused on removing the camping equipment from his heavily laden car and setting up camp for the night.

He and his wife Lindy were more than 1600 kilometres from their Mount Isa home on a camping trip with their three young children. Their youngest, Azaria, was only nine weeks old.

But it wasn't the holiday that they'd hoped for. The next day young Azaria would be dead.

She and her four-year-old brother Reagan had both been asleep in the Chamberlains' small tent. Lindy came to the tent to check on Azaria after fellow campers told her they'd heard a baby's cry. When Lindy entered the tent, Azaria was gone. Lindy didn't notice it at the time but there was blood on Azaria's mattress. The alert was raised and a police search was instigated.

The circumstances of little Azaria's death appeared to be clear-cut. Indigenous trackers were called in to assist and found dingo tracks leading up to and away from the tent. The trackers followed the tracks into the scrub where they found an indentation in the sand. They suggested that it could have been made by Azaria's body being temporarily placed on the ground by a wild dog.

Dingos had long been a threat in the area. For two years prior to Azaria's disappearance, Uluru chief ranger Derek Roff had been pushing for a cull of the wild dogs in the name of public safety. His requests had been ignored by the authorities. What's more, the day before Azaria was taken, a dingo had approached and bitten another camper at the site.

Azaria's body was never found. However, based on eyewitness reports and strong circumstantial evidence, the coroner heading the inquest into her death found that Michael and Lindy Chamberlain were not responsible for the death of their child.

But that wasn't the end of it. Political and public sentiment turned against Lindy Chamberlain. Rumours started up that maybe Lindy had been responsible for Azaria's disappearance. The authorities chose not to dispute the rumours; after all, stories about dingo attacks were bad for the tourist trade.

A second inquest was called. That led to a criminal trial, at which Lindy was found guilty of murdering her daughter. She was sentenced to life in prison.

A few years later the conviction was overturned, but it wasn't until 2012 that Azaria's death was officially recorded as having been the result of a dingo attack. This marked the end of a 32-year legal journey that included four inquiries, a trial, two appeals and a royal commission.

Lindy was innocent. She had always been innocent. Her erroneous prison sentence will go down as one of the greatest miscarriages of justice in Australian history.

Lindy Chamberlain's sentencing was based on weak forensic evidence, which was ultimately shown to be wrong. There was no weapon, no motive and no body. All the witnesses at the camping ground corroborated Lindy's story of innocence.

So, what went so horribly wrong?

The whole terrible story can be attributed, to some degree, to a self-interested Northern Territory government. It was concerned that a court-proven dingo attack could impact their tourist industry. The rest of the blame can be attributed to the bias of many Australians. In the absence of facts, both the authorities and the people came to their own conclusions.

In the lead-up to Lindy Chamberlain's trial the story gained national press coverage. Australia was a nation divided regarding Lindy Chamberlain's guilt or innocence. Facts were scarce, yet Australians held strongly opposing views anyway. Here are three comments taken from but a few of the countless hate-inspired letters that Lindy Chamberlain received at the time:

> 'Lindy, you should be hung up on the nearest tree. 99.5 percent of the people know you are guilty.'
>
> 'Murderer, murderer… You murdered the baby because it wasn't normal.'
>
> 'If you did not kill your baby then your son did.'

As vicious as these comments are, I remind you that they were written before the trial had even taken place!

Human imaginations generate theories. Those theories then become ill-conceived beliefs. Here are some of the bizarre reasons proposed for Azaria's disappearance:

- The Chamberlain's oldest child, Aidan, had done it and his mother was trying to take the blame.
- The Chamberlains had paid people to fake Azaria's death.
- Azaria had been sold into the Asian slave trade.
- A giant bat had taken her.
- An Indigenous woman had taken her.

Another theory that gained traction at the time was that the Chamberlains had sacrificed Azaria as part of a dark satanic ritual. This crazy theory probably started because the Chamberlains were practising Seventh-day Adventists. Family friend Dr Lyell Heise later summed it up when he said that the Chamberlains' religious beliefs would have been considered as strange and the clergy of the Seventh-day Adventists (which included Michael Chamberlain) as phonies. Religious intolerance is yet another incubator of bias.

The trial did little to change the situation. On each day of the trial, TV news footage was broadcast nationally. The cameras recorded Lindy Chamberlain as she entered and left the Darwin courthouse. Lindy was acutely aware that she would be judged by Australians simply by the image that she projected on the small screen. If she was seen smiling, then the public would judge her as uncaring and heartless. If she was seen crying, then she would be accused of seeking sympathy by acting and playing up to the cameras. So, despite her deep inner emotional turmoil, Lindy forced herself to maintain a steely gaze as she threaded her way through the film crews each day.

But it didn't work. The public branded her as uncaring. They questioned how a woman who had recently lost her child could appear to be so steely and cold. 'Where were the tears?' they asked. They branded her as guilty solely from her appearance on TV.

What these people didn't see was the true intensity of Lindy's grief. Those close to her observed it when she was away from the cameras. The public was judging her based on brief and edited snippets of news footage, which represented but a tiny fraction of her 24-hour day.

As I said earlier, every distorted conclusion that bias, assumption and WYSIATI delivered in the story of Lindy and Azaria Chamberlain can also be brought to bear when making investment decisions. I've seen it time and again over the years – those who undertake short cuts when investing typically justify their actions (or lack of action) with the words, 'I bought that stock because I had a gut feeling about it'.

Gut feel? Our gastrointestinal tract isn't capable of making investment decisions! Gut feel is shorthand for 'I didn't bother (or was incapable of) performing any form of research'. Translated more simply, it means, 'I'm actually clueless'.

When you hear someone deliver an investment recommendation based on gut feel, be scared. Be really scared. Gut feel is nothing more than laziness and bias in full flight.

Confirmation bias

So, you've come to your biased conclusion. Where to from there? More specifically, how do you treat any new facts that are subsequently served up? What if the new information runs counter to the conclusion that you've already drawn?

Well, that's a problem, isn't it?

Author F Scott Fitzgerald wrote, 'The test of a first-rate intelligence is the ability to hold two opposing ideas in the mind at the same time, and still retain the ability to function'. Hey, Mr Fitzgerald, that might sound like an absolute pearl of wisdom, but the reality is that few people are capable of living up to that lofty ideal.

Psychologists tell us that, when people attempt to concurrently hold two or more conflicting beliefs, they suffer from a form of mental stress called 'cognitive dissonance' (there's another one for the list at the start of this chapter). We require consistency in order to feel comfortable. So, what do people do with new information that conflicts with their previously formed conclusion? They reject it, of course!

People – and I include both you and me here – typically ignore or discredit any additional information that fails to confirm their established belief. But they accept any new information that confirms that established belief. In fact, they actively seek confirming information.

The programmers who write the software behind computer search engines and social media platforms are acutely aware of our desire for confirmation. They design digital platforms that serve up content consistent with our beliefs. Algorithms detect a user's preferences from their prior online activity, which shapes what is served back to them. This means that their beliefs – whether they are right or wrong – are less likely to be challenged, and so they are more likely to remain engaged. This maximises their screen time and so delivers higher advertising revenues to the digital platform. Users happily continue within their own digital cocoon of personalised 'reality'.

This all has a big social downside. If the user's initial beliefs and prejudices are increasingly reinforced, those beliefs can depart dramatically from the real world. In its most sinister form, this can result in radicalisation.

The human frailty to seek confirming information is rife in financial decision-making. Hell, hardened stock analysts do it all the time. Based on limited research and established biases, they can easily form a favourable investment view regarding a particular stock. Then they seek evidence to support that selection, and they reject information which doesn't support it. Then, being financial types, they can deliver a pretty convincing argument as to why their analysis is sound, particularly to those who know far less about finance. And that's why I don't accept the financial recommendations of others without checking things out for myself.

We all have a tendency to fall into this trap, whether we are financial analysts or not. Have you ever considered why you highlight text or jot down notes when you're reading a book or an article? The fact is that, nine times out of ten, you do it because it confirms something that you already believe. People consider a writer to be clever when they agree with what they have written and stupid when they don't.

I mentioned earlier investors who take their investing cues from strangers on social media. They seek each other out in order to reinforce their biases. This has no place in investing.

The rational decision-maker should follow this maxim attributed to John Maynard Keynes: 'When the facts change, I change my mind.' Skilled investors keep an open mind even after they believe that they've come to a conclusion. Unfortunately, most investors don't.

While bias facilitates quick decision-making, investors don't need to make hasty decisions. The stock market will always be there tomorrow.

Chapter 4

The Crowd

'In crowds it is stupidity and not mother-wit that is accumulated.'
– Gustave Le Bon

In the previous chapter I stated that many of the characteristics that enabled our predecessors to survive and procreate don't necessarily serve us well as investors. Case in point: we are the ape that imitates, and imitation is often the wrong way to behave when interacting with the financial markets. But there is a reason that we do it.

For millennia, before we had the written word, imitation facilitated the transfer of skills and knowledge from one generation to the next. It also helped to keep us safe. Mindless imitation allowed us to follow others who appeared to be fleeing danger even if we hadn't identified that danger ourselves.

So, imitation is a good thing. Right?

Yeah… sort of. But not when the crowd that you are imitating happens to be wrong. And when it comes to the stock market, the crowd is often wrong.

We don't think straight around money

Before I start unpacking the whole crowd thing, I want to discuss how bad some of our financial decisions can be even without a crowd to follow. A great example of what I'm talking about is a study in which 91 people were asked, 'Six months from now you require a new washer and dryer costing $1200; would you rather:

- make six monthly payments of $200 before you take delivery
- make six monthly payments of $200 beginning upon delivery?'

Eighty-four percent of respondents preferred option two; that is, most wanted to defer payment.

The same 91 people were then asked, 'You are planning a one-week vacation to the Caribbean six months from now costing $1200; would you rather:

- make six monthly payments of $200 before the holiday
- make six monthly payments of $200 beginning upon return from your holiday?'

Sixty percent of respondents preferred option one; that is, most wanted to bring payment forward. Most people gave a different response despite the fact that, from an economic perspective, it's exactly the same question.

An economically rational person should answer 'option two' to both questions. It's desirable to defer fixed payments for as long as possible.

That aside, why the different response to the same question? Researchers concluded that emotion clouded sound financial decision-making. The washer-and-dryer purchase was seen as a boring, utilitarian purchase. Many people resent having to replace broken whitegoods, so they seek to delay payment. But the holiday purchase was perceived differently. Respondents preferred to pay for it in advance so the debt wouldn't be hanging over them while they were away enjoying themselves. The holiday was perceived as a reward, and rewards are typically received after a sacrifice has been made, not before.

It's interesting, but none of this remotely compares to the emotional challenges that the stock market throws up. If people – like those in the aforementioned study – are capable of making dumb decisions around money when the economically rational answer is so obvious, then imagine what they are capable of doing when information is sketchy, absent, unobtainable or downright wrong! Because 'sketchy, absent, unobtainable and downright wrong information' describes the stock market very well. Hence, the stock market is the mother of all amphitheatres for the display of irrational behaviour.

Fear of missing out

Let's face it, we don't get a lot of pleasure watching someone else make a killing on the stock market. It's a powerful incentive to throw caution to the wind and blindly jump into the market with them; to act on a 'hot tip' even when it's delivered by a perfect stranger; and to trust false narratives delivered by nouveau riche newcomers who have been lucky enough to buy a stock that's been run up in price. The 'investment' focus then shifts to one thing and one thing only: the rising share price.

If people around you are making easy money then it's hard to resist joining in. And when greed kicks in, the brain disengages! It's called FOMO, or 'fear of missing out', and it's an extremely powerful and motivating emotion.

The Brooklyn Bridge

Fear can be induced by many things: a shark's fin circling in the water nearby; the footsteps of an intruder downstairs in the dead of night; your life savings evaporating in a collapsing share market. But here's the thing: the cause of the fear might vary, but the emotional response is the same. Fear is fear, and it feels exactly the same no matter what triggers it. So, the true story that I'm about to tell you is 100 percent relevant to how investors feel (and behave) during a collapsing stock market.

On 24 May 1883 the newly constructed New York and Brooklyn Bridge was opened to a fanfare of celebration. It was the longest suspension bridge in the world – more than a mile long, it spanned the width of the East River, connecting Brooklyn and Manhattan.

Despite the obvious benefits it would bring to the surrounding communities, there was a cloud of doubt over the bridge. First, it was constructed using pneumatic caissons, a relatively new technique that allowed the massive stone suspension towers to be constructed underwater. This, along with the novelty of the bridge's design and its sheer size, raised doubt in the minds of the public; 'untried' can mean 'unsafe'.

Then there were the issues regarding the supervision of its construction. The bridge's original engineer, John Roebling, had died before construction even began. His son – Washington Roebling, also an engineer – took over as construction supervisor, but at an early stage he suffered a paralysing injury at the construction site. The young engineer's wife, Emily, took over and completed the bridge. Time has clearly demonstrated that Emily Roebling was up to the task – the bridge still stands as a powerful testament to that. However, at the time, people questioned her capacity to oversee such an ambitious project.

Undeterred by this cloud of uncertainty, throngs of people swarmed across the bridge in the days following its opening.

Then it happened. After just six days, tragedy.

On Memorial Day, 30 May 1883, there was heavy foot traffic on the bridge. A woman stumbled and fell on the stairs on the Manhattan side of the bridge. Her friend screamed out in distress.

The crowd, primed by concerns about the safety of the bridge, reacted to the woman's screams. To fear-primed ears the screams were interpreted as a signal that the bridge was collapsing. Panic reigned and people bolted like a herd of frightened antelopes.

Stairways quickly became bottlenecks. People clawed at each other to get off the bridge. Bodies were trampled underfoot. Twelve people died and a reported 36 people were badly injured.

But there had been no threat. It had all been imagined, initiated by a scream when a woman simply lost her footing and fell.

In keeping with Plato's theory in *Phaedrus*, humans are driven in part by the same emotional forces that drive other members of the animal kingdom. In the face of danger, even imagined danger, we react first and ask questions later.

Exactly these same emotional forces come into play around money.

How a pastry fetish almost busted a bank

Time for another story. This one is financially oriented.

Banks operate under a system called 'fractional reserve banking'. Under this system, banks hold less cash than they do deposit liabilities. This means that, if every deposit holder arrived at a single bank on the same day and demanded their money, the bank wouldn't have enough cash on hand to pay all of them out. This is not an indication that the bank is in bad financial shape; it's just that most of a bank's funds are tied up in illiquid assets such as home mortgages and business loans, rather than cash in tellers' cash trays.

Not having enough immediate cash on hand is rarely a problem. Banks don't expect all – or even a large proportion – of its depositors to demand their money be returned at the same time.

But what if they did? With insufficient cash to go around, a bank would be forced to close its doors. This is called a 'bank run', and it typically happens when there is a widespread fear among customers that their bank's future is looking shaky. They line up at the bank's door demanding their money be returned before the bank's vault runs dry.

But here's the thing: just like how a bridge doesn't need to be collapsing for people to believe that it is, a bank doesn't have to be in financial trouble for depositors to start demanding their money back. Which leads me to the story.

Professor Robert Bruner from the Darden School of Business describes (in a blog) the possibly apocryphal story of a Hong Kong bank run in 1985. The run was kicked off when a queue of people was seen forming at its front door. More and more anxious depositors joined the queue. The longer the queue became, the more anxious they all became.

But the early members of the queue weren't there to withdraw cash from the bank. They were queuing up for pastries. There was a popular pastry shop next door to the bank. On this particular day there was an extra-large number of customers wanting cakes and pastries, so they had spilled out of the pastry shop and onto the street.

It was only the later members of the line who were queuing up to withdraw their cash. There had never been a bank threat. It had all been imagined.

Now, as amusing as this story is, it's likely that you also would have joined that queue, desperate to withdraw your money. We act first and ask questions later.

The stock market crash of 1987

Let me now tell you of a day that will forever be etched into my memory.

It was Tuesday 20 October 1987. My radio alarm woke me at 7 a.m. with the news that the US stock market had just closed after shedding close to a quarter of its value. It was the biggest ever one-day drop in the history of the US stock market, and it has yet to be eclipsed to this day!

An hour and a half later I exited the lift at my work and walked into the dealing room at Bankers Trust's Melbourne office. Normally a hive of activity, this particular morning the atmosphere in the room was very, very different. The room was immersed in a deathly silence. Dealers, usually animated, were frozen. None could believe the financial carnage that they were seeing on their screens. You could smell the fear in the air.

But that stillness didn't last. When the Australian stock exchanges opened just 90 minutes later, it was like a bomb had gone off.

Wanting to get to the epicentre of the action, I left the office and ventured a short way down Collins Street to the trading floor of the Melbourne Stock Exchange. Nothing could have prepared me for what I was about to experience.

Entering that cathedral-like trading room was the closest I reckon I'll ever get to what a gladiator experienced upon entering Rome's famous Colosseum. It was loud. It was frenzied. Floor traders were desperately clawing at each other in their efforts to offload unwanted stock. The air was filled with primeval cries to sell. But their screams were largely in vain. Buyers were thin on the ground. Market prices were in free fall.

The bloodbath that the Aussie market experienced that day was even worse than what had occurred in the USA. The broad-based All Ordinaries index finished the day down by 25 percent.

After the day's trading was over, I bought a copy of the final edition of *The Herald* newspaper. Here's how respected financial journalist Terry McCrann summed up the events of the day:

> 'We have reached one of the great watersheds in history. The world that comes out of this stock market crash will be a very different world to the one that went to bed last Thursday night.'

Here I was, still in my 20s and less than 12 months into my first job in finance, and I was being told that the world had changed forever.

Let me address what would have happened had an investor ignored the cries to sell that day and remained fully invested in stocks. What would their share portfolio have been worth three decades later? The answer is that, by maintaining a simple no-brainer investment in a broad-based portfolio of Australian shares and reinvesting dividends received, it would have been worth over 14 times what it was worth that day in 1987.

Let me remind you, it was the day that was supposed to signal *the end of the world as we once knew it.*

The October 1987 Crash started me on a relentless search to find out what it is that drives stock market prices. An obvious long-term driver is the growing profitability of the companies that comprise the stock market. Stock market growth is linked to economic and commercial growth. More corporate earnings, more corporate value, bigger share prices. That earnings growth has been and will continue to be erratic but, given enough time, it will also be relentless. To harvest its riches, you simply need to get on board… and *stay* on board.

But that's not the way that most share investors see things. They prefer to focus on other factors that are less relevant but more attention-grabbing. And it's that focus that delivers the price volatility, engenders the raw emotion and leads to all the irrational behaviour we see.

Fear, particularly when it is being dispensed by a crowd, is a siren song that any long-term investor must ignore.

The threat doesn't need to be imminent!

As I've discussed, a threat doesn't need to be real for it to be perceived as real. Our imagination is fully capable of filling in any voids in the facts. Let me share a story with you to help explain what I mean.

I was chatting to the son of a close friend of mine. He was seeking advice about how best to structure his financial future. He told me how he was saving and of his plans to invest regularly into superannuation. He had worked out what he could potentially be worth one day if he devoted his portfolio to shares rather than cash, fixed interest or Bitcoin ETFs. He was looking at managed funds. But which type of managed fund? They have different names to describe them, such as 'defensive', 'growth', 'capital stable', 'conservative' and 'balanced'.

His financial advisor had steered him away from the more conservative options and towards the 'growth' option. That's because growth portfolios typically have a higher proportion of shares, and that was a good thing for a young, long-term investor like him because, in the long run, shares deliver the best returns.

Now the problem here is that portfolios with fewer shares are typically described by funds as 'defensive' or 'conservative', and when you're a bit of a worry wart – like this kid is – then words like these have an attractive ring to them. You see, he was mildly anxious that the stock market might crash. And he voiced those concerns to me.

I tried to ease his concerns by telling him that stock market crashes are an unavoidable part of investing, and that he will likely experience multiple stock market crashes before he reaches retirement age. 'Just ignore them', I told him.

I also suggested that he take a look at Vanguard's interactive Index Chart on his computer (take a look now if it interests you: vanguard.com.au/adviser/en/index-chart). It shows that, despite periodic stock market downturns, the long-term returns from investing in shares have trounced the returns delivered from investing in cash and fixed interest (the conservative or 'safe' options that he was asking about).

Well, it seemed we were done. I thought my young friend was now reassured that having his money invested in the growth fund was the best choice. He shook my hand and was on his way.

(Note that this young man was still in his 20s. Considering his circumstances, and with four decades of investing ahead of him, shares were a suitable option for him. The same might not be the case for you, particularly if you are nearing retirement age. Your specific personal circumstances need to be considered when structuring your own investment portfolio.)

We met again a couple of months later and he proudly told me that his money was invested in the 'high growth' option offered by his superannuation fund, and that meant it was almost 100 percent invested in Aussie and international shares.

But then we met a third time. He admitted to me that he'd recently contacted his super fund and switched his super out of the high growth option and into the conservative option. The conservative option included shares but was also 50 percent invested in cash and fixed interest.

'What?!' I said. 'After everything your financial advisor and I discussed with you. Why did you do that?'

He tentatively admitted, 'I was watching the news when I got home from work a couple of weeks back, and there was this guy on the TV talking about how things in the economy weren't looking so good, and…'

'Stop', I said. 'What about your 40-year investment plan? You haven't even looked down the barrel of a financial crisis yet and you're running scared. Your entire investment strategy was up-ended by one talking head on TV who, truth be known, will most likely be shown with time to have been talking a lot of hot air'.

'But I got worried after I heard what he was saying', my young friend said, 'and the conservative option started to sound a whole lot safer'.

He switched his portfolio back to the growth option again, but I wouldn't be surprised if he gets nervous when the stock market gets a genuine case of the wobbles, as it inevitably will.

So, what's the point of my story? It's to demonstrate that the biggest investment risk you're likely to face isn't actually the stock market. The biggest risk is you.

Now I can hear you saying, 'Well it's very easy for you to speak like that, Michael, but it's my money we're talking about here, not yours. And I don't want to have anything invested in the stock market when the next crash hits'.

Let me spell it out again just in case you missed it. The stock market will be volatile. There will be times when it plummets by 20, 30, 40 or even 50 percent. But, as a long-term wealth-compounding machine, it has no peer.

So, if you want to invest successfully over the long-term, then you need to find a way of dealing with your reactions to its tempestuous temperament. Like Ulysses, you need to be able to tie yourself to that proverbial mast. Trust in the knowledge that following downturns, stock markets recover and then rise again.

Don't listen to your fears or those of the crowd. When you start to get nervous, don't ring your hands. Instead, sit on your hands.

Chapter 5

The Soothsayer Siren

'There are two kinds of forecasters: those who don't know, and those who don't know that they don't know.'
– John Kenneth Galbraith

Humans have been communicating via the written word for about 5000 years now, give or take a millennium or two. However, our ability to communicate via speech significantly predates that. While the spoken word has left no physical imprint on the archaeological record, there is a general agreement among researchers that we have been chatting to each other for orders of magnitude longer than we have been jotting down notes. This means that, for a long, long time, our only means of passing on knowledge was through conversation alone.

It should therefore be no surprise that homo sapiens is the ape that learns through narratives. Yes, we love stories and, clearly, we always have. So powerful are narratives in shaping our beliefs that we are more likely to be swayed by a good yarn than we are by cold, hard data. And that's even if that yarn has more flaws in it than a $20 diamond.

A good example of this is what emerged during the COVID-19 pandemic in the early 2020s. It was rife with conspiracy theories and vaccine hesitancy, all of which was disseminated through social media.

Forget the research and the statistics delivered by experienced infectious disease experts and highly credentialed epidemiologists.

Forget the indisputable reality that thousands of people were dying from the virus every day around the world.

None of these facts stood a chance against the stories being peddled on social media.

An early and popular conspiracy theory claimed that COVID-19 was nothing more than a fiction spread by corrupt and deceitful governments. 'Can't you see', it questioned, 'that COVID just doesn't exist? I've never met anyone who's had it. Have you?'

Another bizarre fiction that gained traction was that COVID-19 was a ruse that would allow governments to inject their population with microchips, allowing their daily movements to be tracked.

People actually believed this stuff. Unfortunately, fake news is just as prevalent in the world of finance. And people believe these fictions as well.

Economic soothsayers

Economists are often called upon to deliver prophetic narratives about our economic future. And, bizarrely, most people unquestioningly believe them.

When I worked as an analyst and writer for a popular investment newsletter, we would receive emails from panic-stricken members. They would typically read something like this:

> 'I saw an economist on TV last night who reckoned that Australia is heading towards an economic crisis. OMG… I'm so scared. Should I sell all my shares? What do you think?'

This was another common one:

> 'Some economists are saying that there's a recession coming. Should I hold off buying any shares until then, when prices will be cheaper?'

My answer was always the same: 'No, you shouldn't.'

I question anyone's ability to read the economic tea leaves. And that includes economists'.

No, that previous statement wasn't strong enough. I don't question it – I *know* they can't. Remember that we are talking about the future here.

Economist John Kenneth Galbraith eloquently stated why people choose to believe the forecasts of economists: 'Wisdom, itself, is often an abstraction associated not with fact or reality but with the man who asserts it and the manner of its assertion.'

Mr Galbraith, I reckon that you're right. The confident economists who appear on TV – the ones who listeners believe to be knowledgeable – are usually fluent in polished econobabble and are wearing a nice suit. But none of that bestows them with psychic powers.

It seems that, if you give someone a microphone, they mistakenly believe that they are capable of answering any question. As British politician Norman Lamont so eloquently said of his favourite economic pundit: 'He is often wrong but he is never in doubt.'

Then there are those economic prophets who have worked out that the safest way to deliver a forecast is to emulate a broken clock. They just keep delivering the same economic forecast – for example, that we are on the verge of a recession. Keep saying it for long enough and one day it will be right!

Now, all this talk might be difficult for you to accept. Many economists certainly sound like they know what they are talking about. And economists devote so much time and energy to what they do. Surely all that effort must be useful in some way?

I'm sorry to say that, no, it isn't.

The crazy thing is that, despite their incapacity to forecast, lots of people still pay attention to them. Big companies employ economists. Politicians parrot the fiction that their economic models spit out. Economists regularly appear on our TV screens.

But I warn you, if your guard slips and you find yourself paying attention to any of their prognostications, then heed the advice of Danish physicist Niels Bohr: 'It is very difficult to predict – especially the future'.

The age of uncertainty

Several years ago, I accepted an invitation to present at a national investment conference. The conference was titled 'Investing in the Age of Uncertainty'.

Before I kicked off my presentation, I questioned the title of the conference. Why had organisers described current times as 'The Age of Uncertainty'? I know that it was probably just a promotional headline, but I felt that the last five words in the title were redundant. The conference title should simply have been 'Investing'. The rest was simply a given because there has yet to be an age when things were anything but uncertain.

I quoted some statistics to the audience from Dan Gardner's 2010 book *Future Babble*. Gardner states that, up to the publication of his book, the phrase 'Age of Uncertainty' had appeared in *The New York Times* newspaper 5720 times, debuting in 1924, and the phrase 'Uncertain Times' appeared 2810 times, first appearing in 1853.

I reminded the audience that public trade in shares, as we recognise it today, commenced in 1602 – when the first company with publicly tradeable stock, the Dutch East India Company, was formed – and that, right from the get-go, investors had to deal with the inescapable reality of operating in an age of uncertainty. Joseph de la Vega recognised this way back in 1688 when he titled his book about 17th-century trading on the Amsterdam stock exchange *Confusion de Confusiones*.

Four centuries down the track and nothing has changed, nor will it.

The 1929 Crash

Bernard Baruch was born in 1870 and gained fame as an insightful, experienced and highly respected financier. He advised US presidents and successive governments during World War I and World War II. Yet, in November 1929, just weeks after the cataclysmic US stock market rout, Baruch cabled Winston Churchill and advised him, 'Financial storm definitely passed'. Baruch of all people should have known that the word 'definitely' should never be applied to either the economy or the stock market.

Not surprisingly, Baruch was wrong. Far from the financial storm having passed, the stock market slumped a further 82 percent from that point in time.

Baruch wasn't the only one making lousy predictions at the time. An article from the Harvard Economic Society stated on 16 November 1929 that, 'A severe depression such as 1920–1921 is outside the range of probability'. Wrong again. The Great Depression followed hot on the heels of the society's announcement.

Consider also the prediction made by the great Yale professor Irving Fisher. He was (until October 1929) one of the most respected financial tipsters in the USA. Fisher announced shortly before the 1929 stock market crash that stock prices 'have reached what looks like a permanently high plateau'. He went on to say, 'I expect to see the stock market a good deal higher than it is today within a few months'. Less than a fortnight after Fisher's prediction the stock market plunged off a cliff. It ultimately reached a point 89 percent below its 1929 peak.

Fisher refused to accept that his call was wrong. In the immediate wake of the crash, he rationalised his pre-crash call by stating that others had it wrong. Unfortunately for Fisher, it did little to restore his reputation. This is what he said at the time (as quoted in the *New York Herald Tribune* on 3 November 1929): 'It was mob psychology and was not, primarily, that the price level of the market was unsoundly high… the fall in the market was very largely due to the psychology by which it went down because it went down'.

Fisher's vain attempt to resuscitate his image fell on deaf ears. And, as it turned out, it took another 25 years before the US stock market regained the level of Fisher's pre-crash plateau – and on an inflation-adjusted basis it took 29 years. Fisher was wrong. Mob psychology simply can't be sustained for a 29-year period!

Bernanke's bloopers

Let's look at some gaffes of prediction that are a bit more recent. (I kid you not, libraries could be filled with books on this stuff.)

The US Federal Reserve is one of the most powerful and influential financial institutions in the world. Ben Bernanke was its chairman from early 2006 to early 2014. And that meant he was top dog during one of the biggest financial crises in recent generations: the Global Financial Crisis (GFC). Not only a respected economist, Bernanke was also an expert regarding the 1929 Crash and the Great (economic) Depression that followed.

Given his position, experience and academic credentials, when Bernanke opined about interest rates, financial markets and the economy, people sat up and listened. Bernanke was often invited to deliver economic forecasts. But what people failed to realise was that Bernanke's crystal ball was no clearer than anyone else's.

In 2007 there was growing concern in the USA about the large number of mortgages being issued to first-time home buyers who had no hope of paying the money back. Dubbed 'subprime lending', the massive number of mortgage defaults that this dodgy lending practice ultimately led to derailed US financial markets in 2008. And it wasn't contained to the USA – the financial fallout spread like a contagion around the world.

Before the fallout from subprime lending was fully appreciated, Bernanke was asked the following question by an interviewer on business news channel CNBC: 'What do you consider to be the worst-case scenario if US house prices were to come down substantially?'

Bernanke responded, 'Well, I guess I don't buy your premise. It's a pretty unlikely possibility. We've never had a decline in house prices on a nationwide basis'.

Well, Ben, you were about to experience one.

Bernanke also later opined, 'We do not expect significant spillovers from the subprime market to the rest of the economy or to the financial system'.

Wrong again, Ben. The fallout from subprime was the catalyst for worldwide economic recessions, numerous bank failures and stock market collapses around the world.

Prior to the economic fallout Bernanke was asked how the US economy was tracking. He responded, 'Employment should continue to expand… The global economy continues to be strong… Financial markets have remained supportive of economic growth'.

Five months later the US economy was in recession. The next year the full force of the GFC hit. It was the most precipitous financial event since the 1929 Crash. Bernanke, like other economists and financial gurus around the world, simply failed to see it coming.

This stuff surprises people. Yet it shouldn't. As seasoned US financier Roy Neuberger wrote, 'I have studied economics a great deal, but not to help me in the market. My experience is that the "dismal science" is not worth a damn as far as the market is concerned'.

Donald Rumsfeld's dilemma

Donald Rumsfeld, the former US Secretary of Defense in the administrations of George W Bush and Gerald Ford, once stated, 'There are things we know we know. We also know there are known unknowns; that is to say, we know there are some things we do not know.'

Those two sentences describe one of the most important skills that you can develop as an investor: the ability to draw a clear line between fact and fantasy, between knowns and unknowns.

Warren Buffett, the chairman of US company Berkshire Hathaway, believes the same. In his 2011 Chairman's letter, Buffett welcomed two new investment officers to the company (Todd Combs and Ted Weschler). As experienced as they both were, he said of them, 'They are aided in their thinking by an understanding of what is predictable and what is unknowable.' Buffett was acknowledging that all investing, even at the highest level, is undertaken in a world of incomplete knowledge, and that it is skilled investors who better appreciate where the line between truth and fantasy lies.

Here are several unknowns that are regularly served up by financial commentators and writers as knowns:

- where the economy is heading (unknowable)
- what future technologies will disrupt today's established businesses (unknowable)

- where the stock market will be next week or next year (unknowable)
- what the future profits of a company will be (at best they can only be estimated, and often they can't be; hence, accurate share valuations aren't possible).

Why I refuse to make predictions

I was once asked if I'd be interested in appearing regularly on television to discuss the economy and the stock market. Within a microsecond I declined the invitation. Asked why, I replied, 'Because I'd answer every question honestly and viewers wouldn't like it.'

Here's how a typical interview with me might have panned out:

> *Interviewer:* 'We have Michael Kemp in the studio tonight to discuss the day's events on the stock market. First of all, Michael, what was behind the market's ten-point rise today?'
>
> *Me:* 'Can't put my finger on it. Nothing specific. A ten-point rise is insignificant anyway. It doesn't actually mean much.'
>
> *Interviewer:* 'Well then, where is the market likely to head from here?'
>
> *Me:* 'I have no idea. Nor does anyone else, for that matter.'
>
> *Interviewer:* 'Anything more… that you… ah… want to add?'
>
> *Me*: 'Nope.'

The increasingly frustrated interviewer might choose to change tack:

> *Interviewer*: 'OK then, let's move on to the Aussie dollar. It was up against the US dollar overnight. What drove the rise, Michael?'
>
> *Me:* 'No particular reason.'

You've got the idea by now. I'd never be asked back on the show again. You see, these shows demand that commentators always deliver confident, decisive answers, even when decisive answers don't exist.

A great example of what I'm talking about occurred a few months into Melbourne's second COVID-19-induced lockdown. A decent chunk of the workforce was sitting idle at home. But, that day, better than expected jobless figures were announced. A beaming Federal Treasurer informed us that over 110,000 new jobs were created across Australia in the prior month.

Truth be known, the news wasn't as favourable as it appeared. The reported number was a statistical anomaly due to the way employment was defined. But, that aside, it was still a case of the numbers coming in better than expectations. It meant that economists and politicians were taken by surprise. And, being a pleasant surprise, you'd expect that to be good for the stock market. But, as George Charles Selden said in his 1912 book *Psychology of The Stock Market*, 'However important some single factor in the situation may appear to you, it is not going to control the movement of prices regardless of everything else'.

And that was the case here. The favourable employment figures weren't enough to lift the stock market. It fell by 1.3 percent on the day.

Why the fall? Well, potentially for a billion and one reasons. You see, there were over a billion shares traded on the Australian Stock Exchange that day. It wasn't an unusual volume. But, like all trading days, people were both buying and selling for a wide variety of reasons. (Otherwise, there wouldn't be any trade, would there?) The 1.3 percent decline was the net result of all those reasons.

The forces that move the stock market are incomprehensibly numerous and complex. They can't be distilled down into one simple causal relationship. So, the singularly positive jobs numbers were drowned in an ocean of other market-impacting factors. Just don't ask me what they all were or the degree of influence that each carried!

Let's now get back to how commentators would typically reflect on this situation when asked for their opinion. If the stock market had gone up that day, rather than down, then all the stock market commentators would have proclaimed in unison, 'The stock market rose strongly today on the back of better-than-expected jobs numbers.' Each commentator would have then signed-off that evening satisfied that they'd delivered the news as it happened.

But things didn't turn out that way. As I said, the stock market actually fell. The dilemma for the commentators was that they now had to find a different reason in order to explain the fall.

So, what did they say that night instead? It doesn't matter. It wasn't the correct answer anyway.

This should remind us that the reasons behind the stock market moving are far from obvious, even when convenient and credible reasons are served up on a plate for commentators to parrot.

Here's another one. Financial commentators love the first Tuesday of every month. That's when the Reserve Bank of Australia reviews interest rate settings. There are days when the central bank lifts interest rates and the stock market falls. Commentators will say on those days that, due to higher interest rates, investors will now demand higher yields on their share investments. For higher yields to be delivered, share prices must fall.

But what about days when the central bank lifts interest rates and the stock market rises? The commentators will then say that the central bank did this on the expectation of strong future economic growth. And, if economic growth is going to be strong, then this will be good for the stock market. And that's why share prices rose!

(The market's response also depends upon what expectations were prior to the announcement. But this reinforces the fact that the market is a multifaceted beast. It has many moving parts and singling out just one reason for a move delivers the false message that it can be easily explained.)

Here's one to watch out for; it's used regularly by commentators when the market falls on a slow news day. When the commentator can't find an economic event to pin the move on, they will then say that the market fell today due to 'profit-taking'.

People don't question the credibility of the commentator or whether the explanation that they just delivered is valid. As long as it sounds right and it was delivered in a confident manner, then they digest it.

As US psychologist Amos Tversky once noted, 'People accept any explanation as long as it fits the facts.'

So, why do these market professionals spin these stories? It's simple. They do it to save face. Imagine yourself facing the prospect of an imminent appearance on the late news. You have to come up with a plausible narrative in order to explain the day's events. So, you will apply your analytical ability not to analyse but rather to rationalise.

Analysis is rarely possible in these circumstances. The roots of causation are far too complex to identify. So, forget analysis. Rationalisation is the only option!

Some keep the score

OK, so I've delivered plenty of examples of people delivering bad forecasts. But does that paint the full picture? Maybe there *are* experts out there who are capable of delivering reliable forecasts.

Fortunately, there are researchers who have bothered to investigate this exact question. They've recorded the forecasts that so-called experts have delivered and then checked later whether their forecasts came to pass. In a now-famous study, US academic Philip Tetlock recruited 284 political and economic experts to deliver forecasts regarding anticipated political and economic trends and events. Over a multi-year period, Tetlock collected a monumental 27,450 judgments made by his 284 'experts'. Tetlock found that their predictions were worse than random guesses. He critically stated that better results could have been delivered by 'a dart-throwing chimpanzee'. He also found that those soothsayers with the loudest voices were the ones most likely to be wrong.

Psychologists Amos Tversky and Daniel Kahneman would have agreed with Tetlock's findings. In their paper 'On the psychology of prediction', they found that, 'The very factors that caused people to become more confident in their predictions also led those predictions to be less accurate'.

You will be well served to periodically remind yourself that, when it comes to economic forecasting, there is no relationship between being an 'expert' and being confident, articulate or well dressed (the qualities many people use to judge an expert). Notwithstanding, the prediction industry is huge. It sees hundreds of billions of dollars spent annually on an activity that delivers no benefit to either society or to investors.

Most economic predictions fail to eventuate. And events that are never predicted commonly do eventuate. So, why do people keep delivering forecasts, and why do people keep paying attention to them?

In light of all the evidence, why do forecasters keep forecasting?

Now, I can't get inside the head of every forecaster, but I'd suggest that many keep forecasting because they simply can't resist having their egos stroked. And, as long as there are people who continue to listen to them (as there always will be), then they will continue to opine about that which cannot be opined about.

I honestly believe that all that ego-stroking leads many forecasters to start believing their own fallacious hot air! And that brings to mind a well-worn investment joke. It's so relevant to the discussion that I couldn't leave it out:

> 'An oil prospector, on his way to Heaven, is met by St Peter at the pearly gates with some bad news. "You're qualified for residence", St Peter said, "but, as you can see, the compound reserved for oil men is packed. There's no way to squeeze you in." After thinking for a moment, the prospector asked if he could just say four words to the present occupants. St. Peter thought it seemed harmless enough, so the prospector cupped his hands and yelled, "Oil discovered in Hell." The gate immediately opened and all the oil men ran out of the compound to head for the nether regions. Impressed, St Peter invited the prospector in. The prospector paused, then said, "No, I think I'll go along with the rest of the boys. There might be some truth to that rumour after all"'.

Alfred Cowles, founder of the Cowles Commission for Research in Economics, came up with the best reason that I've heard as to why people put their faith in economic fortune tellers. After extensive research, which failed to find any useful advice in numerous popular stock tipping and prediction sheets, Cowles concluded that, 'Even if I did my negative surveys every five years, or others continued them when I'm gone, it wouldn't matter. People are still going to believe that somebody really knows. A world in which nobody really knows can be frightening'.

There it is. We don't know what the future holds so we look to others to tell us. But they don't know either. They just sound like they do. Which means that their confidence alone is enough to satisfy many of those who are listening.

The line between fact and fiction is often indiscernible

The past and the future are as different as night and day. History is fact. The future is unknown. That might sound painfully obvious but, trust me, for many people it isn't. For many it's a very blurry line that separates history from the future.

You see, history is delivered as a narrative. And the future is typically delivered as a narrative as well.

It's the same old thing. People love narratives. So, when they hear a prophecy wrapped up in the form of a convincing story, then they are likely to believe it.

To give you an idea how powerful narratives are, consider this. I know an intelligent guy who appreciates every single word that I've said in this chapter, yet he still builds his own narratives regarding the future of the economy. And he places faith in narratives delivered by economists, especially when they align with his own preconceptions. The fact is that economic and market forecasters will long be free to continue delivering their false narratives. And few will ever bother to check later whether their past narratives came true or not.

Journalist Patrick Commins said it well in his final article for the *Australian Financial Review*:

> 'Every disclosure document comes with the disclaimer: past performance is no indicator of future performance. I believe every market prediction should come with a mandatory preamble: The future is inherently unknowable, but here's my best guess…'

The take-home message

So, what should you take from all of this? It's that you shouldn't base any investment decisions on economic or general stock market prognostications – neither your prognostications *nor anyone else's*.

So, how should you deal with the whole forecasting question? The only way that you reasonably can. Simply ignore all forecasts about the economy and the stock market.

Don't make exceptions. Ignore them *all*.

Understand that investing is the art of making definitive calls in an uncertain world. And, while that might appear to be a difficult thing to accept, I have some great news for you: you don't need to make predictions, or embrace those of others, in order to invest successfully.

Chapter 6

The Market Timing Siren

'I don't know anyone who can do it successfully, nor anyone who has done so in the past. Heck, I don't even know anyone who knows anyone who has timed the market with consistent, successful, replicable results.'
– John Bogle

Stock markets never stay still. They climb. They fall. They climb again.

All of this perpetual motion raises a very important question: is it possible to make money by sensing where the market is heading next – that is, to buy when the market is low and to sell when it is high? Some believe that it's possible. Others say that it isn't.

So, who is right? Is market timing a myth or a money maker? We are going to take an in-depth look at the question in this chapter.

What market timing isn't

In our investigation into whether market timing is possible, it helps to firstly define what it isn't.

Market timing isn't about knowing – or even judging – where the market is headed over the short to medium term (days, weeks or months). I've never seen anyone who can predict with that degree of precision and I'm confident that I never will.

That might sound like a strange thing to say. Surely if you are going to take a view on where the market is heading then you need to have a time frame for when that's going to happen?

Not exactly.

Market timing is not about *knowing* for sure where the market *will be* at a certain point in time in the future. It's more about *judging* where market prices *are currently* in relation to long-term value norms. Is it currently expensive, or is it currently offering value? If you can identify when the market is at an unsustainably high or low level, market timing is more about positioning your portfolio accordingly, and then sitting on your hands and waiting for things to change.

So, it's more a determination of present value relative to long-term norms than it is a precise prediction regarding its future movements. And, the more that market prices are out of whack with what you believe to be the long-term norm, the more faith (but never certainty) you can place in your judgment being rewarded at some time in the future.

Market timing is not an activity that you can perform every day the stock market is open. Even advocates of market timing would suggest it only be attempted when the market is at price extremes – that is, when stock market prices are exceptionally high or exceptionally low compared with historic norms.

And therein lies another problem. Significant market extremes might only occur several times in an investor's lifetime. And it's difficult to become good at something when you don't experience it very often!

Market timing is definitely not a precise science. It can never be about picking the exact top or bottom of the market. In other words, it's not about identifying the crest of the market just before it begins to fall or identifying the bottom of the market just before it begins to rise again. Nailing things that precisely can only be attributed to luck. As investor Bernard Baruch famously said, 'I made my money by selling too soon.'

Despite the discussion so far, it's important to realise that many experienced investors deny market timing is even possible.

So, with those qualifications now under our belt, let's take a look at the case for and against market timing.

The case against market timing

Let's kick off with the case against market timing. This is the side where the weight of evidence lies.

The disbelievers state that market timing isn't possible because the future can never be known. They point out that financial markets are slaves to an unfolding news cycle. News means news. And that means that the market's justifiable level can't be known until right… *now*!

They also argue that extreme market gyrations are driven, in large part, by extremes of investor emotion. And emotions are difficult forces to either read or predict. Sentiment can turn on a dime.

They go on to add that anyone who successfully times the market is simply lucky, and that luck should never be confused with skill.

All hail the skill of the market timer

A while back I received an invitation from an Australia-wide investors' group to attend a lecture delivered by 'a master of market timing'. Being hailed as a 'master' is quite a glowing accolade, so I decided to look up the presenter's investment record.

He had made a big call by reducing his fund's exposure to the share market just prior to the COVID-19-induced sell-off in early 2020. However, in the years preceding that call, things had been pretty dismal for this money manager. His fund had been operating for seven years. From its inception up to the fortuitous pre-COVID call – a period of six and a half years – the fund had significantly trailed its chosen benchmark (the S&P/ASX200 Total Return Index).

He made one call that proved to be a winner. But, getting out just before a stock market crashes is only ever half the story. It is equally important to get back into the market before it climbs again. Sitting on too much cash while the market is recovering can be a massive drag on long-term returns.

So, let's now take a look at what our 'master of market timing' did after that COVID-induced decision to sell.

Unfortunately for him – or, should I say, for his investors – the stock market recovered both quickly and strongly. But he was caught flat-footed holding way too much cash. He missed the recovery. And that meant his fund had to go into public-relations recovery mode. After the market had fully recovered (plus some) the fund declared that the stock market recovery was a lot stronger than they had expected. In their own words, the market 'had reached levels that they could never fathom'.

The 'master of market timing' had just gone straight to the bottom of the class.

I'll quantify the degree of their disappointment with some numbers. The fund underperformed its benchmark index by 35 percent over the twelve-month period from May 2020 to May 2021. The index climbed by more than 28 percent. The fund delivered a return of negative 6.6 percent.

Overall, and since the fund's inception, it has significantly underperformed its chosen benchmark. Investors would have been better served by putting all their money into a low-cost index fund for the entire period. This fund manager's one-off successful call is a bit like the poker player who's been losing all night but, just as you arrive at the gaming table, he produces a royal flush. All hail the master of poker!

There is a second aspect of this tale that I need to highlight. Remember, it was a national shareholder association that was promoting this fund manager's capacity to time the market. So, be on your guard. It seems that anyone or any group – even a group that puts itself out there as an investing authority – can fall prey to the siren song of market timing.

Another market-timing fund manager

Speaking of fund managers who are promoted as market timing authorities, let me tell you of an Australian second-tier fund manager whose self-promotion has no bounds. He has stated publicly that 'If we [fund managers] aren't here to time the market then what are we here for?' (My response to him is that investing in solid assets that potentially deliver strong future returns might be on the top of my list, and you don't need to market-time in order to deliver that.) He went on to claim a personal capacity to market-time.

So, I checked his investment record.

At the depths of the GFC, he went on the public record advising investors to stay out of the market. He warned that it was way too dangerous a time to invest.

Wrong. The market rallied, rising strongly from that point.

As I write these words, the funds that this manager controls continue to lag behind their chosen benchmark. What's more, they are trailing the benchmark over any period that you choose to select and by a significant margin for each of his funds.

Not discouraged by his underperformance, this manager continues to mock anyone who promotes a buy-and-hold strategy (that is, where no attempt is made to market-time).

As John Maynard Keynes argued in a letter to FN Curzon back in 1938 (more on that in a moment), a simple buy-and-hold investor will typically outperform any market timer who grossly misjudged the market's gyrations. The thought of market timing is certainly an attractive one. But it's possible that, for the two fund managers just mentioned, they are searching for fool's gold at the end of fictitious rainbows.

Now, I'll admit that the stories I've mentioned so far don't prove or disprove whether market timing is possible. As they say, one swallow (or two in this case) doesn't make a summer. So, the question remains – is Keynes correct? Is market timing nothing more than another of the stock market's siren songs? Or, to date, have our two fund managers simply been unlucky, and they'll likely perform better in years to come?

Let's consult some financial experts on the matter. I call to the stand, for the case against market timing, John Maynard Keynes.

The masterful Baron Keynes thought not

On 18 March 1938, economist John Maynard Keynes wrote a letter to FN Curzon, the acting chairman of insurance company National

Mutual. Curzon had taken on the role of acting chairman in Keynes' absence.

Keynes' letter was triggered by Curzon's recent criticism of Keynes' investing style. Specifically, Curzon felt that under Keynes' stewardship the insurance company had too much exposure to the share market. Curzon intended to reduce this exposure by selling shares in the companies that Keynes had previously recommended. He was spooked by the recent collapse in the US share market; 12 months earlier the Dow Jones Industrial Average had been 60 percent higher. The market's fall had impacted the National Mutual portfolio harder than its competitors' portfolios due to the persuasive Keynes' advocacy for a high exposure to shares.

But Curzon was outgunned. Keynes was the more insightful investor. Here are three extracts from Keynes' letter to Curzon in defence of his investment strategy:

> 'I do not believe that selling at very low prices is a remedy for having failed to sell at high ones. The criticism, if any, to which we are open is not having sold more prior to last August. In the light of after events, it would clearly have been advantageous to do so. But even now, looking back, I think it would have required abnormal foresight to act otherwise.
>
> '... Then came the American collapse with a rapidity and on a scale which no one could possibly have foreseen, so that one had not got the time to act which one would have expected. However this may be, I don't feel that one is open to any criticism for not selling after the blow had fallen. As soon as prices had fallen below a reasonable estimate of intrinsic value and long-period probabilities, there was nothing more to be done. It was too late to remedy any defects in previous policy, and the right course was to stand pretty well where one was.
>
> 'I feel no shame at being found still owning a share when the bottom of the market comes. I do not think it is the business, far less the duty, of an institutional or any other serious investor to be

> constantly considering whether he should cut and run on a falling market, or to feel himself open to blame if shares depreciate on his hands. I would go much further than that. I should say that it is from time to time the duty of a serious investor to accept the depreciation of his holdings with equanimity and without reproaching himself.'

These words eloquently state Keynes' views about market timing: that it is difficult if not impossible to do.

Keynes' recommendation to not sell at the time of this exchange proved to be correct. At the time of his letter, the US market was at a low point. One year later it was 20 percent higher. Ten years later it was more than 40 percent higher. Keynes was vindicated in his stand against Curzon's attempt to time the market.

The Magnificent Six

In 2016 I was invited to deliver a presentation to a group of investors titled 'How to Time the Market'. Instead, I titled my presentation 'Market Timing and other Fairy Stories'.

So, let me share with you the stories that I told my audience that night. There are plenty of financial heavyweights who have declared themselves to be market-timing sceptics.

The first slide that I showed was a quote from investment veteran John Bogle (also used at the start of this chapter):

> 'I don't know anyone who can do it successfully, nor anyone who has done so in the past. Heck, I don't even know anyone who knows anyone who has timed the market with consistent, successful, replicable results.'

Bogle was well placed to identify a successful market timer, should such a person exist. His career in finance spanned eight decades. He was one of the most respected figures in finance in the second half of the 20th century and into the early 21st century. In 1999 *Fortune* magazine named him one of the investment industry's four 'giants' of the 20th century. Yet Bogle didn't believe that market timing was possible.

After kicking my presentation off with that single slide showing Bogle's quote, I thanked the audience for inviting me to present, and then I went to take my seat. *Why not?* I thought. Bogle was better qualified to address the question of market timing than I was.

But, hey, these people had come out on a cold May night. I knew they deserved a bit more of a show than just one slide. So, I returned to the lectern and continued with my presentation.

Next up I showed the titles of a couple of the books that I'd seen in my travels. The purpose of my slide was to highlight some of the crazy beliefs that were out there.

First up there was the book titled *All About Market Timing: The Easy Way to Get Started.* Hmmm… easy, hey?

Then there was the next book titled *The Ultimate Book on Stock Market Timing: Geocosmic Correlations to Trading Cycles.* Hmmm… astrology, hey? I'm not sure how studying celestial bodies would help to get a handle on the market. But let's try to keep an open mind and push on.

Next in my presentation I wheeled in my 'dream team' of stock market heavyweights. I showed slides of each expressing their personal views on market timing. I had already mentioned how John Bogle felt about market timing but, to my dream team, I now added five more players:

1. Warren Buffett, acknowledged as the most successful investor of all time
2. Benjamin Graham, Warren Buffett's mentor, often described as the 'father of security analysis'
3. John Maynard Keynes, the most influential economist of the 20th century and a great investor in his own right
4. Peter Lynch, who, as the manager of the Magellan Fund at Fidelity Investments, averaged an amazing annual return of just shy of 30 percent over the period from 1977 to 1990
5. John Pierpont Morgan, the world's most powerful and influential financier in the late 19th and early 20th centuries.

I told the audience that I'd be happy to put my team – the 'Magnificent Six' – up against any team that they might choose to debate the subject of market timing. And, in a classic case of 'don't shoot the messenger', I then told them that the opinions I was about to express weren't mine. They belonged to six of the greatest investment heavyweights of all time.

As I said, we had already heard from John Bogle. So, let's now hear from the other five members of the team:

1. **Warren Buffett:** In 1987, at the Berkshire Hathaway Annual General Meeting, Buffett told shareholders, 'I have never met a man who could forecast the market'. Buffett had long held this view because he also said many years prior to that, 'I am not in the business of predicting general stock market or business fluctuations. If you think I can do this, or think it's essential to an investment program, you should not be in the partnership'.
2. **Benjamin Graham:** 'It is our view that stock market timing cannot be done, with general success, unless the time to buy is related to an attractive price level.'
3. **John Maynard Keynes:** 'The idea of wholesale shifts is for various reasons impracticable and indeed undesirable. Most of those who attempt it sell too late and buy too late.'
4. **Peter Lynch:** 'I'm always fully invested. It's a great feeling to be caught with your pants up.'
5. **John Pierpont Morgan:** When asked by a reporter what the future direction of the stock market will be, he replied, 'It will fluctuate'.

Was I biased in presenting these views against market timing? Was I simply cherry-picking evidence to support a view that I already held? Maybe I was. But it is extremely hard to ignore the opinions of such well-credentialed financial heavyweights. Remember, they said it, not me.

For market timers to be successful (as opposed to lucky) they need to possess some sort of sense that things will change, that the market is presently out of kilter. Let's explore further why that is so hard to do.

We just don't see things coming

Just months before the Japanese attack at Pearl Harbor, which heralded the entry of the USA into World War II, Captain William D Puleston, the former Director of Naval Intelligence, stated, 'The Hawaiian Islands are overprotected… the entire Japanese fleet and air force could not seriously threaten Oahu'.

Three days prior to the attack on Pearl Harbor, the Secretary of the Navy, Frank Knox, said, 'No matter what happens, the US Navy is not going to be caught napping'.

On the morning of the Japanese attack, the officer in charge of radar, when told by a radar operator that at least 50 planes were approaching, responded, 'Well don't worry about it… it's nothing'.

Examples of behaviour like this aren't isolated. They are rife throughout all facets of life, including investing.

Unlike tsunamis and extreme weather events, stock market crashes don't come with a warning that they're about to make landfall. Joseph de la Vega lived through and wrote about the Dutch stock market crash of 1688. In his book *Confusion de Confusiones*, he described the general mood among investors immediately prior to the crash: 'On the Exchange, a goodly supply of money and abundant credit were available… a vigorous spirit of enterprise… there was favourable news'. In other words, both de la Vega and investors generally were unaware of the imminent crash.

Henry Hall experienced first-hand the blind optimism that consumed investors in the USA prior to the 1907 crash. He described it as follows: 'The old, old story of the conditions forerunning a crisis was repeated in all other particulars'.

Fred Kelly tells us in his review of broker's reports in the four months leading up to the 1929 Crash that: 'Optimism is the keynote'.

Similar comments describe the mood of investors, brokers, analysts and commentators prior to every past stock market crash that you care to look at.

I would liken investors prior to a crash to a boat full of revellers floating down the Niagara River. Unaware of the imminent danger, they blindly party on as their boat gets ever closer to the thunderous falls. As economist John Kenneth Galbraith wrote in *A Short History of Financial Euphoria*, 'The euphoric episode is protected and sustained by the will of those who are involved'.

Remember that it's not just novices who behave this way. The professionals are up there dancing and partying just as hard as everyone else prior to any crash that you care to examine.

This happens because present conditions colour our perception of how the future will be. We believe that the current state will be maintained and that the future will simply be an extrapolation of the present. We discount the possibility of change. Yet the reality is, as the Greek philosopher Heraclitus stated, 'nothing endures but change'.

Ironically, after change does inevitably occur, many explain it away as having been obvious before the fact. But, if an imminent stock market crash were obvious to lots of people, then it would have already crashed. Think about it!

Why we don't see stock market crashes coming

How often do you hear people claiming to have seen the last crash coming?

I have experienced four market crashes in my investing life. Three I didn't see coming. One I did. Here's my track record:

1. 1987 – I didn't see it coming.
2. 2000 – Dot.com (Dot.obvious).
3. 2008 – I didn't see it coming.
4. 2020 – I didn't see it coming.

Now that's an honest self-admission. But you need to be wary of self-admissions. That's because people are prone to hindsight bias. Voiceless *before* the crash, they claim to have seen it coming *after* it occurred.

So, am I committing the same crime in claiming that I foresaw the bursting of the Dot.com bubble? Absolutely not. I was squawking like a chicken for months before the bubble finally burst. Just ask my friends.

My reasoning behind Dot.com being overcooked was straightforward: it was the outrageous prices that were being placed on all the worthless Dot.com start-ups. The signs were in plain sight for those who were bothered to look. Clearly, many weren't looking.

In order to anticipate a crash, you need to identify when things are unbalanced – that financial norms are being breached… and by a significant margin.

We often don't know why crashes occur, even after the event

If the tea leaves are difficult to read before a market correction, then surely things must become clear after the event, right?

Not necessarily.

Take, for example, the October 1987 Crash in the USA. The stock market collapsed by 23 percent in a single day (19 October). It was the biggest one-day move in history (in percentage terms).

Twenty-three percent! Surely the reason behind such a large collapse must be a case of Captain Obvious – if not before, then certainly after the event.

No, it wasn't!

In the four months following the record collapse there were six independent investigations to determine its cause. I'll list the bodies that conducted the investigations:

1. The Brady Commission
2. The Commodity Futures Trading Commission
3. The U.S. Securities and Exchange Commission
4. The U.S. General Accounting Office
5. The New York Stock Exchange
6. The Chicago Mercantile Exchange.

A whole variety of explanations were offered, and that is telling in itself: their findings were inconsistent. Individuals will voice their own theories as to why the October 1987 Crash occurred. But the fact is that no defining, generally accepted, singular cause has ever been delivered.

So, I ask the obvious question: if six independent investigations (which included hours of expert opinion) couldn't determine the cause of the biggest one-day crash in history, even *after* the event, then what hope does anyone have of identifying an imminent crash *before* the event?

The simple fact that the US stock market collapsed by 23 percent in one trading day indicates that it was a huge surprise. A widely held view that it was going to occur is an unsustainable one because such a belief would have resulted in a crash already happening.

American economist and academic Robert J Shiller surveyed professional investors following the 1987 crash in an effort to better understand what drove their thinking that day. The survey results showed that there was no news story or rumour that triggered the respondent's decision to sell. Most respondents said that their actions were a response to the behaviour of those around them. Theirs was a reaction to, rather than an appreciation of, what was going on.

I'd liken their behaviour to a herd of grazing antelopes. One member of the herd senses danger and darts off. The others followed, not because they sensed any imminent danger but because the other antelopes were on the move.

It wasn't just the US stock market that crashed in October 1987. Stock markets around the world crashed in sympathy. The Australian stock market fell by 25 percent on the day following Wall Street's collapse.

It seems that the sound of those antelope hooves can cross oceans.

A 1988 study from the Massachusetts Institute of Technology (MIT) explored the possible catalysts behind a large number of significant stock market movements. They looked at the 50 largest postwar one-day moves in the US stock market, then they searched for precipitating news stories in *The New York Times*. The question posed was, 'Big news and big moves: are they related?'

Here is the conclusion: 'Our results suggest the difficulty of explaining as much as half of the variance in stock prices on the basis of publicly available news bearing on fundamental values'.

This fact has long been recognised. Joseph de la Vega wrote in 1688 that the stock market can rise or fall due to the 'opinion on the stock exchange itself. For this last reason the news [as such] is often of little value, since counteracting forces [may] operate in the opposite direction.'

In other words, the relationship between news in the street and stock market movements isn't as clear-cut as you might expect it to be. Stock market corrections can just as easily occur on slow news days.

It's difficult to leave the party

Imagine now that you are a market timing disciple – that is, you believe it is possible. So, you are on the lookout for a potential market correction. You are like a passenger on that metaphorical boat heading towards the edge of Niagara Falls. You aren't mindlessly partying like all the others. Instead, you are up at the bow of the boat, alert and on the lookout for potential danger.

Your hope is to sell your shares and move to cash before the crash occurs. But the market is still climbing, so you don't want to sell too early and miss out on any potential gains. You are torn between greed and fear. You are basking in the rise of your share portfolio, but the risk is that you might be fully invested at the top with not enough time to get out.

In describing the difficulty of timing an exit from the market before it collapses, I can do no better that Warren Buffett from his Chairman's letter in Berkshire Hathaway's 2000 Annual Report:

> 'Nothing sedates rationality like large doses of effortless money. After a heady experience of that kind, normally sensible people drift into behavior akin to that of Cinderella at the ball. They know that overstaying the festivities… will eventually bring on pumpkins and mice. But they nevertheless hate to miss a single minute of what is one helluva party. Therefore, the giddy participants all plan to leave just seconds before midnight. There's a problem, though: They are dancing in a room in which the clocks have no hands.'

Crashes typically hit landfall with no warning. Hey, it's not even obvious when a crash does arrive that it's actually the start of a crash. That's because significant corrections don't always kick off with a singular gut-wrenching plunge like October 1987. More often they are like the proverbial slow trainwreck.

The true dimensions of nearly every crash can only be determined *after* they have occurred. And, clearly, that information is unavailable in real time, when decisions about what to do need to be made. Financial crises more typically unfold day by excruciating day. It's no easier to make a decision today about remaining invested (or not) than it was yesterday or the day before yesterday.

Financial crises have their origins and their outcomes intimately intertwined with human behaviour. And that's a very complex thing to understand. As Sir Isaac Newton famously stated after dropping a bundle in the South Sea Bubble of 1720, 'I can calculate the motions of heavenly bodies, but not the madness of people'.

The case for market timing

OK, enough with the negatives. It's time to deliver the positive case for market timing. Evidence is thin on the ground, but I'll try my best to dig some up for you.

First of all, let's talk about identifying market highs – that is, just before the market corrects significantly on the downside.

I said earlier that I saw the Dot.com crash coming. I didn't know when, but I was confident that it would eventually happen. Why specifically Dot.com? And why didn't I see the other financial crises coming?

Because Dot.com was in a class of its own. It was *absolutely nuts*.

Investors (and I use that word loosely) were so enamoured with any meritless, capital burning start-up with '.com' attached to its title that they lost any sense of commercial or investing reality – that is, if they had any sense of that in the first place. It was impossible to value these companies by conventional means because few actually generated any profits and there was significant uncertainty as to which ones ever would. Start-ups were classified according to their 'cash burn rate' – how quickly the money that greedy, eager investors had contributed was being flushed down the toilet by the 'company' they had invested in.

I couldn't comprehend the valuations that investors were putting on these things. I mean, what is something worth that is chewing through money and has little to no hope of turning the situation around? For most the answer was less than zero. (Clearly Amazon, which was founded at around this period, is an exception. But no one appreciated its future growth. Over 90 percent of Dot.com companies failed. Picking future winners was essentially a lottery.)

No, I had no problem realising that Dot.com was going to end in tears.

But it's a different story anticipating when the share prices of solid, profit-making companies are about to be cut in half, as they were in the GFC of 2008 and the COVID-induced plunge in early 2020. Overpricing prior to those crashes (indeed prior to most crashes) is usually more difficult to pick.

For those of you who weren't investors through Dot.com, let me give you a little taste of what it was like.

Dot.com craziness

In the late 1990s the internet, while not exactly a new technology, was new to most people. Its global adoption had been growing exponentially. Clearly it offered exciting new business and communication opportunities.

The local high street ceased to be the sole marketplace for goods and services. Many businesses, and retail businesses in particular, were going global. And what a boon it appeared to be. Most of the costly infrastructure required had already been set up by others. Businesses didn't need to pay to build the internet, establish a postal service to deliver the goods that they sold, or create a banking system to facilitate payments. All were already in place and paid for by others.

New Dot.com companies were popping up every day. Investors weren't deterred by the fact that few were making money. All of them were priced for success. Ultimately, most failed.

Investor enthusiasm had little to do with business fundamentals; it was skyrocketing share prices that was drawing investors in. The USA's tech-heavy Nasdaq composite stock index – which covered the bulk of Dot.com companies – rose by a staggering 400 percent over the final five years of the 1990s.

It peaked in March 2000. Then the bubble burst. The Nasdaq collapsed by a massive 78 percent over the course of the next two and a half years.

Australians weren't immune to Dot.com fever. An Aussie market darling at the time was digital services company Melbourne IT. It was floated on the Australian stock market in 1999 at a listing price of $2.20. Its share price then proceeded to multiply sixfold over the course of the next few months. After the bubble burst, its share price collapsed by a massive 93 percent within the space of a year. (Melbourne IT did turn out to be a viable business, although with a much-reduced share price.)

The share prices of many Dot.com hopefuls went to zero. Their fictional business models simply evaporated into the ether.

So, how did the worldwide Dot.com fallout impact the general stock markets (that is, the non-Dot.com companies)? While the tech-heavy Nasdaq fell a hefty 78 percent from peak to trough, the non-tech-based Dow Jones index fell by a lesser 26 percent over the same period, and the Aussie All Ordinaries index (which contained relatively few Dot.com stocks) fell by a significantly smaller 10 percent over the same period. It's not possible to state how much of that 10 percent fall, if any, was due to the pricking of the Dot.com bubble. Either way, the big losses in Australia were pretty much restricted to Dot.com stocks.

I stayed well clear of Dot.com companies. As I said, it was easy for me to do that because I have a rule not to buy companies that have yet to make money. Dot.com didn't mean that I avoided the stock market during that period; I remained heavily invested in other segments of the market.

I remember my emotions at the time. I was fascinated by the whole thing, enthralled by the way people were behaving. You see, while the period and the players were different, I had read of similar behaviour in history books. Dot.com was like living through a chapter of Charles Mackay's 1841 classic *Extraordinary Popular Delusions and the Madness of Crowds*. It was as if I was watching a film for the first time, but I knew how it was going to end.

To me it had always been a bubble ready to burst. I didn't know when it would burst. But I knew that it would burst.

Picking market lows

I've already said that I can't pick when the general stock market is peaking and about to crash. In that respect I guess I feel similarly to Keynes when he wrote to Curzon that he felt 'no shame at being found still owning a share when the bottom of the market comes'.

But I feel differently about what to do in the wake of a stock market crash. After the crashes of 1987, 2008 and 2020 I invested with conviction.

Financier Henry Clews described this approach in his 1908 book *Fifty Years in Wall Street*. Clews observed that some seasoned investors became interested in the stock market at times when others were shunning it:

> 'If young men had only the patience to watch the speculative signs of the times, as manifested in the periodical egress of these old prophetic speculators from their shells of security, they would make more money at these intervals than following up the slippery "tips" of the professional "pointers" of the Stock Exchange all the year round… I say to the young speculators, therefore, watch the ominous visits to the Street of these old men. They are as certain to be seen on the eve of a panic as spiders creeping stealthily and noiselessly from their cobwebs just before rain.'

I question Clews whether many of these old men are identifiable 'on the eve of a panic'. But I can certainly picture them in the wake of a crash.

For me this is the essence of market timing. I can't pick tops, but it is easy to identify when investors are in a state of panic in the wake of a crash. The best time to invest is beyond that, when a sense of total despondence is reached. I saw that in early 2009 in the wake of the GFC.

So, why is it that most don't feel confident to invest after the market collapses – that, rather than seeking out buying opportunities (at lower prices), they choose to avoid the stock market altogether? It's because people are overly influenced by the availability heuristic. That is, they place far too much weight on what is happening to them in real time. They believe that the present state of affairs will persist. In the wake of a crash they are experiencing anxiety, despair and financial pain. They believe that, by getting out of the market and staying out, their pain will go away.

None of this is surprising. Let's face it, it takes very little to get people anxious about money. I remember on one occasion, when I was working as a stock analyst, I received an email from a woman who was absolutely freaking out because her Coca-Cola Amatil shares were trading at a price 10 percent below what she had paid for them. I'm not talking about being mildly concerned; she was absolutely freaking out.

Then, of course, there's the social factor. Groupthink perpetuates the general mood of anxiety following a stock market crash. Remember that line of people outside the Hong Kong pastry shop who initiated a bank run? Remember those people stampeding on the Brooklyn Bridge following a single woman's screams? Who's to say that you won't get caught up in the rush to sell your own shares the next time the stock market experiences a meltdown?

Is Warren Buffett a closet market timer?

Earlier in this chapter I quoted investment great Warren Buffett, who said of market timing, 'If you think I can do this, or think it's essential to an investment program, you should not be in the partnership'. Buffett was denying a capacity to market-time.

I've mentioned the Buffett quote again because I want to share with you a conversation that I had with a friend of mine a number of years ago. Like me, he is also very interested in investing. On this particular day we were in my car talking about the markets. My friend said, 'Buffett claims that no one can successfully market-time. Well, he's a hypocrite. He times the market. He always buys heaps of stocks in the wake of a crash.'

Now, I don't believe that Warren Buffett is a hypocrite. It was more a case of my friend misreading the situation.

Market timers attempt to trade on general shifts in the stock market. In that sense they would equally hope to profit from timely buying and selling of a broadly defined index fund as they would from buying and selling single stocks.

Buffett doesn't do that. To him, the condition of the general market is certainly of interest. But it isn't the primary driver of his actions.

What Buffett does is study individual companies. Once he identifies a company that interests him, he sets a price that he would be willing to pay for it. If the stock market is offering it at a higher price than his desired price, then he won't buy. But he is prepared to sit, wait and hope that one day it will be offered at a price that suits him.

And, clearly, in the wake of a crash there are many stocks that are being offered at cheap prices. That triggers Buffett's buying. So, to an observer, Buffett appears to be market timing.

This has been confirmed by Buffett himself. On 16 June 1993, Buffett, along with eight other CEOs, was invited to the White House for lunch with US President Bill Clinton. Following the two-hour presidential lunch, Buffett was interviewed by reporters, and a reporter asked him whether the stock market was currently overvalued. He responded: 'I've never been a good judge of the markets. I try to evaluate specific businesses. If I could evaluate a few specific businesses every year halfway correctly, I'd look at it as a successful year. I've never made any money guessing which way the market's going.'

Buffett isn't alone in holding this view. For example, over three centuries ago, Sir Richard Steele, co-founder of the magazine *The Spectator*, wrote, 'Nothing could be more useful, than to be well instructed in his hope and fears; to be different when others exalt, and with a secret joy buy when others think it in their interest to sell.'

Buffett's is a fine but important distinction. Buffett considers himself to be an opportunistic stock picker, not a market timer.

Was Buffett's mentor, Benjamin Graham, a closet market timer?

Earlier in this chapter, I quoted Warren Buffett's teacher and mentor, Benjamin Graham, who wrote 'It is our view that stock market timing cannot be done, with general success, unless the time to buy is related to an attractive price level'. It sounds very much in keeping with Buffett's comment above, that investing is about the determination of a fair price to be paid for an individual company rather than for the market as a whole.

Yet, in his book *The Intelligent Investor*, Graham wrote that, 'Sound procedure would call for reducing the common-stock component below 50% when in the judgment of the investor the market level has become dangerously high'. Here Graham is referring to the market level being high, not to the price of an individual business.

So, how does one, as Graham is asking us to, judge that 'the market level has become dangerously high'? Graham doesn't tell us specifically. In his own words, it comes down to 'the judgment of the investor'.

Judgment, hey? Clearly, everybody judges things differently. So, Graham's recommendation is certainly no panacea.

Is it possible to learn how to market-time?

The answer to the question 'Is it possible to learn how to market-time?' appears – at least to me – to be both 'yes' and 'no'.

I say that because I agree with Graham. The predominant ingredient here is the judgment of the individual, and judgment is heavily reliant on personal qualities – qualities that you might have or you might not have. And personal qualities are difficult, if not impossible, to teach.

Financial judgment is dependent on the way that you process information. You must process it in a relatively independent manner (not to be overly influenced by the opinions of those around you) and in a comparatively rational manner.

By independence I mean the capacity to keep social influence to a minimum. The course of action that you take must be the result of your own well-considered beliefs, not those of others. A capacity to think independently has a lot to do with who you were coming out of the womb; it doesn't lend itself well to instruction. But it's not enough just to be an independent thinker. There are plenty of independent thinkers out there who believe that the world is flat and that extraterrestrials built the pyramids.

Let me explain how all of this applies to financial markets.

Deciding whether the stock market is underpriced or overpriced at any particular time isn't purely a scientific or mathematical consideration. Numbers and metrics have some, but limited, value. It's not like determining whether it's hot or cold by looking at a thermometer. So, how is a judgment made, then?

First, it's important to appreciate that financial markets are driven by an indeterminable number of factors. Most are unidentifiable and unmeasurable. Complicating things further is that the factors that are identifiable (and likely those that aren't) are constantly changing with respect to their intensity and their degree of influence.

But, what if occasionally one of these factors became the predominant influence? And what if you could identify when this was happening? Well, there do appear to be occasions when you can. These times are when the emotions of market participants become both extreme and largely unified.

The problem that you face at these times is that humans – and remember that you are one – take their cues from the actions and beliefs of others. As I explained in chapter 4, you are likely to find yourself subconsciously following the lead of those around you. And while that's fine in most social settings, it isn't with the stock market. Being influenced by a crowd primed with emotion is the antithesis of an environment in which to make sound investment decisions. As a London attorney observed of stock market participants in Exchange Alley during the height of the speculative South Sea Bubble in 1720, 'I had a fancy to go and look at the throngs… and this is how it struck me yesterday; it is nothing so much as if all the lunatics had escaped out of the madhouse at once.'

So, the capacity to judge the state of the stock market necessarily starts with a capacity to block out social influence (as best you can).

Next comes the training part – in other words, the development of a capacity to judge when 'all the lunatics have escaped out of the madhouse at once'.

I can't begin to emphasise how important an extensive reading of financial history assists your judgment here. Read about financial booms and busts. Develop an appreciation of how people were thinking and behaving at the time. Go way back. There is over four centuries of stock market history to explore. You will begin to realise that the story associated with each boom and bust is the same. Only the characters change.

Armed with the anchor that an education in stock market history can deliver, you will start to appreciate the concept of mean reversion. What do I mean by mean reversion? Don't worry, I have devoted an entire chapter to mean reversion later in the book.

My own feelings about following the crowd

So, how do I personally fit into this discussion?

As I said, I'm better at identifying depressed markets than euphoric ones. I genuinely feel, as Warren Buffett has often stated, that I am better at being 'greedy when others are fearful'.

I find it relatively easy to do that because I have never felt an urge to do what others are doing. For example, I have always preferred individual sports to team sports or 'to do my own thing'. As a teenager in the army cadets, when our drill sergeant barked out the order to 'left wheel', I'd occasionally deliberately wheel right and then march away in the opposite direction to the platoon. (Thank goodness there was never a war!)

But, saying that, I'm also a realist. I'm a human being, so I can't be totally immune to social influence.

But that's me. Everyone is different. You need to make a call regarding your own sense of individuality. But, until you face a true financial crisis, with real money on the line, self-assessment is often a difficult thing to undertake.

Let's try anyway and have a dress rehearsal of how you might react in a stock market crash.

How might you have reacted if you'd been around in 1929?

Let's now subject you to a test. Don't worry, only you will know how you've performed. But I do want you to try to be totally honest with yourself.

Over the next few pages, I'm going to describe how the US stock market crash of 1929 unfolded. I'll be focusing on the three-year period from September 1929 through to July 1932. I want you to transport yourself back to 1929 and imagine yourself among it all. I want you to judge how you might have felt and behaved as your stock portfolio was decimated by the crushing decline of the US stock market in 1929 and the few years that followed.

Let's start our hypothetical emotional journey in September 1929. The stock market is absolutely rocking. The market's key index, the Dow Jones, has almost quadrupled over the past five years. Everyone has been making lots of easy money, even those who don't have a clue about investing. Confidence about the future of the stock market is at a fever pitch.

If you were invested in stocks, then you'd probably be patting yourself on the back for being so clever. After all, the 'market experts' have been in agreement with the investment decisions that you've been making. They describe it as the dawn of a new era for US enterprise, one that promises a future of unrelenting prosperity for all.

As confident as you feel about having made all the correct decisions, there is something that you fail to recognise: it's that the experts aren't actually agreeing with you. Rather, your view has been strongly shaped by theirs.

Case in point, you have just read an article in the August 1929 edition of *Ladies' Home Journal* titled 'Everybody Ought to Be Rich'. The article is based on an interview with prominent New York businessman

John Jakob Raskob. Raskob proposes that the path to becoming rich is through ownership of common stocks. He argues that, despite the strength of the stock market over recent years, 'we have scarcely started'.

Then there's highly respected US economist and stock market commentator Irving Fisher. He has just proclaimed that stock prices 'have reached what looks like a permanently high plateau'.

You consider yourself to be better informed than the average investor. You read widely and, during the course of that reading, you note that prominent economist and businessman Roger Babson is calling the market differently. Babson believes that the market is currently overpriced. But, in a classic case of the boy who cried wolf, Babson has been delivering the same pessimistic call for years. He actually started selling stocks five years earlier. These early sales meant that Babson had failed to fully capitalise on much of the run-up in stock prices over recent years. So, you choose not to pay any attention to Babson. He's an idiot, you tell yourself. You've made better choices than him, so why would you even consider selling now based on his advice?

You prefer to agree with financial heavyweights Raskob and Fisher. Their positive message is in keeping with your experience so far. With experts like them backing your view, what could possibly go wrong? You tell yourself that it's just onward and upward for the market from here.

Or am I wrong here? Would you have run counter to the advice of the experts and the behaviour of the general investing public? Would you have sold among all that enthusiasm and confirmation? I doubt it. But let's move on.

Just days later, Black Thursday hits.

On Thursday 24 October 1929 the US stock market opened down a massive 11 percent. It's a big shudder, but by the end of the trading day the market has steadied and largely recovered. After the dust settles, the day's losses are modest. At the close of trade, the index is down a reassuringly small 2 percent.

Newspaper reports attribute the intraday market recovery to the actions of Richard Whitney, the vice-president of the New York Stock Exchange. Armed with a large pool of money provided by several prominent New York bankers, Whitney stepped onto the trading floor of the New York Stock Exchange amid the strong selling. As the market was plunging, Whitney placed a bid to buy 25,000 shares of U.S. Steel at $205 each. His bid was well above the prevailing market price. He then did the same for other blue-chip stocks. His actions injected a dose of confidence into previously fearful investors. The market steadied, reversed and then recovered most of the morning's losses. Whitney was hailed the hero of the day and dubbed the 'White Knight of Wall Street'.

After reading about Whitney's actions in the newspaper, you decide that everything is going to be fine with your own stock portfolio. Your confidence is confirmed over the next two days of trading.

The market is steady on Friday and Saturday. (Yes, the stock market used to be open on a Saturday.) It seems that everything is OK again. So, you are content to maintain your investment portfolio. No need to sell and no spare money to buy!

Or am I wrong here? Would you have liquidated your entire portfolio and converted to cash? Would you have sensed something about the stock market that the vice-president of the New York Stock Exchange failed to sense? I doubt that very much. But let's move on anyway.

Two days later, on Black Monday (27 October), the market collapses by 13 percent. The next day the market collapses by a further 12 percent.

Your stock portfolio is now down by almost a third of its value from where it was just eight weeks ago. So, what do you do now? You ask yourself what the market is going to do tomorrow. Will it rise or fall? You develop a growing realisation that you have no idea.

You regret not selling eight weeks ago when the market was at its peak. In fact, it hurts just thinking about it. You desperately want the market to return to that level so that you can sell and convert to cash. You need a plan of action. Fuelled with regret, your plan is to hang on and to sell when (if) the market returns to its September high. Hope is now driving your decision-making. (History has since shown us that the market didn't return to that September high for another 25 years.)

Rather than climb, the market just keeps sliding. It falls another 14 percent over the next two weeks. Your stocks are now worth half what they were just ten weeks earlier. The emotional pain is now so intense that the only way you can deal with it is to try to switch it off. Everything is starting to become surreal. Half of you wants to scream out loud; your other half simply wants to deny that it's even happened.

So, what do you do now? You oscillate between two plans. One part of you wants to sell; you hope that will remove the pain of loss and the torment of uncertainty. But another part of you can't stand the thought of selling. Ten weeks earlier you felt rich. If you sell now, then you will destroy any chance of regaining that feeling. What's more, if the market recovers to its prior level, then you will punish yourself for selling now.

Your hope that it will recover is boosted when the famous pre-crash pessimist Roger Babson declares in late 1929 that the price decline is over and that stock prices will rally in the new year. You didn't accept his pre-crash prediction, but you want to accept this recent one. His prediction now feeds your hope, so you desperately want to embrace it.

And recover the market does. From that mid-November-1929 low, the stock market climbed by a massive 48 percent over the next five months. The economic mood in early 1930 is calm. Interestingly the editors of *The Times* singled out the Antarctic exploration of Richard Byrd, and not the October crash, as the most important news story of 1929. Your confidence returns as Wall Street prices climb.

It's April 1930 now. You tell yourself that you made the right call to hang on and not to sell back in November. You held your nerve. You declare yourself to be the master market timer!

Or am I wrong here? Would you have sold a few paragraphs back (before I told you that the market bounced back by almost 50 percent in the five months following the October crash)?

The market has now rebounded by 50 percent. If you still own stocks, do you sell now or do you hang on?

Have you made your decision? OK, let's move on.

A few weeks later the newspapers report that Richard Whitney, the recently appointed president of the New York Stock Exchange, has just delivered an address to a bunch of financiers at the Algonquin Club in Boston. You recognise the name; Whitney is the guy they dubbed the 'White Knight of Wall Street' after he steadied the market during the early stages of October's plunge, the guy who bought up big on the floor of the New York Stock Exchange. 'Hey, that guy is smart', you tell yourself. And he's a man of action. He's shown that he's prepared to back his judgment. What's more, he's now been appointed as the president of the New York Stock Exchange.

Because you value his opinion about the stock market, you read the newspaper article containing snippets from his recent speech at the Algonquin Club. You hope that it will deliver clues about where the market is heading from here.

Whitney's address doesn't deliver any prophecies – in fact, he denies an ability to prophesy in his opening comments – but you don't see that as a negative. All you are looking for is whether Whitney is optimistic or pessimistic about the current state of the stock market.

In his speech Whitney recounts the prevailing investor sentiment leading up to the 1929 crash. The following are Whitney's actual words from his address: 'The decline in share prices which ended in the panic began as early as mid-September. At first however the movement contained no suggestion of panic whatsoever.'

In other words, people didn't see the crash coming. Whitney's reflection makes you feel better. You don't feel so stupid about not seeing it coming yourself. And you were smart enough to hang on for the subsequent rally.

Whitney goes on to describe the mood on the weekend following Black Thursday and immediately preceding Black Monday and Black Tuesday (28 and 29 October) – in other words, immediately following his 'White Knight' actions that helped to steady the market. He stated that, 'Public opinion had been startled, but also seemingly reassured. Many people believed that the stock market crisis was over'. He also described investor sentiment a fortnight further on from those three 'crisis' days in late October: 'The final rally which marked the end of the panic set in forcefully on November 14th. Normal conditions returned to Wall Street… so passed the Panic of 1929'.

There we go. Whitney believes that the panic has passed. When he delivered his address, the market had recovered somewhat.

After reading Whitney's recent thoughts, what should you do with your share investments now? Well, you hang on, of course. The stock market has recovered strongly from its post-crash low, and all the financial heavyweights are in agreement that the crash can now be filed in the annals of history. It's definitely onwards and upwards from here.

So, what actually happened from that point in time? The market fell massively. In fact, it fell by a further 81 percent!

By the time the market hit rock bottom in July 1932, it had collapsed by a gut-wrenching 89 percent from its pre-crash September 1929 high. It means that, if you had held over the course of the two years following Whitney's speech, you would have woken up every morning wondering if this was the day that the pain would end. It was a long, slow train wreck of monumental proportions.

Whitney had delivered no insights. The experts and market commentators had delivered no insights. No one knew that the market was about to recommence its descent following that initial strong rebound. And the whole time that you were searching for some sort of assurance that things were going to turn around, all that you were experiencing was financial death by a thousand cuts – for two long years!

So, why do people endure this pain?

People tend to hang on when markets are falling for two main reasons. First, they don't like to accept the crystallisation of a loss; they remain anchored to the lofty prices that existed prior to the fall, and they yearn for those high prices to return. Second, market movements unfold in real time; so, as the market continues to sink, each day is lived in the hope that the bottom has been reached and a recovery is about to begin.

The reality is no one knows what the next day will bring. There is no crystal ball. Events merely unfold with no information regarding the future direction.

But in the wake of a crash, clearly not everyone 'hangs on'. Many take fright and sell.

Many investors were forced to sell in the wake of the 1929 Crash. This is because many bought their shares using borrowed money (referred to as 'investing on margin'). Their lenders wanted the money to be repaid, so they forced investors to liquidate their holdings to repay the loans before the market fell any further. Thousands of once 'paper-rich' individuals had their wealth wiped out overnight.

Why getting out of the market can be a hazard to your wealth

I have always taken a long-term approach to investing. I typically don't sell in the wake of a crash, but nor do I experience heartache when it happens. I do experience an elevated emotional state, but it isn't due to any perception of loss; rather, it's due to the opportunity to buy stocks cheaply.

Let me explain using an analogy. As an Aussie who spent a lot of time at surf beaches when I was a kid, I remember some oft-repeated adult advice: should you get caught in a strong rip, don't swim against it; rather, go with the flow and work with its force.

Well, there's a natural force in investing in stocks. It was well documented by Edgar Lawrence Smith in his classic 1924 book *Common Stocks as Long Term Investments*. Smith argued that, because most companies retain a proportion of their profits and reinvest those profits back into their businesses, then there is a tendency for company share prices to rise over time.

Obviously, this is a general rule that doesn't apply to every single company on the stock market. Some companies, for a variety of reasons, experience a falling share price over time (most commonly due to falling profitability). But, when companies are considered as a group, then it does apply. Their combined retention of profits sees the general stock market trending upwards over time. If you require confirmation of this, then just take a look at how the stock market has performed since 1980 (as measured by the All Ordinaries index).

The All Ordinaries index since 1980

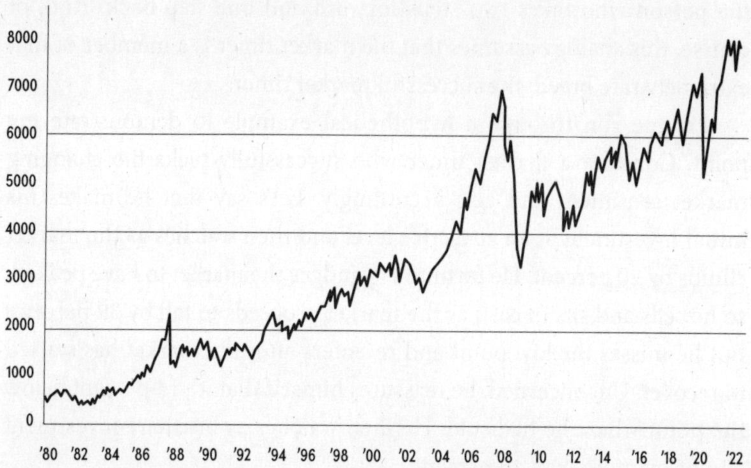

Now, while retained profits exert an influence on the long-term direction of the stock market, they are far from the sole influence on stock prices. As we know, stock markets can head in any direction in the short to medium term. But, like the swimmer who works with the force of the ocean, the long-term investor has the underlying force of retained profits assisting them. And for the market timer, who sells and converts to cash, that beneficial force is lost until such time as they re-enter the market.

This concept underpins the buy-and-hold investment strategy, which is the antithesis of the market-timing strategy. The buy-and-hold investor ignores all the ups and downs of the market and simply continues to hold.

It's wise to remember the advice delivered more than a century ago by the wealthy US financier Russell Sage. During a period of persistently declining prices Sage was asked by a novice whether stock prices would rally. The laconic Sage replied, 'they always have'.

The drag of CGT

Let's now look at another force working against the market timer: capital gains tax (CGT). The payment of CGT means that the successful market timer, who repeatedly exits and re-enters the market, is like the person who takes two steps forward and one step back. And, of course, this analogy assumes that the market timer is a member of that extremely rare breed: the successful market timer.

Let me run through a hypothetical example to demonstrate my point. Consider a market timer who successfully picks the changing market sentiment and acts accordingly. Let's say that he makes his initial investment at an attractive level and then watches as the market climbs by 20 percent. He fortuitously judges the market to have peaked, so he sells and sits in cash as the market proceeds to fall by 32 percent. But he misses the low point and re-enters after the market has started to recover. Unconcerned, he reassures himself that it's 14 percent below the point where he had sold. He then watches as his share investment climbs by more than 45 percent.

He considers himself a market timing genius. He has correctly picked the market's direction on all three legs of the investment journey so far. He feels that he hasn't put a market-timing foot wrong, and he scoffs at his flat-footed friend who remained invested for the entire period and had to endure the worrisome downward correction that he had largely avoided.

So, let's now compare their respective investment outcomes. Let's say that both invested $10,000 in a broad-based index fund when the stock market was at 3000 points. Fearing an imminent market correction, the market timer sells within 12 months and converts to cash as the market peaks at 3600 points. He pays $940 in CGT (assuming a marginal tax rate of 47 percent including the Medicare levy). Sitting out of shares for the entire market fall, the market timer also misses out on two dividend payments totalling $320 (after tax). After hitting its low point, the market starts to rise again. The market timer misses the inflection point but gets back in when the market is at 3100. He reinvests his $11,060 and watches as the market recovers strongly and surpasses its previous high. Two years later the market timer sells when the market reaches 4500 points and pays $1174 in CGT. He now has $14,880 in the bank.

Now to the buy-and-hold strategist. He didn't try to time the market but remained fully invested for the entire period. His shareholding would now be worth $15,000. He would also have received an additional $320 in dividends. In total he is $440 better off than the market timer. (The market timer would have received an additional small amount of interest while sitting in cash but also would have had to pay brokerage fees for his trades.)

Now, I acknowledge that in this example the market timer ends up holding cash and the buy-and-hold strategist is still holding shares. However, if the final objective is to own a portfolio of a certain value, then the distinction is redundant. I also acknowledge that I have used a high marginal tax rate in the example. But it doesn't change the fact that the drag of CGT is a feature whatever the tax rate. In fact, I have favoured the market timer in this example – he barely put a foot wrong. Such precision is rare and, could I suggest with the subtle changes in market direction described here, is more likely the result of luck.

A parting comment about market timing

As Warren Buffett has famously stated, those investors who hope to profit from the errors of others need to be fearful when others are greedy and greedy when others are fearful. The problem is that most people can. Not. Do. That.

For most people, if not all, a capacity to market-time is nothing more than a wishful fantasy. While many are seduced by the concept of market timing, the reality is that, when other market participants are losing all sense of value in a frenetic bull market, they get caught up in all the enthusiasm as well. And, when a financial storm hits, they are equally influenced in their actions by the mindless, terrified masses.

Let me sign off this chapter with a great saying. Remember it whenever you are tempted into believing that you, above all others, have a sense for where the market is heading: market timing is like chocolate-coated arsenic – it's seductive but lethal.

Chapter 7

Sirens Painting Pretty Patterns

'The human understanding is of its own nature prone to suppose the existence of more order and regularity in the world than it finds.'

– Sir Francis Bacon (1561–1626)

Neuroscientists have long recognised that homo sapiens seeks to identify and interpret patterns to an extent that outstrips all other species. This characteristic has, to date, delivered humans an evolutionary benefit. Searching for patterns has helped us to decipher order from chaos. It has allowed us to scan the horizon to anticipate the weather and to search for food. It has allowed us to judge, to assume and to hypothesise. And it has allowed us to survive, prosper and pass our pattern-seeking genes on to our offspring.

Humans seek answers in patterns. Put simply, we just love patterns.

But there is a downside to all this pattern-seeking behaviour: we see patterns wherever we look. What's more, we apply significance to patterns even when significance isn't warranted. For example, the leaders of Roman and Babylonian civilisations used to consult with haruspices. They were people trained to divine the future by inspecting the shape and position of entrails from sacrificed animals.

Even today fortune tellers divine our future by studying the patterns made by leaves on the bottom of teacups and of the skin creases on the palms of our hands. Psychologists use the Rorschach test to delve into a patient's psyche by asking what thoughts they have when they look at random ink blots on a page. We see the man in the moon, images among the clouds and human faces on the trunks of trees. We play dot-to-dot with the stars in the night sky, and we use the lines drawn to generate images of water-bearers, lions, fish and scorpions.

We even have names for pattern-seeking behaviour. Apophenia is a desire to seek patterns in random information. Pareidolia describes our tendency to see familiar objects (such as faces or human forms) in unrelated objects (such as tree trunks and bizarrely shaped vegetables).

It all sounds like a bit of harmless fun. But it definitely isn't harmless when it comes to the serious business of investing. It seems that there are plenty of investors out there who practise apophenic behaviour when it comes to their bank balance.

Let's take a look.

Randomness often doesn't look random

High-level investing demands deductive logic – that is, drawing conclusions based on logic and reasoning. A comprehensive range of facts needs to be gathered; then, those facts need to be intensely analysed. This demands an enormous amount of mental effort and a significant amount of time in order to be performed properly.

But the fact is that people shy away from things that are difficult. So, rather than undertaking a process of deduction, we prefer to undertake a process of induction. Inductive reasoning sees us form conclusions from observation. It's easier, it's quicker, and it requires less effort.

It's for this reason that many investors are quick to draw conclusions from observing graphs and patterns. But, as discussed, this risks giving relevance to patterns that are devoid of meaning.

Before I wrote the following words, I tossed a coin ten times. Below is the outcome in the exact order that heads (H) and tails (T) appeared:

H – T – T – T – T – T – T – H – T – T

What you see is a 'one-try' result. I didn't repeat the exercise in order to achieve a result that best suits the following discussion.

When asked what the result of ten tosses might look like, most people would describe something close to alternating heads and tails. They might include a couple of heads in a row or a couple of tails in a row, recognising that perfect alternation would be rare. But few people would expect the result that I achieved above: eight tails from ten tosses and six tails in a row! Surely the coin must be biased in some way, right?

No, it wasn't. Such is the nature of randomness.

If I had instead tossed the coin 1000 times or 10,000 times, then the result would have been closer to an anticipated 50:50 split. Such is the law of large numbers. But, even then, a precise 50:50 split is unlikely.

The fact is that true randomness rarely appears to be random.

The flying bomb

In the final year of World War II, Londoners faced a new and terrifying German weapon. I can remember my mother, who lived in London throughout the war, describing it to me.

It was a flying bomb propelled by a pulse-jet engine. I remember my mother calling them 'buzzbombs'. The name referred to the noise that they made as they flew over London towards their target. Armed with a crude guidance system, they were launched by the Germans from the coast of France. Once over London their control system sent them into a steep dive. The fuel flow ceased and they went into freefall. When the pulsing propulsion system went quiet it indicated to those below that an impact was imminent.

The first incarnation of flying bombs, the V-1, was far from a precise weapon. Most landed within a 30-kilometre circle of their intended target. Several months later the Germans replaced the V-1 with the long-range V-2 rocket. It was much faster than the V-1, travelling at the speed of sound. The V-2 was essentially the world's first long-range ballistic missile. As far as the Allies were concerned the V-2 was basically unstoppable. But its primary disadvantage, as far as the Germans were concerned, was that it was even less accurate than the V-1.

So, now you have the picture. The rockets were effectively landing in a random fashion across London. It was similar to the distribution of darts on a board thrown by a bad dart player.

Of course, the random nature of where the bombs were landing at the time was fully appreciated by the Germans, but not by the English. What the English did notice, as the attacks progressed, was that certain areas of London suffered more hits than other areas. They came to believe that the working-class East End, which sustained an inordinate number of hits, was being targeted by the Germans, while other areas of London were being spared. But, as we all now know, that wasn't the intent of the Germans.

Following the war, statistician RD Clarke showed that the bombing patterns were totally compatible with a random distribution. The English had misinterpreted the bomb clustering in a similar fashion to how one might attribute meaning to the result of the coin toss I shared with you earlier.

The simple fact is that people are innately prone to seek order even when there is none. And it's essential to appreciate this fact when investing.

Technical analysis

I now want to talk about an investment technique called 'technical analysis'. For the purpose of this discussion, it's essentially the same thing as 'charting'. It involves drawing conclusions from the price graphs and trading volumes of commodities and securities (such as shares).

There are plenty of devotees out there. It's a serious business.

Technical analysts have long been employed by stockbrokers and investment houses around the world. Courses and books on how to undertake the practice are plentiful. As well, there are countless stock trading software programs, based on technical analysis, that are available for use by home traders.

True devotees of technical analysis believe that everything a trader needs to know is embodied in the price and trading volume data. What they are essentially doing is studying lines and patterns on charts.

Patterns… hmmm.

You can see where I'm heading with this, can't you? So, I'm going to go in hard and early. I suggest that our oft-misplaced pattern-seeking behaviour is on full display here.

The search for meaning

A pivotal research paper was delivered by statistician Holbrook Working back in 1934 exposing the predisposition of investors and traders to place unwarranted trust in patterns of stock and commodity prices. Working studied historical commodity price data on charts. He identified many of the repetitive shapes and patterns that chartists use in order to draw their conclusions.

But then Working took his analysis one step further. He plotted the magnitude of price change from one transaction to the next. He found that the magnitude of change was random. Working also generated charts from random sequences (that is, they weren't real) and presented them to professional commodity traders. The traders couldn't distinguish Working's fictitious charts from real ones.

Working's findings aren't unique. Maurice Kendall, a professor of statistics at the London School of Economics, studied the price patterns of a range of stock prices and commodities covering an extended period. He was unable to identify any structure, meaning or predictive significance from the historical prices.

Harry V Roberts, a statistician at the University of Chicago, used a computer to generate random numbers that varied within certain limits. The need to place price boundaries recognised the fact that the last traded price of a stock or commodity influences the next traded price, particularly in the absence of significant company news. Roberts wanted to find out if studying past prices provided information that could be used to generate profits. He found that the methods chartists employed were a waste of time.

I could keep going with confirming study after confirming study, but I'll stop there.

You see, much (if not all) of our faith in charts is likely to be little more than a by-product of our innate pattern-seeking behaviour. Are the head-and-shoulders formations that technical analysts observe on stock charts nothing more than the financial equivalent of the man in the moon? Are the triangular formations on stock charts as irrelevant as the identification of a triangle within the shield of the constellation Orion?

I am not saying that there is no such thing as pattern formation in financial markets. There is… well, sort of. I'd prefer to describe it as a search for correlations.

The fact is that over recent decades ultra-smart mathematicians using algorithmic code and massive computing power have unearthed otherwise indiscernible correlations and market pricing inefficiencies. Termed 'quants', they've made themselves into billionaires doing it. (I talk more about how they've gone about things later in the book.)

Quants have shown that studying historical price data can be a useful exercise. But casting an imaginative eye over a price chart is not the way to gain the type of financial edge that they are looking for.

Now, I know they are fighting words, so I expect immediate pushback from the charting fraternity. But I'd suggest that many chartists are zealots when it comes to their 'craft', and it's almost impossible to instil an alternate belief in the mind of a zealot. I have heard their case. I have considered their case. I have read my fair share of books on charting. But, after having done all of that, I believe that the words of 17th-century English philosopher John Locke are appropriate here: 'madmen put wrong ideas together, and so make wrong propositions, but argue and reason right from them'.

Technical analysts who employ charts are free to argue their defence. But I believe that the proposition from which they argue is wrong. And, as there is no better example of that than this, let me share with you some extracts from an article written by a chartist who describes herself as 'an internationally respected professional technical analyst and author'.

A price target set by an 'internationally respected technical analyst and author'

Back in 2010, I read an article published in a popular daily business newspaper. The article was written by a chartist who, after studying a historical price chart of a listed Australian company, advised readers of the company's investment potential. I was so intrigued by the conclusions that I felt compelled to save the clipping.

The writer described the price advances, declines and patterns that the company's share price had made over the prior 14-year period. There was copious use of words and terms such as 'spiral', 'pinnacle', 'steady sideways path', 'oscillating', 'reversal triangular', 'exhausted', 'pullback resistance', 'barrier lines' and 'momentum divergence'. The writer concluded that, in the first half of 2008, 'the momentum divergence and a barrier created by the new path trend produced a fairly sharp downturn to seek support from the base of the trend'.

Now, all this pattern narration is fine and well as long as it delivers some useful information.

The stock was trading at around $12 at the time of the article. And here is the writer's investment recommendation following an intense study of that 14-year-long squiggly share price line:

> 'The longer-term potential gained from the triangle [the shape pertaining to more recent movements] indicates upside towards $15 and possibly through $20 later on. The risk within the long-term path would be a drop below $10 to test the $9 area support, with the danger back to the lower limits of the trend around $7.50.'

There it is. All bases covered. The stock was either destined to climb to the sky or plunge by 40 percent. Happy investing!

To me, much of this activity fails to pass the pub test. I see charting as little removed from the interpretations delivered by haruspices in Roman times based on their examination of the entrails of dead animals.

In saying that, am I denying that there are any successful traders out there? Not at all. In fact, there are. But they don't seek their trading edge by doodling on sheets of paper or placing bets based on false signals delivered by proprietary charting software.

My advice to you is to put an extra chunk of wax in each ear when sailing past the siren-infested island of Charticus!

Chapter 8

The Siren Song of Stock Picking

'There is general agreement among researchers that nearly all stock pickers, whether they know it or not – and few of them do – are playing a game of chance.'
– Daniel Kahneman

Aussie baby boomers will remember the fervent rivalry that once existed between Ford and Holden drivers. AFL supporters know all about the competitive friction that exists between Collingwood and Carlton supporters. For centuries wars have raged between those with differing religious beliefs. And so the list goes on…

Passionately held dichotomies of opinion can be seen in many walks of life. In the world of finance, it's a case of technical analysts warring with fundamental analysts.

In the previous chapter I discussed technical analysts. They believe that everything required to make successful trading and investing decisions is embodied in the charts.

Fundamental analysts (also referred to as 'stock pickers') seek their investment inspiration elsewhere. They acknowledge that shares are nothing more than small slices of large businesses. So, the key to investment success, they say, is to approach investing as a potential business owner would.

Fundamental analysts study business sectors. They scour trade reports and financial statements. They hang on the words of CEOs. They seek out companies with growth potential and shun those which are in decline.

Like technical analysts, fundamental analysts also watch stock prices, but they do it for an entirely different reason than technical analysts do. They don't seek patterns and trends. Rather, they are on the lookout for opportunities either to buy stocks cheaply or to sell them for more than they believe they are worth. In order to do that, fundamental analysts form their own, independent view about what a company's shares are worth. Then they compare their valuation to the price at which those shares are trading on the stock market and, if they spot a promising company being offered at a cheap or fair price, then they might be tempted to buy it.

By building a portfolio comprising the shares of sound companies purchased at attractive prices, they hope to achieve a superior investment return to that achieved by an investment in the broader stock market. In financial parlance, through their effort and skill, they seek to achieve 'alpha'.

But, is this possible? Does fundamental analysis actually work? Can you tell ahead of time how a company is going to perform? And can you tell whether the current share price is a favourable one?

Now, considering the absolute shellacking that I gave to technical analysis in the last chapter, I know what you're thinking right now: that I've chosen my team and it must be the fundamental analysis, stock-picking team, and that I'm about to now tell you all the reasons stock pickers are winners.

Well, you'd be wrong! Just take another look at the chapter heading: 'The Siren Song of Stock Picking'. And take another look at the Daniel Kahneman quote at the beginning of the chapter.

The fact is that most stock pickers are like the novice violin player who has just pulled the Stradivarius out of its case for the very first time. He tucks the instrument under his chin, drags the bow across its strings and then, just as the first agonising screech is heard, tips one ear to the telephone in anticipation of a call from Carnegie Hall.

You see, even if stock picking appears to be a supremely logical activity, it's a long, long road from the logical to the possible. I apologise to all those Tony Robbins aficionados out there but let's not get our capabilities mixed up with our possibilities. Look, there are some skilful stock pickers out there, but they are as few and far between as world-class violinists.

Let's dig a little deeper.

The three stock prices

As I see it, three different prices can be pinned on a stock.

First up there is the market price. That's the price that a stock last traded at on the stock market. It's easily definable and it's indisputable.

The other two prices take a bit more explaining.

The second price is a consideration of what the stock is *really* worth. Now, you might say that, surely, what a stock is really worth is the market price. After all, that's the price that you can sell it for (if you own it), or the price that you need to pay (in order to own it). So, why the distinction?

I agree that the market price defines its worth if you want to buy or sell it right now. But what if you aren't about to buy or sell right now? Bear with me here.

If you are planning to hang onto a stock rather than sell it now, then what a stock is worth today can be viewed in an entirely different way. Your stock is now worth what it will deliver back to you during your period of ownership. That worth will come in the form of dividends during your period of ownership plus the ultimate sale price when you come to sell it. Unfortunately, because you don't have a crystal ball, you can't possibly know for sure right now what those future amounts will be. Added to the problem is the uncertainty of inflation – you don't know what those future amounts will be worth in today's dollars.

All that uncertainty will evaporate one day – that's the day you sell and you get to look back at your investment's performance. Then you will know for sure what this second price is. But you don't know today.

Now let's talk about the third price.

In the absence of a time machine to transport you into the future to find out what the second price is, analysts estimate (today) what those future cash flows *might* be. They then use them to calculate the price they'd be prepared to pay for that stock today. Analysts refer to this as the 'intrinsic value'.

It involves crystal ball gazing, and that means it's never going to be a rock-solid price. It's based on estimates and judgments regarding the future. The skilled stock picker is banking on their estimates being closer to the mark than most others are. It's like that game of throwing coins towards a wall – the person whose coin lands closest to the wall is the winner. Or, in this case, the analysts with the best estimates (today) are the winners (in the future).

You might have already heard of the term intrinsic value. It's regularly thrown around by professional investor types. They often mistakenly use the term with great confidence and authority. They say things like, 'The intrinsic value of ACME Inc. is $2.50 per share. And, since it's trading on the stock market at only $1.35, then I strongly recommend it as a buy!'

The problem is that, for analysts to calculate these intrinsic values, they have to come up with lots of estimates and assumptions about an uncertain future. And that means a stock's intrinsic value is a pretty rubbery figure at the best of times. For example:

- What are the company's future prospects?
- Are its competitors a threat?
- What technologies are on the horizon that might impact its business?
- Where are interest rates heading? (Interest rates are one of the many influences on share prices.)
- Where are its costs of production heading?

And on… and on… and on.

Of course, none of these things can be known with any certainty, and that's why analysts can only ever use estimates. And we know how reliable they can be! Analysts then throw all these uncertain judgments and estimates into a simple mathematical formula to come up with their estimate of intrinsic value – that is, our third price.

In this sense intrinsic values are a fiction generated within the minds of analysts. And that's not such a reliable thing. Investors have long known that investment judgment is coloured by bias and emotion. Englishman John Houghton wrote, as far back as 1694, that shares 'rise and fall according to hopes and fears'.

There is a very, very high chance that time will show most analyst-derived intrinsic values to have been very, very wrong. Put another way, if you lined up 100 analysts and asked them what a quoted stock is really worth, then you could potentially end up with 100 different intrinsic values.

Even so, intrinsic values tend to cluster. That's because analysts are strongly influenced in their determination of intrinsic value by two main things:

1. the prevailing market price
2. the intrinsic values that other analysts are coming up with.

Analysts are like schoolkids cheating in an exam: they look over their shoulder to check out what intrinsic value the other guys are coming up with before they come up with their own. Do you blame them? After all, there is safety in numbers. It's better for an analyst's reputation if, when they are wrong, everyone else is wrong with them. As John Maynard Keynes wrote in *The General Theory of Employment, Interest and Money* (commonly referred to simply as *The General Theory*), 'Worldly wisdom teaches that it is better for reputation to fail conventionally than to succeed unconventionally'.

But the fact is that, in order to be a genuine winner at the game of fundamental analysis, you have to back your own judgment, not that of others. That judgment needs to come from a base of superior knowledge and superior analysis.

It's a really tough gig to become the best. And it's only the best who end up playing at Carnegie Hall.

Skill and practice. Skill and practice. Skill and practice.

The average punter's view on stock picking

If a stranger came up to you in the street and asked you to lend him $100, it's extremely unlikely that you would. But, if a good friend asked you the same question, then there's a fair chance that you'd open your wallet.

Why the different reactions? After all, it was the same question: 'Can you lend me $100?'

Effectively it's all about risk, and the risk here is that you don't get paid back the $100.

What if a friend of a friend asked you to lend him $100? Maybe it is the first time that you've met this guy. But, hey, he couldn't be too bad, could he? After all, he's a friend of your friend.

You might perceive the risk to be less than lending to a perfect stranger. But you are likely to feel hesitant. You might consider lending him the money. But, equally, you might refuse.

What if the same friend of a friend now told you that, in return for the $100 loan, he'd pay you back $1000? That sounds far more appealing, doesn't it? You're more likely to give this offer serious consideration.

Why the different reactions? Again, it was the same question.

Because it's now also about return. The potential now exists for a big return on your money.

These simple examples distil what investing is all about. It's about giving up a quantifiable amount of money today in the expectation of receiving a larger amount back in the future, and also giving consideration to the risk associated with the deal. Investing is all about risk and reward; it's a balancing act whereby you want to minimise the risk and maximise the return.

But here's the bind: coming up with a precise measure for both risk and return is extremely difficult. In fact, in most situations it's impossible. It usually boils down to judgment.

I now want to direct this discussion to the valuation of shares. Conceptually, a share is worth the present value of all the cash flows that ownership of that share will deliver back to you in the future. There are two principal cash flows that you will receive after you buy it: the future dividends that it pays you and the price that you eventually sell it for when you relinquish ownership. Because you can't reliably predict any of those future payments, you must rely on a judgment of what they might be.

But you're not finished yet. You must now adjust your estimates of those payments for two further factors:

1. the riskiness of the investment (the higher the risk, the less likely that you will receive the future payments; you acknowledge this by placing lesser values on payments that are riskier)
2. inflation (the higher the anticipated inflation, the lower the value you will place on future payments).

The difficulties here are that risk is a nebulous concept and inflation is unknown. Despite these difficulties, analysts have to push on in order to come up with their independent stock valuations (intrinsic values). Now, the tools and concepts analysts use to value stocks that I have discussed have been around for centuries. Even so, most investors aren't bothered to use them when they invest.

For now, that's all I want to say about stock valuation. It's not my intention with this book to turn you into stock pickers. My job is done if you now have a better appreciation of the fundamental concepts. (If you are interested in gaining a deeper understanding of how to value stocks then I'd recommend that you read my second book: *Uncommon Sense: Investment Wisdom Since the Stock Market's Dawn.*)

The story of MMM

The following story shows how caution can be thrown to the wind when dreams of massive returns outweigh what might be otherwise obvious risks.

MMM was a Russian 'investment company' headed by a guy called Sergei Mavrodi back in the 1990s. Sergei spent millions on Russian TV promoting his company. He delivered his message through a fictional MMM shareholder called Lyonya Golubakov. Lyonya, by investing in MMM, had discovered the key to immense wealth. A gullible investing public was told that, by investing in MMM, a 3000 percent annual return could be delivered.

Lots of people bought the story. At its peak MMM had around 2 million shareholders and was taking in around US$11 million of new money per day.

So, what did the company MMM actually do? It did nothing! It had no operations, no earnings, no investments and no financial strategy. But nor did it pretend to do any of those things. All it did was collect people's money! When polled, virtually all of the shareholders admitted to having no knowledge of what MMM did.

So, what was the main reason behind people buying shares in the company? It was because they saw the share price rocketing. The shares were issued in February 1994 and by July 23 of the same year they had climbed from $1 to $65.

The Russian government began investigating MMM in mid-1994. Warnings were soon issued to the public and the stock collapsed from $60 to 45 cents within a period of two days.

Now you'd reckon that would have been the end of the story. But it isn't. This story just keeps getting better – or, should I say, worse! So, I feel compelled to share the sequel with you.

Despite getting caught peddling a scam, Movradi just wouldn't lie down. He blamed the price collapse on government interference. He promised that the share price would recover and that MMM shares would soon be issued in the USA and Europe. Some of the public believed him and buying picked up in August.

However, soon after that, Mavrodi was charged with tax evasion.

Still Mavrodi fought on! Russian law provided immunity from conviction for members of parliament for all but serious crimes. So, Mavrodi ran for parliament. His media blitz told voters that he would save MMM and thereby return investors their money. They believed him and he won the election. He also saved himself from a jail term.

At the celebration of his election victory, Mavrodi made a statement that MMM wasn't going to be resurrected. He walked away with his fortune intact.

Mavrodi's immunity was nullified in 1995 and he was arrested in 2003 after eight years on the run. He did a brief stint in prison and is now a free man.

It's a tall story that couldn't happen to you, right?

Of course it could happen to you. I could write a book containing stories just like that one, and I could fill it with investment scams and stories that have happened in Australia alone. Otherwise intelligent people are easily duped. (The big one that's happening as I write this book is crypto scams. People are providing fraudsters access to their bank accounts after being shown fake profits from early 'trades'.)

The bottom line is that, if you have no appreciation for the true value of what you're buying, then you leave yourself wide open to being scammed.

The father of security analysis

Let's hear again from Benjamin Graham, Warren Buffett's mentor. Graham was a stock picker to his bootstraps. Deep into his classic 1934 tome *Security Analysis*, Graham poses the question as to whether stock analysis is a worthwhile undertaking. His answer to the question, which is perhaps the most insightful comment in a book that has no shortage of insights, is that stock analysis has value 'only in the case of the exceptional common stock', and for stocks in general it must be considered 'either as a somewhat questionable aid to speculative judgment or as a highly illusionary method of aiming at values which defy calculation and which must somehow be calculated none the less.'

Let's dissect what Graham is saying here. The godfather of stock pickers is telling us, almost a century ago, that he believes stock picking is a futile process when applied to most companies – that its usefulness is limited to 'the exceptional common stock'. But it would seem that most Graham devotees have missed this finer point. Nearly all listed stocks have analysts dedicated to cover them. Graham believed this to be an unnecessary and futile exercise.

So, how do you identify exceptional businesses? Unfortunately, they don't come with an asterisk attached. It requires a deep appreciation of the internal operations of the company being researched. In other words, it takes years of experience and hard work to know what you are looking for and what you are looking at. And, as Francis Wrigley Hirst wrote back in 1911, 'Those who understand a business or an institution best are those who have made it or grown up with it'. Based on Hirst's assessment an analyst's aim should be to understand a business as well as its founding CEO does or did.

Once the analyst identifies that great company, then comes the need to get a handle on what it is worth – the intrinsic value determination. The intrinsic value is then compared to the price that it is trading for on the stock market (the market price) to determine whether the stock market is offering it at an attractive price or not. Stock picking is essentially a constant search for opportunity.

The stock picker cannot hope to determine the value of any business without an intimate understanding of its operations. And that is where novices regularly get tripped up.

Stock valuation formulae

Allow me a slight diversion here regarding stock valuation, or intrinsic value calculation.

There are various valuation formulae that analysts use to 'calculate' an intrinsic value for the stocks that they study. The analyst plugs estimates – which they are able to derive because they understand the business – into their preferred intrinsic value formula. There are many such formulae. They might appear to be different, but the fact is that almost all are algebraic variations of the same mathematical concept: the discounting of future cash flows.

I won't delve into things much further, but anyone with a moderate level of mathematical acumen can get their head around these formulae within an hour (or probably minutes if they are a savant!).

The problem is that the novice investor, on discovering any one of these formulae for the first time, believes they have found the magic key to unlock the secret door of investing. But understanding these formulae offers the novice no meaningful benefit and certainly no investing edge. The formulae require inputs, which are essentially intelligent estimates. The player who wins at this game is the one who comes up with the best estimates. And the best estimates are born from an extreme amount of hard work and superior (might I say unique) insight.

Without the effort, the insight and sound estimates, the formulae are worthless, and the intrinsic values that they deliver are nothing more than fool's gold.

But I'm ready to start investing – I've read all the Warren Buffett books!

Unless you've been living under a rock, you'll probably know that US investor Warren Buffett has made quite an impression on the investment community over the past several decades. He's generated massive returns for the shareholders of Berkshire Hathaway, the company that he heads. Not surprisingly, countless investors around the world have dreamed of emulating but a fraction of his success.

Buffett's investment principles are easy to track down, so I'm not going to describe them in any detail here. But I do want to list ten of his commandments (my term, not his). Buffett has often stated that the companies he seeks should possess the following characteristics:

1. long track record of adding value
2. durable competitive advantage
3. easy to understand
4. strong and passionate management
5. possess pricing power

6. financial strength (sound balance sheet)
7. strong cash flow
8. high and persistent return on equity (ROE)
9. strong and positive 'owner's earnings' (more useful than reported net profit)
10. trading at a fair or cheap price.

So, why doesn't everyone simply apply these principles and make a motza? I've just discussed why.

Even the founders didn't know what they were sitting on!

Most shareholders care little about understanding the businesses that they invest in. Rather, they view their companies as price-fluctuating stock codes. But John Maynard Keynes was a member of that rare group of investors who did understand how real businesspeople (as opposed to shareholders and analysts) think. He wrote in *The General Theory*:

> 'A large proportion of our positive activities depend on spontaneous optimism rather than on a mathematical expectation, whether moral or hedonistic or economic. Most, probably, of our decisions to do something positive, the full consequences of which will be drawn out over many days to come, can only be taken as a result of animal spirits – of a spontaneous urge to action rather than inaction, and not as the outcome of a weighted average of quantitative benefits multiplied by quantitative probabilities.'

What Keynes is saying here, if we relate his words to the founders and builders of businesses, is that most aren't driven solely by economic considerations. Often, they are simply driven by a burning desire to develop that type of business.

Shareholders are typically blind to this. Their world is a more mercenary one.

Like Keynes, Buffett appreciates this distinction well. Case in point: he likes to buy companies that are still being managed by their founder. But that's not to say that Buffett invests in start-ups. Investing in companies in their formative years is a gamble. Buffett appreciates that.

To demonstrate what I'm talking about, let's take a look at three household names. No one would deny that Apple, Google and Nike are great businesses today. So, I suspect that you will be surprised by what I'm about to tell you.

Let's kick off with electronic product producer Apple. The stock market loves Apple. Its share growth has been explosive. So, it's no surprise that people fantasise about having bought Apple shares years ago when its shares were much, much cheaper than they are today. To demonstrate, I googled 'What would I be worth today if I'd invested in the Apple float?' and almost three million results came up!

At the time of writing, and since being floated on the US stock market back in 1980, its share price has multiplied by a massive 1640 times (allowing for stock splits). It means that $1000 invested back then would now be worth $1.64 million.

But wait, there's more. That's just the share price. That figure is a gross understatement of how rewarding an investment in Apple would have been. We should also factor in the dividends that it has paid along the way. If you'd received – and then reinvested – those dividends back into more Apple shares, then your returns would have been turbocharged way beyond 1640 times.

Apple's colossal climb seems obvious to us now but, for years, its future success was far from certain. In its formative years Apple's future was as precarious as a snowflake on a hot summer's day. Not even the three founders of Apple – Steve Jobs, Steve Wozniak and Ronald Wayne – realised what a great success Apple would eventually become. In fact, not one of them had enough confidence in the company's future to hang onto their founding shares.

By 1985 Steve Jobs had reduced his stake in Apple to just one solitary share. After being unceremoniously sacked from Apple's board, he maintained that token ownership so that he could keep an eye on how things were going inside the company that he founded.

Fellow co-founder Steve Wozniak (who developed Apple's first computer) also sold his stock early on. In 1980, when Apple shares were first offered to the public through its IPO, Wozniak owned 8.7 percent of the company. Today, a shareholding of that magnitude is worth $197 billion (and yes, that's billion with a 'b'). While Wozniak is certainly no pauper today, most of the dividends that he receives are from companies other than Apple.

The third co-founder, Ronald Wayne, sold his 10 percent stake in Apple just days after the company was founded back in 1976 for the princely sum of $2300. Wayne has since stated that it was 'the best decision with the information available to me at the time'. He has also stated that he could see 'significant bumps along the way and I couldn't risk it'. Wayne was right about the significant bumps: for years Apple was a dodgy investment. In 1997, a full 21 years after it was founded, Apple was on the brink of bankruptcy.

So, if Apple's founders opted out early and its future continued to be uncertain for a couple of decades, then I can now confidently say two things to you:

1. It's unlikely that you would have invested in Apple early on (and, in fact, it's unlikely that you would have even known it existed).
2. Even if you had bought Apple shares in the initial 1980 stock offering, it is extremely unlikely that you would still hold them today. All the bad news coming out of the company over the years would likely have seen you run scared and ditch your shares long ago.

Let's now turn our attention to Google (Alphabet Inc.). Today, the company is a $1.3-trillion tech powerhouse. But it wasn't always like that. Just one year after creating Google, co-founders Larry Page and Sergey Brin were prepared to sell their company for less than $1 million.

The sale didn't proceed because the prospective buyer claimed that their asking price was too high.

Today, through their part ownership of Alphabet, each of the co-founders is worth about $80 billion. Lucky that they didn't sell!

Do you now wish that you had bought Alphabet shares 20 years ago? It's unlikely that you would have. At the time, neither of its founders appreciated what their business would one day be worth, so why should you have?

A very similar story can be told of Phil Knight, the founder of Nike. In 1964 Phil Knight kicked off his business by selling sports shoes from the boot of his car. This modest enterprise was to become the sportswear powerhouse Nike. Nike's corporate road has been an extremely rocky one since its humble beginnings. It almost went broke several times. In 1970 the company was suffering a severe cash flow problem. At the time, Knight tried to sell 30 percent of the company in an effort to raise $300,000. No one was interested. An employee and his mother pitched in a combined $300. That was it! The company is now worth $135 billion.

Let me finish with the following quote from US investor Joel Greenblatt, which sums up this chapter beautifully:

> 'Choosing individual stocks without any idea of what you're looking for is like running through a dynamite factory with a burning match. You may live, but you're still an idiot.'

Happy stock picking!

Chapter 9

Sirens in Pinstripe Suits

'Statistically a broad-based stock index fund will outperform most actively managed equity portfolios.'
– Paul Samuelson

By now you might be feeling a little disheartened. You're probably starting to appreciate how difficult it is to excel at this investing caper.

Well, you could always call in the cavalry if you feel that you're not up to the job. You see, there are guns for hire out there. They are trained professional investors called fund managers. Just hand your money over to them and they will invest it for you. For a fee, of course.

At first brush that seems to make a lot of sense. After all, we get our cars serviced by mechanics, our teeth looked after by dentists and our houses built by qualified tradespeople. So, why not get our money looked after by professional fund managers?

I hope to answer that question in this chapter.

It's a zero-sum game

So, how good are fund managers? And how much do they charge for their services?

I'll get to their ability in a moment but, on average, retail fund managers charge a fee of around 1 to 1.5 percent of funds under management. That means, if a fund manager controls a $900 million fund, then they will get around $9 million to $13 million in annual fees.

You can see why the name of the game for these guys is size. It takes a manager little extra effort to manage a $2 billion fund compared to a $1 billion fund, yet they would receive double the fees.

Consider the fees generated by Australia's superannuation industry. Australians currently have $3.4 trillion invested in super. This delivers a fee feeding frenzy for fund managers, with $34 billion extracted from investor's accounts annually.

As you can see, professional investing is big business.

It's a negative-sum game

I now want you to consider a hypothetical world where there are no fund managers. In this world investors don't undertake any stock analysis. Each investor is simply paid a share of the total profits delivered by all companies listed on the stock market.

Every dollar of corporate profit ends up in investors' pockets and each investor's share of those profits is determined solely by the size of their investment. There are no winners and no losers, no investors who outperform the market and none who underperform it.

Imagine, now, that this world is invaded by fund managers. The invaders tell the resident investors that they will now start selecting the best stocks for them in an effort to outperform the average market return, and for their services they will charge a fee. In order to convince the residents of the benefits of this new arrangement, each fund manager stands in turn and addresses the crowd of investors. Each fund manager promises a wonderful new world where their stock-picking skills will deliver higher future returns to all who choose them as their fund manager.

Upon completion of their marketing spiel, one wise old resident yells out from the back of the crowd, 'Each of you has promised to deliver us better returns than we were receiving before you came along. But the only source of income here is the profits that our companies have been distributing to us for years. Yet you plan to extract your fees from those profits before you distribute the remainder to us. So, how can we all be better off? It seems to me that, as a group, we are going to be worse off to the tune of all the fees that you charge us!'

Well, of course, such a hypothetical world doesn't exist. But the message the story delivers is real. The fees that professional fund managers charge must come from company profits before those profits are distributed to investors. (Of course, there are also many other costs that the stock investor must bear. Broking fees, corporate lawyers, auditing accountants… and so the list goes on.) This is exactly why investment legend John Bogle stated, 'It's not a zero-sum game. It's a negative sum game'. Fund managers know this – that, considered as a group, investors have to be worse off. So, their marketing message focuses very much on their individual capacity to deliver superior performance when compared to the other fund managers.

But not all can be winners. Investors, therefore, need a way to measure fund manager performance so that they know which fund manager to choose. Rightly or wrongly, this is typically done in two main ways:

1. by comparing a fund's performance against a general stock market index. You likely hear about these stock indices every night on the finance news. The best known in Australia are the S&P/ASX 200 and the All Ordinaries index. Both measure the combined performance of the biggest companies on the Aussie share market
2. by comparing their investment returns to the investment returns delivered by their peers.

Unfortunately, both of these measures have significant failings. But, rather than acknowledging these failings, fund managers employ them to their advantage.

So, let's lift the lid on this whole con game.

First up, let's take a look at Aussie equity funds (those that invest mainly in ASX-listed shares). They typically benchmark their performance against a general stock market index such as the S&P/ASX 200 or The All Ordinaries index. In doing this the fund managers are comparing the returns that they achieve against the return delivered by the broader stock market.

To find out how they perform based on this yardstick, let me now introduce you to SPIVA.

SPIVA

Now, it was never my intention to confound you with financial jargon. So, a bit of jargon busting is required here. SPIVA is an acronym for S&P Indices Versus Active [managers].

It was dreamed up by S&P Dow Jones Indices. So, who is S&P Dow Jones Indices? To quote their own website, they claim to be:

> '... the world's leading resource for benchmarks and investable indices. Our solutions are widely considered indispensable in tracking market performance, evaluating portfolios, and developing investment strategies.'

As well as constructing indices that are used by share investors and fund managers around the globe, S&P Dow Jones Indices has also compiled over 20 years of data looking at the performance of more than 10,000 actively managed funds (you know, the guys and girls who all claim to be market beaters). The SPIVA results, which are posted on the S&P Dow Jones website, make for some very interesting reading.

Let's kick things off by looking at the performance of active fund managers over the past five years. Basically, their performance has been atrocious. In every country and continent studied, more active funds underperformed their respective broad-based stock market index than outperformed it. And, in each country looked at, the percentage of managers who underperformed the benchmark was substantial.

Canada should hang its head in shame: 96 percent of its active funds underperformed the index. In the USA, 85 percent of active funds underperformed the index. In Australia the underperformers totalled 74 percent (83 percent over the past 15 years).

In their defence, these results are measured after their fees have been extracted. The benchmark indices against which the active fund managers are being compared aren't impacted by this drag. But, even before fees are deducted, more active fund managers underperform the benchmarks than outperform them. What's more, fees are an essential consideration for investors; after all, it's post-fee dollars that end up in investors' pockets.

As the wise old resident in our earlier hypothetical investment world yelled out from the crowd, 'It seems to me that, as a group, we investors are going to be worse off to the tune of all the fees that you charge us!' And that has proven to be the case in the real world. The research tells us that the great majority of fund managers can't even generate enough alpha (outperformance) to cover the fees that they charge.

To demonstrate this fact, look no further than the additional research undertaken by S&P Dow Jones Indices. They generate data on what they call 'Institutional SPIVA.' This research adds back the fees that managers charge to their investment returns. By measuring the investment results of managers before fees are deducted, their results can be directly compared to the market indices. Here are their year-end 2021 findings for US institutional fund managers: '78% of both large-cap institutional accounts and large-cap mutual fund managers underperformed the S&P 500 Index over the 10-year period ending December 31, 2021.'

But it gets worse…

Can you pick an active fund based on their record?

Faced with these sad statistics, I can hear you right now saying, 'OK, so if around 80 percent of active fund managers underperform the benchmark, that must mean 20 percent outperform. So, I'll simply choose one of the outperformers and invest my money with them'. This now leads me to the second method that is used to assess fund manager performance: comparing their performance to that of their peers.

We feel comfortable with the concept of peer performance comparisons. Case in point, they are commonly employed in sports in the form of league tables; the cumulative performances of football, baseball and basketball teams are recorded throughout a season and then used to construct a league table. Not surprisingly, league tables are also constructed to compare the performance of active fund managers.

'So', I hear you say, 'hand me that league table. I'll soon find out which funds are in the top-performing 20 percent. I'll invest my money with the winner'.

Hang on… not so fast.

You see, the winner's podium is more like a revolving door than it is a podium. SPIVA looked at the top-performing 25 percent of fund managers in any given five-year period, and they found that less than half of them appeared in the top half of performers in the following five-year period. That's in keeping with chance playing a significant role in the determination of their position on the table.

The late, great John Bogle studied the annual investment performance of 681 US funds over the ten-year period between 1982 and 1992. He found that the top-performing fund in any single year was, on average, 100th in the following year. The average rank of the second-best performing fund was 383rd in the following year. And the average rank of the top 20 funds in the subsequent year was 284th.

Don't worry that Bogle's research is related to US funds. His results are in keeping with SPIVA's findings about Australian funds. In fact, it's a universal finding.

SPIVA's figures show that only one-fifth of the Aussie-run funds that found themselves in the top quartile in any year repeated their top-quartile performance in the subsequent year. Put another way, past results have shown there to be a greater than 80 percent chance that the 'top' fund in any particular year failed to shine the following year.

It doesn't matter what period of past performance you look at. Attempting to select a future winner by scanning last year's league table is pretty much akin to a crapshoot. The statistics that I have just listed are indicative of chance outcomes, not of skill. But you won't hear that fact acknowledged by the funds. Funds that find themselves at or near the top of the league table in any year love to advertise the fact heavily in their marketing brochures. So, what's going on here?

Despite SPIVA's findings, which show league tables are meaningless, fund managers continue to acknowledge them, because they know that Joe Public places faith in them. So, the funds are capitalising on a lucky placement at or near the top of a league ladder in any given year by falsely advertising it as evidence of their skill.

Dissecting luck from skill

It's easy to find out who the number one tennis player in the world is at any point in time. Elite tennis tournaments are constantly being played around the globe. Players are awarded points based on their performance at each tournament. These points are then used to construct a 'live' scoreboard with the world number one, whoever it is at that time, placed on top.

The fact is that sports league tables are far more useful than those used to display fund manager performance. We rarely see tennis players win a grand slam at Flushing Meadows or Roland-Garros who were 150th or 300th in the rankings the year before. It can happen, but it's rare. However, as already discussed, we regularly observe massive annual shifts in rank occurring with fund managers. Why the difference?

It's because the position on sports league tables is strongly correlated to skill. Such a correlation is virtually absent with fund managers.

Let's explore this some more. A world-number-one tennis player has a reasonable chance of reaching the finals of any tennis tournament that he or she enters. It isn't guaranteed, but there is a good chance. Case in point is Roger Federer, one of the greatest tennis players of all time. At one stage of his career, Federer spent 237 weeks as world number one. Nothing lucky about it; he was the best. Persistence like this characterises an activity where skill is a major determinant in the outcome, and 237 weeks straight of being on top spells persistence with a capital 'P' and skill with a capital 'S'.

Now, I'm the first to admit that luck can play a role in sporting outcomes. The let cord on match point. The serve that just nicked the outside of the service line in a crucial tie breaker. Even so, skill remains the predominant factor.

Time now for a story.

Occasionally I play golf with my son. Not often, just occasionally. Neither of us will ever pose a threat to Tiger Woods. It's not actually about golf; I simply enjoy getting out there on a sunny day and having a few laughs with my son (usually about our lousy golf swings).

During the course of one game, we caught up to a group of four golfers who were playing in front of us. Demonstrating impeccable golfing etiquette, they propped at the tee-off area and invited us to play through so that they wouldn't hold us up. Now, that meant I had to tee-off with an audience of five: my son and the four strangers.

If you had any appreciation of my golfing ability, then you'd understand that my tee-shots can end up anywhere. They could advance just ten feet in front of me. Or, I could swing and miss the ball altogether! So, with my gallery of spectators looking on, I kept my eye on the ball, swung my club back in a deep arc and let it rip.

After completing my shot, I timidly cast my gaze ten feet ahead to check where the ball had landed. But no, instead, it was tracing a perfectly straight line down the fairway as it disappeared into the distance. It was the best golf shot that I'd ever played in my life. And likely ever will be.

I just stood there looking straight ahead. I was too scared to turn around and look back at the others behind me. They would have seen the look of amazement on my face.

Then I heard one onlooker behind me whisper to the others, 'Gee, he's good'.

After my son played his shot, we marched off down the fairway.

To this day, if you asked any of those four strangers whether I was any good at golf, then you would undoubtedly receive the wrong answer. Their misperception regarding my golfing ability would have been based on a single observation.

You see, where luck is a major factor in determining outcomes, consistency is absent. I could have attempted that shot another 100 times and not repeated it.

So, let's summarise what I've been saying here:

- Where skill is the major influence on outcomes, consistency becomes obvious (like Roger Federer).
- Where luck is the major influence on outcomes, inconsistency is obvious (like fund managers).
- Where skill is the major determinant of outcomes, a single observation is possibly an indication of future outcomes (Roger again).
- Where luck is the major determinant of outcomes, a single observation is a very poor indication of future outcomes (unfortunately, this one is me playing golf, but it's fund managers as well).

If skill were the principal determining factor behind a fund manager doing well, then you'd expect to observe it repeated in subsequent years. And that we don't see. Put plainly, it's because luck is the principal determinant, which begs the question: is all investing (based on stock picking) purely luck?

For most people the answer is yes, it is. However, as you read on, you'll begin to understand that investment skills can be brought to bear by some rare and exceptional individuals.

So, can we quantify how much luck is involved in investing?

Can we get a handle on how much luck and how much skill determines the results displayed by professional investors? Not precisely. But research does provide us with a feel for things.

Nobel Memorial Prize–winning economist Eugene Fama and fellow researcher Professor Kenneth French undertook a novel experiment in order to study this very question. The two researchers used data based on the performance of more than 3156 actively managed US funds over a 22-year period from 1984 to 2006. When considered as a group, they found no statistically significant evidence of market-beating skill. And that was *before* fees were extracted.

Of course, studying average results doesn't prove that skilful fund managers don't exist. The presence of genuine skill or complete incompetence could have been masked by the large number of fund managers in the group. So, Fama and French searched for evidence of the exceptional, both good and bad.

In order to investigate how much of the observed performance could be attributed to chance, the researchers generated two graphs. The first showed the range of outcomes delivered by real-life fund managers. The second showed the range of outcomes generated from 10,000 random computer simulations (known to be pure chance). Then they superimposed the two graphs.

The two lines – the first real and the second randomly generated – were almost identical. Their study suggested that the results achieved by active fund managers could be explained almost entirely as being the result of chance.

But there were two small areas of their superimposed graphs where the two lines weren't perfectly aligned. The researchers concluded that, while luck was the principal influence, there was a minor part of investment outcomes that luck couldn't explain. They suggested that this was the result of a small number of managers demonstrating skill and a small number of managers demonstrating incompetence.

So, does this study offer us a glimmer of hope that there are some market-beating fund managers out there? And, if we had some way of identifying them, then could we profit from their skill?

Alas, for a number of reasons, Fama and French's findings are of no practical benefit when it comes to identifying management skills. First up, their study was retrospective, and that doesn't solve the problem that you have to identify the skilful *before* you invest your money. Problematically, there is no way of identifying them early on, before they outperform. That would be like knowing the outcome of a horse race before the race is run. By the time you are able to identify the outperformers, they could well be retired, in the twilight years of their careers, or the fund they once managed might not exist anymore.

And don't forget that, even for the skilful, luck remains the predominant determinant of outcomes. Even if you had a way of identifying their skill at an early stage (which you don't), then bad luck might be the principal determinant of their future results.

And finally – and this is the absolute clincher – Fama and French quantified the excess return that the most skilful group appeared to be achieving over the long term and it was a meagre 0.5 percent annually. It's important to remember that Fama and French used returns *before* fees to generate these findings; after deducting their sizable management fees, this token outperformance was totally wiped out.

Don't get me wrong. There are investors out there who are capable of outperforming the market when observed over extended periods. But such individuals are *extremely* rare – so rare are they that Fama and French's study failed to identify them. Also, outperformers don't necessarily operate in the funds management business, preferring to harness their skills for their own benefit.

I'll be talking more about these exceptional individuals later on.

Time to hear from the fund managers

As they say in the classics, there are two sides to every story. The story so far has been based on some pretty heavy-hitting research, but we have yet to hear from the fund managers. After all, they aren't going to take this sort of talk lying down, are they? It's bad for business!

Fund managers prefer to interpret the league tables differently. They are in the business of attracting fresh money to their funds. They like it that so many ill-informed investors place their blind trust in the tables. So, when a fund is awarded the apparent honour of being last year's top performer, then the fund's marketing department starts salivating.

They know that the investing public doesn't appreciate any of the research findings that I've mentioned in this chapter so far.

But the public does watch TV, listen to the radio and read the newspapers. It means that when the top fund manager is interviewed on the small screen, or they are mentioned in the newspapers, potential investors sit up and pay attention. In fact, I would suggest that few of the financial journos who write the articles extolling fund managers' results understand the numbers themselves. Given that these league tables are typically published annually, it means that fund managers are awarded bragging rights for an entire year (until next year's lottery is drawn).

By way of example, I was more than a little amused by a newspaper article that I read a couple of years back. It was written by a budding fund manager and part-time media commentator. He was talking about his own fund and his article embodied a fair deal of 'artistic licence': 'Investors need to be careful not to over-allocate toward passive strategies which could gradually erode their capital. Active management was key'.

He offered no confirming evidence for his statement. But he did offer a way for readers to identify the best managers: 'Look up the best performers in the past year. Or, of course, you could ask me how I do it'.

Well, we've already dealt with the problems associated with looking up the best performers in the past year. Clearly this guy missed the memo. But what of his suggestion to ask his humble self how he went about outperforming the market?

I didn't need to ask him. Five weeks later his fund reported its past performance. Since inception it delivered an average (geometric) annual return of 2.59 percent. This was before management fees were extracted (which were hefty). After fees, the average annual percentage return to investors in his fund had a '1' in front of it.

So, how did his fund's performance compare to its chosen benchmark? He used the ASX 300 total return index, which delivered an annual average return of 6.14 percent over the same period.

Hmmm... that's quite a difference. He didn't mention that in his self-promoting newspaper article.

Let me share with you another example of what I've been talking about. A couple of years ago an Aussie investment fund was hailed by the financial press as being in a league of its own. For the financial year ending June 2021 it delivered its members a return of 93 percent while the general stock market index (ASX 200) delivered a positive return of 25 percent for the same period. A prominent newspaper declared the fund's youthful founder to be a 'wunderkind'.

In order to achieve a return like that, this fund had to go out on a very long limb. The assets that it held had to differ greatly from the constituents of the benchmark index. The trouble with this strategy is that the long limb that the fund climbed out on could prove to be the wrong limb to be out on in subsequent years.

It astounded me that finance commentators, who should know better, were committing exactly the crime that I have been talking about in this chapter: they were hailing pure luck as profound skill. I ask, had no one read the SPIVA research?

So, how did the wunderkind go in the year that followed? In the financial year ending June 2022 his fund crashed. It delivered a catastrophic negative 71.18 percent. That year the broader Australian share market delivered a far more palatable negative 10 percent. After fees – yes, hefty fees were still charged in the losing year! – investors who had rushed into the fund on the back of glowing newspaper reports had close to three quarters of their money wiped.

Since the fund's inception (which includes the freak good year) investors would have been far better served if they had simply placed their money in an index fund.

How am I going so far?

OK, have I convinced you yet? At the very least I hope that you will now view league tables for fund managers in a very different light.

If not, then you're an extremely tough nut to crack – you remind me of Greek philosopher Dio Chrysostom's declaration almost 2000 years ago: 'Why oh why are humans so hard to teach, but so easy to deceive'.

Identifying investment skill

Given everything that I've said so far, how does a layperson know whether the professionals that they turn to are serving up hot tips or hot air? League tables are useless. Advertising blurbs are self-serving. Even the newspapers are quite capable of dishing up fake news. And, unlike watching a skilled sportsperson or musician in action, you can't gain any sense of a fund manager's skill simply by watching them in action. Think about what they do all day: sitting at their desk reading reports and plugging away at their computer. What is there to judge?

In the absence of any meaningful performance benchmarks, some people turn to the irrelevant in order to judge the capability of fund managers. For example, they might not like the way that the fund manager stutters when interviewed on TV. Or they might not like her hair. Or he's too old. Or she's too young. Or maybe it's the way the fund manager speaks: that he sounds articulate and impressive when asked a question on TV. The viewer might not understand what he was talking about, but he did appear to be knowledgeable, didn't he? And that was such a nice suit he was wearing.

The real answer to the question of how skill can be identified is far more obscure than anything that I've talked about so far. Importantly, it boils down to the investment process that is employed by the fund manager. They need to employ a process that delivers them a genuine edge. This process won't guarantee investment success all the time; in fact, successful fund managers often get it wrong. They accept this, appreciating that their sport is played in an arena largely characterised by chance. But they have discovered an edge that will tip the odds of winning in their favour, provided that they play for long enough. They appreciate that the aim of the game isn't to win every point; rather, it's to win the long game.

But here's the catch. Two things need to happen for a layperson to identify that skill:

1. The fund manager needs to invite them into their office, sit them down and explain in detail what their modus operandi is.

2. The layperson needs to possess the smarts to know that particular modus operandi will actually work.

It has nothing to do with appearances. The layperson must be able to genuinely recognise that such an edge exists. And let's be honest here, if you are able to identify that skill in another person then you aren't a layperson – you must be truly skilful yourself. And, if you are skilful, then why not employ that skill for your own benefit?

Complicating things even further is that the skills that deliver success change over time. Truly skilful investors need to periodically reinvent themselves in order to remain on the cutting edge of their game. Processes that have defined skill in the past eventually become widely known and, when that happens, they no longer provide an edge.

Why experience isn't being transferred into skill

Maybe, despite all the facts that I've presented, you are still struggling to believe what I've been saying. Don't worry. It's entirely normal for you to think that way. In fact, it's innate.

Psychologist and Nobel laureate Daniel Kahneman has offered an explanation why we underplay cold, hard evidence, especially when it is presented in the form of statistic-based facts. He has stated that our mind is strongly biased toward causal explanations and does not deal well with mere statistics.

The causal explanation here is that we expect work and effort to invariably be converted into skill. And, in most pursuits, it is. So, why aren't all those clever and hardworking financial analysts and fund managers being rewarded for their efforts?

Kahneman has also answered this one. In his book *Thinking, Fast and Slow* he wrote that two basic conditions are required to develop a skill:

1. plenty of practice
2. an environment that is sufficiently consistent.

Both of these conditions are met in many, many areas of life. Take, for example, skilled surgeons, musicians, carpenters and tennis players. After hundreds, if not thousands of hours, they learn how to incise, pluck, hit or swing much more skilfully than your average Joe. Their environment is sufficiently consistent to convert their practice into skill. Consider also the consistent environment that a golfer operates in:, that little white ball that they aim to whack over the horizon sits perfectly still while they wind up their swing (although wind and other playing conditions on the day will also affect the result).

Alas, consistency is not a feature found in the financial markets. Financial experts might put in the hours, but they are operating within an environment characterised by chaos. Their playing field is unfolding before their eyes, and every decision they make is ultimately judged in an environment that was unknown to them when the decision was first made.

Consistency is all but absent. Only those investors who can identify 'snippets' or 'small windows' of consistency among all that chaos have any hope of achieving favourable outcomes through the application of skill. And most investors, including most active fund managers, are incapable of identifying any snippets of consistency that they can profit from.

How has this reality impacted my own thinking?

I kicked off my investing career decades ago, all bright-eyed and bushy-tailed. At the time I appreciated little of what I've written about in this book. Back then I felt that, with enough hard work and accumulated knowledge, I was assured of outperforming the market averages.

I now think differently; or should I say that I now have some basis upon which to form a realistic opinion on the matter. I've now had a long exposure to the financial markets. I've studied accounting, economics and corporate finance. I've worked in banking and stock broking. I worked for nine years as a stock analyst and even longer as a finance writer. I've written books about investing, including one on the history of stock valuation. I've given lectures on finance both in Australia and overseas. I ran an investment portfolio that bettered market returns over the multi-year period when I made the calls. My personal stock portfolio has delivered seven figures of excess absolute dollar return when compared to market returns.

Yet, I consider none of it to be a big deal. And that's because none of it proves that I earned one single dollar of skill-determined outperformance.

With that background, let me now share my belief regarding my own efforts to select individual stocks. After a lifetime of effort, I now feel like the old greyhound that John Bogle describes in his book *Enough*. He tells of a conversation between a preacher and a retired greyhound. The greyhound was not too old to continue racing, had been successful and was treated well, yet it had chosen to quit. 'Why?' the preacher pressed. The greyhound replied, 'I just quit because after all that running and running and running, I found out that the rabbit I was chasing wasn't even real'.

Just like the old greyhound, I have come to realise that the outsized returns I had believed I was chasing might not have been real. Maybe I'd simply been lucky. So, like the greyhound, I stopped running. I cashed in my chips and sunk the larger proportion of my share portfolio into index funds!

Chapter 10

The Siren Song of Tech Stocks

'The stock market must make its values first and find its reasons afterwards.'
– Benjamin Graham

Before we get into the meat of this chapter I just want to pause and reflect on the Benjamin Graham quote above. In doing so, let's perform some mental gymnastics.

A company's stock price is driven in large part by investors' judgments and perceptions of how that company will perform in the future. But we can only ever live in the present. The future can never be known.

Let me stress this point because it's essential for investors to appreciate. The stock price of a company is driven by investors' perpetually unfolding and changing views about the company's future. And because of this, stock prices must perpetually be viewed through a forward-looking lens. Each investor holds their own unique set of perceptions about that future. But it is the combined views of all the investors who interact with that stock which deliver the stock prices that we observe.

Some of these perceptions will be rational. Many will be irrational. Some will be even downright crazy. You can't get into the minds of these investors. So, the forces driving stock prices are largely unidentifiable and unquantifiable.

It means that stock prices must always be viewed with a sense of suspicion. Prices are less a foundation than they are shifting sand. Yet most investors place implicit trust in stock prices. Maybe it's because, for every fleeting moment that they are displayed, they are, in that moment, real.

I get it. But what investors do next with those market prices is totally unjustifiable. In a form of reverse financial engineering, they fabricate justifications for that price. Whether that justification has any basis or not is irrelevant to them. All that matters is that they now have a justification for the price that *sounds* credible. And, if it sounds credible, then it is usually accepted as fact. Never suggest to these believers that their price-justifying narrative might be wrong because hell hath no fury like an irrational investor scorned!

Humans behave this way because, as I explained back in chapter 7, we are inductive animals. We observe and then we explain. Along the way the truth can easily be corrupted.

Skilled investors behave differently. They employ deductive reasoning. They question generally held beliefs. Their conclusions are based on as sound and logical reasoning as they are capable of generating.

This is a difficult process for most people to undertake because deductive reasoning demands an enormous amount of mental effort. What's more, this Socratic form of behaviour can be flagrantly anti-social, something that most people prefer to avoid (both consciously and subconsciously).

Rather than employing deductive reasoning, by employing the far simpler (but incorrect) inductive reasoning, crazy stock prices don't need to be questioned. Feathers won't be ruffled. Criticism for expressing an alternative view won't need to be endured.

And there is no area of the stock market where corruption of reasoning is as easy to identify as in relation to tech stocks.

What do I mean by tech stocks?

If you mention 'tech' most people tend to think of digital platforms such as Facebook, Twitter, TikTok and Instagram. They might also think of smart devices, online services and the countless apps that we increasingly use today. Asked when the tech era kicked off, many would respond that it is a recent phenomenon associated with the widespread uptake of the internet, the availability of cheap computing power and the release of the smartphone.

But I disagree. Tech has been a thing for centuries. You could even argue millennia. Let me put tech into a broader perspective.

Author Yuval Noah Harari argues that homo sapiens has come to dominate the world because we are the only animal with the capacity to cooperate flexibly in large numbers. Add to that our capacity to imagine and to conceptualise. This has allowed us to convert our ideas into an overwhelming number of social and economic benefits that range from advancements in the delivery of medicine to improvements in housing, nutrition, transportation and communication. All of this has been facilitated by our ability to pass on ideas through speech and the written word. Communication has enabled us to capture and then to build on knowledge passed on from those who came before us.

Within this context, I don't see tech as unique to our generation. Today's tech is but one point on a long and evolving journey of tech. Of course, the journey hasn't always progressed at the same rate. So, let's put that into perspective as well.

Homo sapiens has been around for about 300,000 years. We started communicating with each other through speech between 50,000 and 100,000 years ago. We developed agriculture about 10,000 years ago. The advent of agriculture saw hunter-gatherer tribes diminish and town-based communities grow. For thousands of years technological advancement was sloth-like, bordering on static. The shoots of true scientific advancement didn't really start to sprout until about 400 years ago. That was when human technological advancement took off.

The Age of Enlightenment

So, what changed several centuries ago to spur on the rate of technological progress?

First, from the middle of the 17th century through to the end of the 18th century, there was a revolution in the way that we perceived the world. Referred to as the 'Enlightenment', the 'Age of Enlightenment' or the great 'Age of Reason', it was a period of rigorous scientific, political and philosophical discourse that was to change the world forever.

Leading into and closely intertwined with the Enlightenment was the 'Scientific Revolution'. It was a period of advances in mathematics, physics, astronomy and biology driven by great European thinkers such as Nicolaus Copernicus, Galileo Galilei and Isaac Newton.

Then, among all of this, the Industrial Revolution kicked off.

Many historians mark the dawn of the Industrial Revolution with Thomas Newcomen's development of the steam engine in 1712. While the concept of steam power wasn't new, Newcomen developed the first practical way of replacing power previously delivered by muscle, wind and flowing water with a machine. Steam power delivered the advantage that production could now be scaled up to levels never seen before. Large factories could now be built in cities. The Industrial Revolution had begun.

Was this period the dawn of tech? Maybe it was. But it can equally be argued that tech predates the Industrial Revolution.

Tech through the ages

We need to be careful drawing precise lines in the sand here. After all, before Newcomen first cranked up his steam engine, humankind had already developed:

- the lever (several millennia BC)
- the nail (a few millennia BC)
- the navigational compass (China 2000 years ago, Europe 12th century)
- paper (2nd century)

- the optical lens (13th century)
- the printing press (1430s)
- the mechanised clock (15th century)
- the refracting microscope (1608).

I'd argue that all in the preceding list are significant technological discoveries. Now let's take a look at a (by no means complete) list of technological advances that have occurred since the steam engine:

- 1731: sextant
- 1802: electric light
- 1804: steam locomotive
- 1826/27: photography
- 1837: telegraph
- 1850s: ocean telegraph cable
- 1850s: refrigeration
- 1876: telephone
- 1885: motor car
- 1902: air conditioning
- 1903: aeroplane
- 1906: radio
- 1927: television
- 1935: radar
- 1936: modern computer
- 1938: nuclear fission
- 1939: jet-engine-powered aircraft
- 1947: microwave
- 1947: transistor
- 1957: satellite
- 1958: laser
- 1961: silicon chip
- 1961: human space travel
- 1965: fibre-optic data transmission
- 1969: internet
- 1970s: personal computer

- 1975: digital camera
- 1992: smartphone.

This list is much broader than the common view of 'tech'.

And it's the same with biotech. Like all tech, biotech has long been a story of progressive evolution. Here are just a few medical developments that have occurred over the past two centuries:

- Edward Jenner developed the first vaccine in 1796 when he inoculated a 13-year-old boy against smallpox.
- Modern anaesthesia has been around for almost two centuries.
- Scottish scientist Sir Alexander Fleming discovered the first life-saving antibiotic agent way back in 1928.

Today we view inoculation, anaesthesia and antibiotics as routine medicines that don't represent technological breakthroughs, but all were cutting-edge biotech in their day. Each was as groundbreaking as anything that is being currently developed.

And that's the point, isn't it? Yesterday's extraordinary becomes today's ordinary.

Case in point, can you imagine the excitement in 1866 when the first successful transatlantic telegraph cable was laid? Prior to then, communication between London and New York relied on ships crossing the Atlantic Ocean. After the ocean cable was laid, communication time was slashed from 10 to 14 days down to a few minutes. In 1866 this was the stuff of science fiction. Today it's the stuff of museums.

And can you imagine the excitement when, on 4 September 1882, Thomas Edison delivered electric power to homes in Manhattan? Kerosine lamps were relegated to hallway cupboards and second-hand shops. Progressively homes were illuminated with bright electric light for the very first time.

No, stop right there… think about that for a minute. People were being lifted out of the semi-darkness for the first time in history. Electric light was an absolute sensation. Yet today, flicking a light switch has become a totally emotionless exercise.

I pose the question: is today's new tech any more amazing than past tech? I don't think so. Cutting-edge tech has been thrilling us for centuries.

Pushback

Several years ago I experienced first-hand a failure to consider tech in an evolutionary or historical sense. It was during the course of a telephone conversation that I was having with one of the founders of a funky new app-based investment platform. Of course, investing is investing no matter how you serve it up. This guy's offering wasn't particularly life changing. But he was talking as if he'd just invented the wheel.

Even so, I listened politely to what he had to say – that was, until he said something that demanded my interjection. He stated that tech was an entirely new phenomenon.

Well, you can appreciate how I responded to that one! I offered my view on tech, but he totally rejected it.

I don't really blame the guy for thinking the way he did. He shares this belief with plenty of others. What's more, people have been thinking the same way as this guy for centuries. In 1697 Daniel Defoe, author of *Robinson Crusoe*, suggested, 'Past Ages have never come up to the degree of Projecting and Inventing… which we see this Age arriv'd to'.

That's fair enough. Defoe was most likely right. But that was 1697, a time when witches were still being burnt at the stake and the fastest form of land transport was the horse. Technological advancement has sped up considerably since Defoe's time. And no doubt, as Moore's Law predicts, things will continue to speed up from here.

In 1895 French polymath and author Gustave Le Bon wrote, 'The present epoch is one of those critical moments when man was undergoing a process of transformation'. Le Bon described two forces that he saw as driving this: first, a transformation of religious, political and social beliefs, and second, 'the creation of entirely new conditions of existence and thought as the result of modern scientific and industrial discoveries'.

Personally, I think Le Bon's comments were a little late to the game. As already discussed, what he described had been going on for a couple of centuries.

In 1843 Commissioner of Patents Henry Ellsworth stated to Congress, 'The advancement of the arts, from year to year, taxes our credulity and seems to presage the arrival of that period when human improvement must end'.

Well, Mr Ellsworth, we are almost 200 years on and human improvement has far from ended.

The belief that we were done and dusted on the tech front was also expressed in 1899 by the satirical magazine *Punch*. The comedy magazine offered a look at the 'coming century'. In a cartoon conversation, a genius asked, 'Isn't there a clerk who can examine patents?' A boy replied, 'Quite unnecessary, Sir. Everything that can be invented has been invented'.

In 1911 British journalist Francis Wrigley Hirst described the technology of the day that was being used to facilitate stock market transactions: 'It is difficult to see, now that the tape machine and the telephone have been perfected, how the invention of aids and facilities to speculation can go much further'.

Of course, Hirst was wrong. And, while he had no way of foreseeing what was coming in the form of computers, the internet, fibre optics and satellites, Hirst should have acknowledged that further technological advances, in one form or other, were likely to come.

There is always danger in predicting what those future technologies will look like. For example, in 1946 Thomas J Watson, founder of the International Business Machines Corporation (IBM) is said to have predicted that the future world will have use for just five computers!

The relationship between tech and the stock market

Hopefully by now I've expanded your perception of tech to a much, much wider embrace of time than just the here and now. So, let's get back to the question in hand: what is the relationship between tech and the stock market? (This is, after all, a book about finance.)

As I have mentioned, the modern stock market kicked off in 1602 when shares of the Dutch East India Company were first offered for public trade. So, let's look at several technologies and enterprises that the public have been able to buy shares in during the four-century time frame since then.

Before we get to specific examples, I want to introduce you to an American economist called Hyman Minsky.

Hyman Minsky and displacement

Hyman Minsky loved thinking about the forces that drive stock market booms and busts. Each boom or bust carries its own unique characteristics, but Minsky identified some common features that tend to crop up each time.

For example, Minsky observed that speculative enthusiasm commonly kicks off with some form of shock to the macroeconomy. He called this event a 'displacement'. Displacements take many forms, as the past four centuries have demonstrated. But way, way up at the top of the list of displacements are new forms of technology. There is nothing like an exciting new idea to embolden investor fanaticism and to stoke the speculative fires.

While a displacement is the spark that gets things started, Minsky hypothesised that fuel is also required to get stock speculation truly alight. He identified that fuel as the widespread availability of cheap money. Typically, this takes the form of low interest rates and a widespread willingness for lenders to dispense that money to borrowers.

Mix the two together and we have ignition!

With the speculative fire alight Minsky then went on to explain how it spreads. Freely available money sees investors borrowing to invest. The infusion of money pumps up asset prices. People start making easy money and this draws more people in.

As stock prices rise further, mounting numbers of speculators are drawn in. More speculators fuel further price rises. A positive feedback loop is established where increased speculation fuels higher prices and higher prices fuel increased speculation. This phenomenon even has a name: 'reflexivity'.

The feedback loop continues to fuel an upward trend in prices. Prices can advance so far that they become disconnected from economic or commercial reality. This type of price distortion can continue for a surprisingly long time. For the inexperienced and the easily influenced, the soaring prices become their 'proof' that the illusion is in fact a reality.

First-time participants become entranced by the experience. Even experienced investors, who have been through similar events before, can become so seduced by rising prices that they also lose any sense of economic perspective. The uninformed majority are so busy 'making money' they are happy to keep partying.

This type of behaviour was famously displayed in a classic misstatement made prior to the GFC back in 2007. Then Citigroup CEO Chuck Prince stated, 'When the music stops, in terms of liquidity, things will be complicated. But as long as the music is playing, you've got to get up and dance'.

Just months later the USA, and much of the world, was facing its biggest financial meltdown since 1929. Prince was still partying. He was sacked.

When to stay away

When a tech darling is soaring there is often a very big giveaway that the party is overcooked. It's when traditional and objective methods of valuation are totally abandoned. When you see creative new methods of 'valuation' in order to justify the unjustifiable then it's only a matter of time before the whole house of cards implodes.

Benjamin Graham identified this investor phenomenon almost a century ago in the lead-up to the 1929 Crash. He wrote:

> 'But the "new era" commencing in 1927 involved at bottom the abandonment of the analytical approach; and while emphasis was still seemingly placed on facts and figures, these

> were manipulated by a sort of pseudo-analysis to support the delusions of the period.'

I'll now draw examples from over four centuries of investing to demonstrate what happens when gullible investors collide with new technologies.

Canal Mania

Picture England in the 1700s. Thomas Newcomen's new steam engine is revolutionising production techniques and volumes. All forms of manufacturing are evolving from what had previously been cottage-based processes to factory-based processes.

But the growing use of coal-fired steam engines introduced a new problem: how do you cart all that coal around the country? After all, coal is heavy stuff. There are no trucks, there are no trains – just horses and wagons. For 5000 years overland transport had relied solely on horse power… literally!

This wasn't the only problem. England's roads weren't up to the job anyway. Let me deliver you a little taste of what England's roads were like back in the 18th century – these are words of agricultural writer Arthur Young from his 1770 book *A Six Months Tour Through the North of England*:

> 'Let me seriously caution all travellers who may accidently purpose to travel this terrible country, to avoid it as they would the devil; for a thousand to one but they break their necks or their limbs by overthrows or breaking down. They will meet with ruts which I actually measured four feet deep, and floating with mud only from a wet summer; what therefore must it be after a winter.'

Young's comments related to England's roads in general but the ruts he describes were on the Wigan turnpike. And, to further emphasise how bad English roads were, the turnpikes were considered to be the best in England at the time. People actually had to pay a toll in order to travel on them.

Enter Francis Egerton, Third Duke of Bridgewater. Inspired by France's Canal du Midi, Egerton put together a team to build England's first industrial-scale canal. It was opened in 1761, and he used it to transport coal from his mines directly to the production centres of Manchester and Liverpool.

At the time, canal barges were powered by horses walking along the water's edge. This new mode of transport delivered massive advantages over road transport. One horse could haul a ton on land, but it could haul up to 30 or even 50 tons when loaded on a canal barge. Fragile finished goods were transported more safely on smooth water than on pot-holed roads. What's more, transport times were slashed.

The duke's new canal saw the price of coal plummet and his profits soar. His success sparked a decades-long period of investment and speculation that will forever be known as 'Canal Mania'.

The mania came in waves. To give you an idea of how rapidly things were moving during the first wave (the early to mid-1790s), the total capital authorised to build canals in 1790 was £90,000, but it had risen 30-fold to £2,824,700 just three years later.

In terms of individual share prices, shares in the Grand Junction Canal rose from £100 to £472.75 in the month of October 1792 alone. But the initial wave of euphoria didn't last. The first bubble burst in 1793 and the share price of Grand Junction collapsed by 80 percent.

There were two further notable price surges in canal stocks over the course of the next 40 years. The final legacy of all this speculation meant that by 1830 a total of 3900 miles of canals had been constructed in England.

But the days of canal building were soon to end. A brand-new type of transport technology had started to capture investors' imaginations.

Railway mania

There's one thing that you can be sure about with new technologies: they are doomed to become old technologies. And that's exactly what happened to canals. Their usefulness died as the railways took off.

Rail first appeared in 1825 with the opening of the Stockton and Darlington Railway in England. But things really got going six years later with the opening of the Liverpool and Manchester Railway in 1831. Even the young Queen Victoria helped to generate public interest in this new form of transport. In the summer of 1842, she was persuaded by her husband, Prince Albert, to make her first railway trip (from Slough to Paddington).

Finding the money to build the new railways wasn't an issue. As with every debt-fuelled asset bubble, the railways were built courtesy of the lowest interest rates in almost a century.

The fuel was there. The new technology provided the spark. Railway mania took off.

Throughout the country, journals and pamphlets proclaimed the railways as a revolutionary technological advance unparalleled in the history of the world. Typical of what was being written at the time, one publication of the day declared:

> 'The length of our lives, so far as regards the power of acquiring information and disseminating power, will be doubled, and we may be justified in looking for the arrival of a time when the whole world will have become one great family, speaking one language, governed in unity by like laws, and adoring one God.'

It reads like an article describing the internet, doesn't it?

Railway mania spread west to Ireland and north to Scotland. The poet William Wordsworth observed, 'From Edinburgh to Inverness, the whole people are mad about railways. The country is an asylum of railway lunatics'.

In his 1846 novel *Dombey and Son*, Charles Dickens lampooned the contemporary fashion for:

> '... railway hotels, coffee-houses, lodging-houses, boarding-houses; railway plans, maps, views, wrappers, bottles, sandwich-boxes and timetables; railway hackney coach and cabstands; railway omnibuses, railway streets and buildings...'

Investing in railways had become a craze among those with access to money. In April 1845 Alexander Baring declared in the House of Lords:

> '... nothing more important could occupy the attention of Parliament than the present feverish state of the gambling events connected with railways. In this case, however, as in many others, it was easier to point out the difficulty than to suggest the remedy.'

The Economist denounced the irrationality of the situation on 25 October 1845:

> 'The market value [of railway scrip] depends, not on the opinion as to the ultimate success of the undertaking, but rather how far circumstances will tend to sustain or increase the public appetite for speculation. Nothing can show this more powerfully than the fact that we see nine or ten proposals for nearly the same line, all at a premium, when it is well known that only one CAN succeed, and that all the rest must, in all probability, be minus their expenses.'

Hmmm… that quote reminds me of cryptocurrencies.

By June 1845, plans for over 8000 miles of new railway were under consideration. Over the following month, new schemes were appearing at the rate of over a dozen a week. Advertisements for railway prospectuses soliciting subscriptions from the general public flooded newspapers. In September 1845, over 450 new schemes were registered, and a single issue of *The Railway Times* contained over 80 pages of prospectus advertisements. Many of the promoters of the new railways appeared interested only in their own personal profit. Unrealistic business models and financial scams were rife, as they had been more than a century earlier during the South Sea Bubble of 1720 (and, more recently, during our own Dot.com and crypto manias).

Many of the pie-in-the-sky railway proposals never got off the ground. About a third of the proposed routes were never built. The companies either collapsed due to poor financial planning, were bought out by larger competitors before they could build their line or turned out to be nothing more than frauds.

Then the Bank of England increased interest rates. The money started to dry up. Railway mania had reached its climax. It was all downhill from there.

An article in *The Times* on 24 October 1845 stated:

> 'A mighty bubble of wealth is blown before our eyes, as empty, as transient, as contradictory to the laws of solid material, as confuted by every circumstance of actual condition, as any other bubble which man or child ever blew before.'

Bicycle mania

It might be hard for you to believe but even the humble bicycle was once viewed as a technological marvel.

Prior to the 1890s bicycles were both difficult and dangerous to ride. I'm sure you've seen what the old penny-farthing bicycles looked like: a massive wheel at the front and a tiny one at the back. No gears. No chain. And a long way to fall to the ground if you got things wrong.

Then, in the 1890s, the bicycle industry went through a period of rapid innovation. A new type of bicycle appeared that looked similar to the ones we have today. Not surprisingly, they were named 'safety bicycles', or 'a safety' for short. People now viewed the bicycle as a serious alternative to getting around on horseback. What's more, costing about two weeks' pay, the new bicycles were widely affordable. They were an immediate hit.

By the spring of 1896 there were close to 20 public companies making bicycles. Within a year, there were more than 100. The bubble that was created wasn't actually about the bicycles; it was about owning shares in the bicycle companies. Their share prices were advancing daily.

In every bubble there are always entrepreneurs who get in early and make a financial killing. Enter a dubious property dealer named Ernest Terah Hooley, who managed to convince a bank to give him a massive loan. Realising that bicycles required rubber tyres, Hooley used the money to buy a company called Pneumatic Tyre for £3 million. He renamed the company the Dunlop Pneumatic Tyre Company and then flipped it for £5 million. The massive success of Hooley's deal captured people's imaginations. Everyone wanted a piece of the bicycle action.

The explosion of new bicycle companies meant that not all were going to survive. The pricking of the bubble came in 1897 in the form of cheap US imports. In similar fashion to Chinese imports today, American mass-made bikes entered the English market. The American bikes were about half the price of British bikes.

The British firms were forced to slash their prices. The drop in revenue was profound. Of a total of 140 British public bicycle manufacturing companies, 40 were bankrupt by 1901. And, over the next ten years, another 60 went bankrupt or got out of bicycle manufacturing altogether.

It was yet another case of a new technology sparking an unsustainable investor frenzy.

Motor cars

For most people cars serve a utilitarian purpose. They sit in the garage or out in the street, largely forgotten about, until they are required to transport you somewhere.

Yes, I know that there are some people who make a big thing about their cars. But that's usually emotion-based and relates to a need for speed, prestige or social acceptance. Today, cars are rarely viewed as the technological marvels that they once were, nor are car companies pursued today with the rampant speculative desire that they once were (with the exception of Tesla, which falls into its own pigeonhole).

Karl Benz patented the first gasoline-powered motor car in 1886. Development from then was explosive. By the 1920s, the USA dominated the automotive industry due to their development of mass production technology. The Ford Motor Company pioneered the moving assembly line, introducing a complete line in 1913 at its Michigan plant. The adoption of mass production lowered production costs and retail prices, which allowed the average American worker to buy into the dream of cheap, far-flung personal mobility.

In *The Industrial Revolution in America: Automobiles*, Kevin Hillstrom and Laurie Collier Hillstrom highlight:

> 'By the end of the 1920s, there was approximately one motor vehicle for every six people in the USA. In 1929 alone, more than 5.3 million passenger cars, buses, and trucks were sold across the country – nearly one million more than had been sold a mere year earlier.'

These figures show what a major force the automobile industry had become – in its own right and through its importance to other industries.

The same was happening in Europe. According to *Encyclopaedia Britannica*, British automotive production more than tripled from 1922 to 1929 (rising from 73,000 to 239,000). Success breeds imitation. New car manufacturers started sprouting like flowers in springtime.

But, like all excessive growth, only the strong survive. Automobiles proved to be no exception. The weak fell by the wayside. As a demonstration of how many car manufacturers have come and gone, look up Wikipedia's 'List of defunct automobile manufacturers in the United States' and brace yourself for a surprise: well in excess of 1000 car manufacturers no longer exist. And the overwhelming majority ceased to exist in the early years of the development of the automobile. The number of active automobile manufacturers dropped from 253 to just 44 in 1929, with about 80 percent of the industry's output then accounted for by Ford, General Motors and Chrysler. Most of the remaining independents were wiped out during the Great Depression, with Packard, Hudson, Studebaker and Nash hanging on only to collapse during the post–World War II period. Remember that this is just the USA!

There were only ever enough places for a restricted number of participants. This is typical where new technologies are involved, with the rationalisation of countless hopefuls down to a successful few. This early and mispriced optimism even has a name: financial economist and author Bradford Cornell coined the phrase 'the big market delusion'.

It describes the situation where every new player in a novel business segment is priced for perfection, as if everyone will be a winner. The reality is that, whether it be railways, motor cars or cryptocurrencies, most end up failing.

Radio

People marvelled at the radio when they first experienced it, and justifiably so; it is truly amazing. Just stop and think about radio technology for a moment. I mean it. Sounds produced in one place travelling through the air for hundreds of miles to reach another place. It's no surprise that a century ago this was considered to be absolutely space-age stuff – except that back then the space age had yet to arrive!

Radio caught the imagination of investors back then in the same way that the internet captured our imagination three decades ago. Radio Corporation of America (RCA) was the tech darling of the 1920s. And, as investors bought into the story, its share price rose by 939 percent between 1925 and 1929.

That price peaked at $568 in September 1929. Three years later it was trading at around $10 to $15. Those who had remained heavily invested in RCA throughout the early 1930s saw their stock portfolios decimated.

But here's the thing: ask those who bought it in September 1929 if they believed it to be worth $568 per share. I'd suggest few would have denied that it was. After all, as I've already mentioned, the stock market price was (for them) proof in itself.

The fact is that RCA was a solid company. It made real profits. It had demonstrable value. And it remained in operation until 1986. But when too many investors buy into an investment story, then the share price develops legs of its own.

The tronics boom

The space and 'tronics boom' from 1959 to 1962 followed hot on the heels of the Soviet Union's successful launch of the first artificial Earth satellite, Sputnik 1, in October 1957. The space race that followed

Sputnik's Earth orbit captured people's collective imagination. The stock market wasn't immune. A proliferation of new space-related stock offerings appeared. Stock promoters found that the inclusion of some garbled version of letters or sounds from the word 'electronics' in any company's name enhanced its attraction. It was the case even when the company had nothing to do with electronics or with space. For example, the company American Music Guild sold record players door to door, but it changed its name to Space Tone before listing on the stock exchange. Its stock rose from $2 to $14 in a matter of weeks simply because its name reflected something to do with the space industry.

Investors argued that 'tronics' stocks couldn't be valued according to traditional methods because they represented a whole new category of enterprise that bore no relationship to the traditional economy. The same fractured reasoning has been offered to justify the prices of overpriced stocks before this and in every overpriced crazy 'tech'-related market since. This flawed logic saw 'tronics' stocks soar to multiples of 50, 100 or even 200 times earnings. But economic reality bit and, in late 1962, 'tronics' stocks came crashing down amid a massive sell-off.

Let's now wind the clock forward to the next generation and show how the folly was repeated again.

Dot.com

Have you ever heard of Knowbot, Archie, Gopher, Magellan, Excite or Infoseek? I could keep going; the list is near endless. They were internet search engines. And, while they had a decade's head start on Google, it's Google that dominates the search engine space now.

Remember Napster? It pioneered the downloading of music from the internet. It went bankrupt. Today we have in its place SoundCloud, Audiomack, iTunes, YouTube, Apple Music and Spotify, just to name a few.

The fact is that it's close to impossible to pick the eventual winners of any corporate race, even after the race has started.

Take the Dot.com craziness of the mid to late 1990s, for example. People like to remind us that it was during this time Amazon was first offered to the investing public, and that it has since grown into the biggest company on the planet. If you'd only got in at the ground floor, and so on. But Amazon's future success was far from obvious at the time, and for every Amazon there were battalions of roadkill – countless companies that are simply no longer with us.

When Dot.com was in full swing it was just like the 'tronics' boom a few decades earlier: facilitating the successful launch of a new company on the stock exchange in the late 1990s simply required 'Dot.com' to be tacked onto the end of any concocted corporate name. It didn't really matter what the company did. A company could have filled a prospectus with pictures of grannies darning old socks, but if the new business venture was called 'Sock-it-to-me Dot.com' then freshly minted shareholders would have thrown millions at it.

Long-time investment guru Warren Buffett was moved to say at the time that, if he were teaching an investment course, he would ask his students, 'How do you value a Dot.com company?' And those who provided him any answer at all he would award an 'F'.

Cryptocurrencies

Wind the clock forward another generation and we have cryptocurrencies. There's no denying that there is something attractively modern about cryptocurrencies. Conventional forms of money and banking have been stuck in a rut for a long time now. Physical currency in the form of hard coins had long been a thing when Jesus Christ was walking the streets of Nazareth.

Cryptocurrencies have been embraced with a frenetic fervour that's scary. As I write these words there are in excess of 10,000 active cryptocurrencies worldwide. But there are just 195 countries! The imbalance is even more ridiculous when you consider that crypto is supposed to be blind to international borders.

Now, it's impossible to pin an intrinsic value on any of them because they don't spin off any income. Rather, their prices at any point in time are a product of social interplay between passionate and largely uninformed buyers and sellers.

But there are those who have come up with inventive ways to justify the prevailing prices of crypto. In keeping with a common characteristic of bubbles, some have found creative ways to value the valueless. (Remember my earlier comments about inductive reasoning.) The 'father of value investing' Benjamin Graham warned us of times like this when he stated, '... even when the underlying motive of purchase is mere speculative greed, human nature desires to conceal this unlovely impulse behind a screen of apparent logic and good sense.'

In May 2021 investment house J.P. Morgan delivered their own version of Graham's 'screen of apparent logic and good sense'. They declared the current fair value for Bitcoin as, '... assuming a volatility ratio of bitcoin to gold... a quarter of $140,000, or $35,000'. The bank predicted in January that Bitcoin could conceivably become an alternative to gold, hitting $146,000 in the long term, but noted that this would be a 'multi-year process'.

As unjustifiable as these statements appear to be, the J.P. Morgan analyst still used language that is usually reserved for stock valuation. The price determination of $35,000 is referred to as 'fair value'. Really! Why is that fair? Show me the proof.

It's no surprise that, 18 months later, the volatile cryptocurrency was trading at an entirely different price than that judged to be 'fair' by J.P. Morgan. By November 2022 it had suffered a 12-month long rout that saw its price collapse by 75 percent. This prompted a change in tune from J.P. Morgan; the Wall Street banking giant came out with yet another inane comment, now predicting that Bitcoin could fall by another 25 percent! That would have taken it to around $12,000. Well, yes it could. It was more likely that it wouldn't. How did the analyst choose $12,000 as their target price? And why bother issuing such statements? Unfortunately, many innocent people take these comments seriously.

The statements and justification are nothing more than gobbledygook born from the imagination of a creative storyteller who has been masquerading as an analyst. This fits John Locke's definition of madmen, who 'put wrong ideas together, and so make wrong propositions, but argue and reason right from them'.

J.P. Morgan wasn't on their lonesome here. Plenty of others were making bold predictions about where Bitcoin was heading, yet not one of them could have realistically known where that was. For example, in September 2021, *Reuters* reported that a new cryptocurrency research team at Standard Chartered predicted that Bitcoin would double in value and hit $100,000 by early next year (that is, early 2022) and that it could be worth as much as $175,000 longer term. Not surprisingly, they were way out on their first prediction. Time will tell how wrong they might be with their second.

As discussed earlier, the term 'fair value' is, strictly speaking, a pretty rubbery determination even when it is applied to the stocks of conventional profit-generating companies. Extending the use of the term to Bitcoin is, in my mind, simply crazy. Something must give. The cryptocurrency craze will come to an end and the vast majority will simply cease to exist.

Rinse, repeat

The examples of enraptured investors falling in love with the latest tech offering need not end here. There are plenty more tales that I could tell. But I think you have the idea by now.

Repeat it has done, and forever it will.

My final comments about tech

I hope that you now appreciate how investors periodically lose their collective minds over new tech. If not, then let's summarise how it happens:

- A new technology is created.
- It's met with broad excitement that it will revolutionise our future (for the better).

- Ways are created for the general public to subscribe to the new technology.
- As people rush in, the sheer weight of money coming in pushes up prices.
- The popularity and price increases associated with the early investments see the birth of countless worthless copycat offerings. Their main (if not sole) purpose is to make their promoters rich.
- Few investors, even professional investors, are capable of determining the true economic merit of the new technology or to pin a realistic value on it.
- People use the rising prices as proof that their investment decisions have been wise ones.
- Reality hits. Prices fall. The myth unravels.

Each story follows the same plot; just insert a different name for the folly, whether that be canals, railways, bicycles, motor cars, electronics, the internet or cryptocurrencies. As Fred Kelly wrote in 1930, 'The game is old but the players are always new'.

I haven't written about the events of 'tulip mania' of 1637 or the South Sea Bubble of 1720. You might choose to look them up if you want to explore this subject further.

Each new generation falls prey to the same folly. The young rarely take advice from those who have experienced similar events in the past. Why? Because the young typically view any form of advice as unwarranted. 'What you are talking about is irrelevant', they declare. 'It's from another age. You are too old to understand'.

But it isn't irrelevant. The one constant that links all of these stories is human behaviour. It hasn't changed through the centuries, nor will it change in the future. By ignoring the lessons of the past, each new generation will learn the hard way: by losing money.

So, how could reading these stories help you as an investor? Hopefully, in the same way that reading about them helped me.

By internalising them. Feeling them. They aren't fiction, so try to place yourself in the shoes of those investors who preceded you. They are real people who were burnt financially.

And, when the next new technology craze hits, and you feel tempted to join the mindless throng, resist the temptation as Ulysses would have done: *tie yourself to the mast.* And make sure that rope is nice and tight.

Chapter 11

The Siren Song of Day Trading

'Don't confuse brains with a bull market.'
– Humphrey B Neill

Every decade or so investors lose their collective minds and create what is referred to as a 'bull market': an enthusiasm-fuelled rising stock market where most stocks tend to climb as one.

Bull markets are like any other craze. A previously disengaged public becomes intrigued with the stock market and just blindly wants to join in. Money is made easily. And that can be an extremely seductive activity.

I like to say that it's a time when novice traders start behaving like frogs. I say frogs because, when it's raining heavily, all the lily pads on a pond rise together. A frog that is jumping from lily pad to lily pad might believe that it is getting higher in the pond through its jumping. The reality is that it would have risen by an equal amount if it had simply remained on the first lily pad.

Like the frog, people view the profits that they generate from repeatedly buying and selling in a bull market as due to their acumen as a trader. They remain blindly unaware that the real reason that they are generating profits is that *everything* is going up. This delusion of skill can even cause people to leave their day jobs and start trading stocks full time. It happened in 2021 with the trading of meme stocks, and while that was a fresh, new experience for many young investors, there is actually nothing new about the activity of day trading.

This sort of behaviour has been going on for centuries. So, let me provide you with seven short sharp examples of this financial folly, which have occurred over the past 300 years.

Oh, sorry, before we start, I just want to say that each of the examples that I'm about to share with you ended exactly the same way: in heartbreaking financial loss for most participants.

1. London's stock market (1697)

London's stock market was booming in 1697. A late-17th-century London investment pamphlet titled *A Proposal for Putting some Stop to the Extravagant Humour of Stock-Jobbing* expressed the writer's concern that stock trading might result in individuals turning away from their occupations to focus on speculation. It added that their neglect of trade and commerce would have a deleterious effect on the wealth of the kingdom.

2. The South Sea Bubble (1720)

The founder of the South Sea Company, Sir John Blunt, wrote of England's speculative stock frenzy commonly referred to as The South Sea Bubble:

> 'The distemper of the times, which captivated the reason of mankind in general, not only in England but in all the neighbouring countries; who leaving the usual methods of labour and industry to gain estates, were all tainted with the fond opinion of being rich at once, which caused many persons to engage much beyond their fortunes, not only in South Sea stock, but in every pernicious bubble that could be devised.'

3. Wall Street's 'scripomania' frenzy (1791)

Within a couple of years of George Washington being sworn in as the first President of the United States, Wall Street was caught up in a speculative frenzy centred on newly created stocks and bonds. Founding Father Thomas Jefferson lamented about the effect this speculation had on the normal economy. He wrote:

> 'The spirit of gaming, once it has seized a subject, is incurable. The tailor who has made thousands in one day, tho[ugh] he has lost them the next, can never again be content with the slow and moderate earnings of his needle.'

In August 1791, Senator Rufus King of New York reported that business had ground to a halt as people rushed to buy scrip:

> 'Mechanics deserting their shops, shopkeepers sending their goods to auction, and not a few of our merchants neglecting the regular and profitable commerce of the city.'

King's words weren't an exaggeration. That same month, Edward Rutledge lamented to fellow Founding Father Thomas Jefferson:

> 'Ships are lying idle at the wharfs, buildings are stopped, capitals are withdrawn from commerce, manufactures, arts and agriculture to be employed in gambling, and the tide of public prosperity almost unparalleled in any country is tarried in its course, and suppressed by the rage of getting rich in one day.'

4. England's railway mania (1847)

Financial journalist David Morier Evans reported at the time of England's railway mania:

> 'The neglect of all business has been unprecedented; for many months no tradesman has been found at his counter, or merchant at his office, east, west, south or north. If you called upon business, you were sure to be answered with "Gone to the City".'

5. Gold fever, Australian-style (1851)

In February 1851, near Bathurst in New South Wales, Edward Hargraves discovered gold. By the end of May, 1000 diggers were braving the elements working the site. Thousands more left paid employment and made their way over the Blue Mountains from Sydney.

Historian Robert Hughes described the phenomenon: 'as though a plug had been pulled and the male population of New South Wales had been emptied like a cistern, in a rush toward the diggings'.

The Bathurst and Sydney newspapers reported that normal business was utterly paralysed: 'A complete mental madness appears to have seized almost every member of the community'.

6. Dot.com (late 1990s)

And now for my earliest personal experience with this sort of behaviour. I was in my early 40s when Dot.com was in full swing, so I remember it well. Being a financial type, my interest in what was going on was intense – not because I wanted to jump in and play the Dot.com game myself, but for exactly the opposite reason. I was intrigued why people were engaging when so many of the companies being served up to investors were nothing more than a financial farce.

There is one aspect about Dot.com that I remember very well. It was the countless nightly TV news reports showing people in all parts of the world, and from all walks of life, who were tossing in their jobs and careers to instead spend their time trading internet and telecommunication stocks.

But it was a short-term career change for all of them. In early 2000 the entire house of cards collapsed.

7. Robinhood and meme stocks (early 2020s)

Robinhood Markets is a financial services company that was founded in 2013. Its claim to fame is that it pioneered commission-free stock trading.

Robinhood was able to offer 'free' trades to its clients because it made its money in other ways. A large part of this was from selling its trade-flow information to third parties. These third parties profited by trading on the information purchased from Robinhood.

The brokerage clients of Robinhood were largely unaware of this. But those who were aware didn't care anyway. All that they were interested in were the commission-free trades. And, boy, did that encourage them to trade. Armed with their chat room intel, millennials got cracking.

They principally traded meme stocks. A meme stock is best thought of as a stock that has become a plaything on social media. Stories posted on social media delivered bold claims about where the share prices of specific meme stocks were heading. Business fundamentals and true investment worth were irrelevant to these traders. If enough punters put their faith in a social media post claiming that a stock was about to go higher, then it often went higher.

Two stocks typified the excesses of the period: GameStop and AMC Entertainment. In late 2020 GameStop's share price was a little over $10. Within months it had soared to a staggering $483! The reality was that GameStop shares were never worth anything like that.

Early on its share price had been driven by something called a 'short squeeze'. Now, I won't get into the nitty-gritty of what a short squeeze is, but it delivered a temporary boost to the share price. But, even after the influence of the squeeze had waned, GameStop continued to trade between $150 to $250 over the course of 2021. The early price surge had provided a 'price reset' in the minds of punters. Despite the stock being worth but a fraction of its traded price, there were now enough welded-on believers to keep the share price buoyant. The economic reality was that GameStop's business operations weren't even turning a profit. It was the chat rooms that continued to support the share price.

And what about AMC Entertainment? It's a movie theatre chain that was founded over a century ago. The share price of this profitless company, at the start of 2021, was a little above $2. The chat rooms got hold of it and, within five months, its share price had rocketed 30-fold. Like GameStop, there had been no change to its business outlook to justify this crazy lift in its share price. All it takes is enough true believers.

The problem with a stock price that is being supported by unfounded social belief is that it's a bit like the Looney Tunes cartoon character Wile E. Coyote after he has just run off the edge of the cliff and is momentarily suspended in mid-air: eventually, gravity (and reality) exerts its influence. If there's nothing of substance to make it stay there, then it doesn't!

Just don't engage

OK, I've described how difficult it is for people to resist the urge to day-trade. Hopefully you won't fall into the trap yourself. Personally, I don't need a mast to tie myself to when it comes to day trading. I appreciate day trading for what it really is, so it's easy for me to stay away. It's for the same reason that I don't buy lottery tickets or frequent casinos.

Trader and author Nassim Nicholas Taleb resorts to stronger measures in order to resist the urge to get involved. In his book *Fooled by Randomness*, Taleb explains how day traders are deceived. While it's social factors that initially draw them in, once they begin trading, their decisions are heavily influenced by irrelevant market news and mindless social media chatter. Emotion and groupthink take over and control their actions. They start reacting to the irrelevant chatter, falsely believing that it is relevant. Taleb demonstrated statistically that the vast majority of the market's short-term price movements deliver no useful information. Yet, he acknowledges that people still react to these price movements anyway.

Taleb had a novel way of ignoring it all. In other words, it's his way of tying himself to the proverbial mast. When working as a trader Taleb chose not to listen to the market noise at all. He believed that his time was better spent reading scientific theory, poetry and philosophy rather than the daily financial news. He argues:

> 'My problem is that I am not rational and I am extremely prone to drown in randomness and to incur emotional torture. I am

> aware of my need to ruminate on park benches and in cafes away from information, but I can only do so if I am somewhat deprived of it.'

This is not how market-obsessed day traders behave. They are too busy dancing to the latest tune to appreciate whether their decisions are sound or not. The problem for them, and for everyone they are dancing with, is that no one knows when the music is about to stop.

Chapter 12

The Siren Song of High Returns

'What ails the truth is that it is mainly uncomfortable, and often dull. The human mind seeks something more amusing, and more caressing.'

– HL Mencken

Not long before I wrote this chapter ABC TV aired a disturbing *Four Corners* program highlighting a sad case of financial fraud. It centred on a large number of vulnerable Aussies who were cheated out of a combined millions of dollars by an elderly con man called Edward Lancaster.

Now, there's nothing new about financial fraud. It's been going on since Con the Caveman was caught scamming naïve Neanderthals back in the Paleolithic period. But the chicanery investigated by *Four Corners* was particularly tragic because many of those who were conned were pensioners who lost their entire life savings.

The victims described Lancaster, the man who had convinced them to invest in a contrived and worthless mining company, as 'a well-presented executive type' and 'an English gentleman'. Lancaster had seduced them. And it's an easy thing to do in the world of investing, where financial knowledge is thin on the ground, and investment fairy tales masquerade as financial wisdom.

So, what lever did Lancaster lean on in order to encourage these pensioners to freely part with their life savings? They were offered the chance to purchase shares in Lancaster's mining company for one cent a piece but told that they were actually worth one dollar.

Stop right there… seriously!

Yes, you read that right. They were told that they could effortlessly make 100 times their money. All that they had to do was to buy shares for a pittance and then wait until the company was listed on the stock market. Then they would all be rolling in money.

They were seduced by the promise of huge returns.

The seduction of supersized returns

I saw this sort of thing first-hand about ten years ago. It was at a trading and investing seminar and expo at the Melbourne Convention and Exhibition Centre – which meant that it was 'investment types' who were being scammed.

A shady guy had slithered in under the front door and into the conference right under the nose of event organisers. He set up a stand selling proprietary options trading software. And he claimed that his software could deliver its users a 200 percent annual return (that's tripling your money every year). The promise of these large returns had created general mayhem around his stand. And there was an army of uniformed salespeople selling the options trading packages faster than a Bondi Beach vendor selling ice creams on a hot summer's day.

I stood there in awe of the magnitude of the seduction. I mean, this was an investing expo. Weren't attendees supposed to possess enough investment savvy to avoid sharks like this?

It seemed not. I pulled out my financial calculator (don't judge me… I don't always carry it) and worked out that this guy's trading software promised to convert a one-off investment of $10 into $35 billion in 20 short years (such is the power of compounding your money at 200 percent per year).

The point that I want to make here is that apparently intelligent people are still vulnerable to financial seduction.

Financial intelligence and general intelligence are not the same thing

A couple of years ago a newspaper article appeared that carried the following subheading: '"I don't do boomer stocks": Gen ASX discovers investing. What could go wrong?' The article was based on an interview with a 23-year-old part-time trader who said, 'Why would you get something like Rio Tinto when you could buy WZR or BET and generate maybe 100 percent return in a year'.

There is nothing new about unrealistic expectations like this. They have existed in the minds of the ignorant since the dawn of financial markets.

This 23-year-old may not have realised it but his actions were akin to that of a gambler. Because, if it were genuinely possible to reliably achieve 100 percent annual returns, then he could turn a humble $1000 into $4500 trillion by the time he hit retirement age.

Ridiculous? Yes, But ridiculous comments require ridiculous responses!

So, what has happened in the brief two years since he made this claim to the newspaper reporter? Unlike Rio Tinto, the company he ridiculed, both of the companies that he recommended have yet to make a profit. That's right, they still are, and have always been, loss-making companies. In that time, BET's share price has collapsed by 50 percent and WZR's by 77 percent, but RIO's share price has lifted and delivered a massive $30 per share in grossed-up dividends over the same brief period.

Unrealistic expectations like those held by the 23-year-old remind me of the parable of the rice and the chess board. Here it is:

> When the game of chess was first presented to a great king, the king offered its inventor any reward that he wanted. The inventor asked that a single grain of rice be placed on the first square of the chessboard. Then two grains on the second square, four on the third... and so on, working through the board, doubling each time until the sixty-fourth and final square was

> reached. The king immediately agreed to what he felt was a very modest reward.
>
> A week later the inventor returned to the king and asked why he hadn't been paid his reward. The enraged king summoned his treasurer and asked why the payment hadn't been made.
>
> The treasurer explained to the king that it was simply impossible – that, by the time you got halfway through the chessboard, the amount of rice required was more than the entire kingdom possessed. And by the time the sixty-fourth square was reached, there would be over 18 quintillion grains of rice required. (That's 1.8 with 19 zeros behind it!)

So, how did the story of the great king and the inventor of chess end? The only way it could: the king had the inventor killed!

These young traders who achieve fleeting success don't realise that their feat of doubling their money can rarely be repeated. It was due to a rare event of good fortune, not skill.

At about the same time that the article of the 23-year-old appeared, I listened to an interview with investment legend Jeremy Grantham. By way of introduction, Grantham has more than five decades' experience in financial markets. He founded Boston-based asset management firm GMO, which has well in excess of $100 billion in assets under management. Not only is Grantham a respected financial historian but he has also been rated as one of most influential investment strategists in the world.

Following is a snippet of the Grantham interview, where he discusses his concern about the current cryptocurrency enthusiasm:

> 'It's pretty hard to stop you with dry historical stories. [Instead, you tell yourself] "That was then. This is now. Get aboard. You dinosaurs don't get it." Well, the trouble is, we do get it. How can I persuade you? There is no way. Just trot out the regular story and one-in-a-hundred might listen. I will sympathise with them when they get cleaned out.'

Novice investors and a booming market are a toxic mix

Let me share a sad story with you.

The story begins when I was woken from a deep sleep by the ping of an incoming text message on my iPhone. The message was essentially a screenshot of a Twitter post that a friend had forwarded on to me. Here's what the Twitter post said:

> 'My cousin-in-law was interested in investing. He opened a Robinhood account. As many of us do, or have done, he got interested in options. So, he began buying and selling options. Fast forward to sometime this past week and his account showed him owing $700k+. How does a 20-year-old with no income get access to that kind of leverage/exposure?'

The emotional stress from the exposure caused him to take his own life.

I went to my computer and searched further. I read that the young man who took his own life was Alex Kearns, a 20-year-old student at the University of Nebraska. In a note left to his family he said he had 'no clue what he was doing' and had 'never intended to take this much risk'.

But the story carries a devastating twist. It appears that he mistook the loss on just one leg of an options trade for the overall balance of his trading account. Sure, one trade had gone sour to the tune of US$730,165. But his account actually had a positive balance of US$16,000.

Now, that's a tragic story. But Alex isn't the only person who has been caught up in these types of get-rich-quick trading frenzies. Stories of easy money being made have a way of attracting armies of stock-trading novices. And it was rife during the period of the COVID-19 lockdowns in 2020 and 2021.

Restaurants were shut. Airlines were grounded. Borders were closed. Government-imposed restrictions saw millions of workers around the world laid off from work, surviving on government handouts and with little else to do except binge-watch Netflix and shop or gamble online. Economists made dire predictions: sustained unemployment. Severe worldwide recessions. A property market crash. Unsustainable levels of government debt. Investors took fright when the coronavirus was first declared a pandemic, with stock markets around the world collapsing.

Unusually, investor fear dissipated as quickly as it had arrived. Stock markets around the world experienced not only their most rapid meltdown in history but, not long after, their most rapid recovery. In the four months between mid-February and mid-June 2020 the US market first collapsed by almost 40 percent and then rebounded by a colossal 51 percent. It was rapid. If you blinked, then you missed it.

But none of this happened in a straight line. Stock markets were volatile. The intraday price swings were massive. The mere fact that this price action was occurring in both directions (up and down), and over such a short time frame, indicated that no one had any idea what was going on.

Enter into this world of uncertainty an army of novice investors.

As the stock market climbed upwards from the depths of its 40-percent plunge, news started filtering out of a mounting wave of young, first-time investors. They were making easy money and bragging about it by posting their stories on social media and chat sites. Their enthusiasm attracted other like-minded first-timers. The growing battalions pushed the stock market even higher.

Their focus was tech stocks, many of which had never turned a single dollar of profit. And their weapon of choice was Robinhood, a US-based trading app. It offered zero-commission trades and a simple, video-game-style interface. The trading frenzy saw 3 million new Robinhood accounts opened in the first three months of 2020.

Three other brokers – Schwab, E-Trade and Interactive Brokers – jointly added another 1.5 million in new accounts in the first five months of 2020. TD Ameritrade reported 500,000 new accounts in the first quarter alone.

That was the US experience, but it was a similar story worldwide.

No profits? Doesn't matter!

As a prime example of the craziness, consider troubled car rental company Hertz. It filed for bankruptcy protection in the USA during the coronavirus pandemic. It's not surprising that it ended up in financial trouble. The COVID lockdown meant that all the hire cars they relied on to generate revenue were sitting idle. It also meant that their US$19 billion of debt couldn't be serviced. When news about its financial trouble broke, its share price collapsed by 80 percent. That was the smart money getting out as quickly as it could.

Then the rookie trading forums got hold of it.

Hey guys, the share price has collapsed. It must be cheap now. Right? Wrong. But, hey, who cares about what the stock actually *should* be worth? It's now become the plaything of the trading forums. A trickle of buy orders quickly became a flood and, less than two weeks later, the share price had climbed by an incomprehensible 900 percent.

There were whoops and hollers of joy and virtual high fives all round as traders congratulated themselves on social media platforms about their brilliance. Some even started to publicly mock 89-year-old investing legend Warren Buffett. Buffett had been sitting on a cash pile of $130 billion as the stock market climbed, yet they claimed their superior investing acumen, which had seen them throwing their respective hundreds of dollars into the market, was clear evidence that Buffett was a 'has-been'.

Ironically, the wily old Buffett had summed up this type of thinking years before in his 1997 Chairman's letter to Berkshire shareholders:

> 'Any investor can chalk up large returns when stocks soar. In a bull market, one must avoid the error of the preening duck that quacks boastfully after a torrential rainstorm, thinking that its paddling skills have caused it to rise in the world. A right-thinking duck would instead compare its position after the downpour to that of the other ducks on the pond.'

In other words, never confuse brains with a bull market.

Now, of course, most of the bragging was coming from the mouths of those who were experiencing the stock market for the first time in their life. It wasn't long before the market stopped minting fresh fools and the price of Hertz shares collapsed again.

The problem is when people are making money – well, in this case, for two weeks they were – it's almost impossible to convince them that they are doing anything stupid. Case in point: at the time, ABC TV reported on a warning issued by the financial regulator about the risks that inexperienced traders were facing. But the same ABC segment also told of the supersized paper profits that some traders had made. Reporting this effectively extinguished their warning.

Some ridiculed the ABC segment. One social media poster wrote:

> '[It] tells people not to invest, then shows people making money. I'm surprised they picked someone who is only up 35 percent. There are a lot of people making more money than that. Hell, my Zip is up 380 percent and I didn't time it that well.'

The sad fact is there is absolutely *nothing* new about this type of ill-considered thinking. Supersized returns have long been the expectation of inexperienced investors.

The famous 20th century economist John Maynard Keynes absolutely nailed it when he wrote in the profound twelfth chapter of *The General Theory*, 'Life is not long enough. Human nature desires quick results; people find a peculiar zest in making money quickly, while far off gains are discounted by the average man at a very high rate.'

The fact is that markets don't climb forever. And, for those gullible investors who are still topping up their glass when everybody else has left the party, it invariably ends in tears.

The person who made the social media post that I mentioned above felt that a 35 percent annual return was low. If such a return was consistently achievable, then consider the following: were the equivalent of $10 invested when stock trading first kicked off in 1602, then today it would be worth over $40 million, trillion, trillion, trillion. That's 4 followed by 55 zeros.

If you can't get your mind around that number then let me help. Currently the entire world economy is valued at a meagre $86 trillion. So, with the sort of moolah that we're talking about here, someone would theoretically have enough to buy trillions of trillions of other planet Earths. That's not trillions and trillions; that's trillions *of* trillions.

Come to think of it, you are going to need that many planets to park all your Lamborghinis!

Dot.com again

Let me share with you my very own Dot.com story to illustrate what I mean about return expectations.

Back in 1999, during the height of the Dot.com boom, new companies were being minted on a daily basis. Whether they were profitable or not really didn't matter. Most weren't. Personally, I stayed well clear. As I said earlier, I maintain an unshakeable rule: no profits, no investment.

But, clearly, not everyone felt that way. One night, at the peak of Dot.com, I got into a heated discussion with a friend of a friend. He clearly had been doing pretty well from buying shares in internet start-ups (well, on paper, anyway). He thought that I was wrong to avoid Dot.com stocks. I thought that he was wrong to buy them.

Well, as we now know, Dot.com crashed. After the dust had settled, I asked my friend how his friend had fared. 'In total he lost $11 million', came the reply.

I never brought it up again.

Over the centuries there have been many frenzied stock crazes just like Dot.com and the one we experienced during the COVID-19 lockdown. They never last for long. As I said, there is nothing new about speculative behaviour – at attempts to make a quick buck. Back in 1870 author Matthew Hale Smith wrote, 'Speculators do not make money, except by a turn as rare as good luck at a gambling table… Of the countless who throng Wall Street from year to year, the great mass of speculators are ruined'.

So, it seems that wiser heads have been warning about the dangers of such behaviour for a long time.

On a positive note, I'm hoping that you will take my message on board. After all, you are reading this book, aren't you?

PART II

GAINING AN EDGE

Chapter 13

What Is an Edge?

'Something that everyone knows isn't worth knowing.'
– Bernard Baruch

In order to outperform an opponent, you need to outplay them, outmuscle them or outsmart them. You have to be better in ways that matter. So, who is capable of reliably achieving outsized investment returns? And what unique characteristics does that person possess?

Is an investing edge obvious to others? Or is it something that is obscure, indistinct, non-specific and only known to the one who possesses it?

Unfortunately, it's the latter. It's obscure and difficult to identify. In fact, truly skilled investors are almost as rare as rocking horse droppings.

People don't like hearing that. People prefer things to be obvious. They want to beat the market. And they want it to be easy.

And, even if it isn't them who does it, they believe (incorrectly) that any articulate, self-assured finance type must possess an edge. They believe that skill and success can be achieved by anyone who studies finance and then puts in a modicum of effort.

Have you seen the 1987 movie *Wall Street*? If you haven't then let me describe the film's main character, Gordon Gekko (played by Michael

Douglas). Gekko is basically a crook who makes millions by trading on inside information. But many people see Douglas's portrayal of Gekko as epitomising the character of a gun stock trader. He is well dressed, sits in a big office and makes bold trading decisions with the rapidity of machine-gun fire.

'Lunch is for wimps', declares Gekko. 'Greed, for the lack of a better word, is good', he boldly proclaims to a packed room of stockholders.

Gekko oozes success. He wins people over with his hubris. 'Yes', say the masses, 'that's what an investing edge looks like'.

I'm sorry to be the bearer of bad news, but that is not what an investor who possesses an investing edge looks like. Nothing like it. In the real world an investing edge is less in-your-face than that. Investing isn't Hollywood. So, let's wipe that image and start afresh.

Before we get into the meat of what an investing edge actually does look like, let's first consider who or what the possessor of an edge is trying to beat.

Your chosen opponent, in the game of investing, actually isn't an individual. Rather it's an amorphous mass of people commonly referred to as 'the market'. To claim victory in this game your aim is to outperform the average performance of all the other investors.

Let's explore how it works.

What is a stock market index?

Stock markets are made up of lots and lots of companies that investors can invest in. These companies are referred to as listed companies because they are 'listed' on a stock exchange. Each country with a stock exchange has hundreds, if not thousands, of listed companies.

Now, keeping track of how all these companies perform (in price terms) was once a difficult thing. Charles Dow, a US journalist, knew that it was easy to follow how the share prices of individual stocks performed on any particular day – just look at how their stock price has changed! But he wanted a measure of how the stock prices of the companies that make up the market moved as a group (commonly referred to as the 'movement of the market'). In order to deliver this measure, in 1884 Dow constructed (with Edward Jones) the world's first stock index. Then in 1896 he created a second index. Dow's second index has become the most famous stock index of all time – the Dow Jones Industrial Average. Affectionately known as the 'Dow', it is still used today. That's despite it now comprising a totally different set of companies than it did originally. (Over time new companies are added and old or defunct ones are dropped.)

Since the Dow was introduced, there have been many other stock market indices created around the world. Those that encompass a sufficient number of large companies are viewed as proxies for that country's entire stock market.

Australia has two favoured general market indices: the All Ordinaries index (the All Ords) and the S&P/ASX200. The All Ords measures the combined price movement of the 500 biggest companies on the Aussie stock market. The ASX200 measures the combined price movement of the 200 biggest. These are both capitalisation-weighted indices, meaning that, the more an entire company is worth, the more its individual stock price movement influences the index.

So, we have now identified your opponent in the game of investing: a suitably broad market index. Now, beating a market index might sound like an easy thing to do. But it isn't.

Why do people assume they are skilled investors?

Time for another story. Imagine that you are watching tennis at Rod Laver Arena. It's a hot Melbourne day in January. The tournament's top two seeds are slugging it out in the final of the Australian Open. Right there in front of you are two of the best tennis players in the world.

And what about you? You play tennis, right?

Yep, you swing a racket at your local tennis club every Saturday afternoon. And you play an admirable game. Heck, just last season you and your 65-year-old partner won the club pennant in the C-grade mixed doubles.

Since you play tennis so well, why not pop down to the court right now and challenge either of the two tennis titans to a game next weekend?

What, you don't want to do that? Why not?

Well, apart from being quickly ejected by court-side security, it's because the contrast between your skill and theirs is obvious. So, there's no need to step onto a tennis court in order to decide that one.

Let's now translate this analogy back to investing.

Two titans of investing over the past several decades have been Jim Simons and Warren Buffett. The scoreboard measuring their success is their bank accounts. In the case of Simons, it's US$28 billion. Buffett has US$100 billion tucked away for a rainy day. Strength is added to Buffett's result when you consider that he's given away 5 percent of his (then) wealth every year since 2006!

But here's the thing. Unlike the spectators at the Australian Open, who know that the players down on centre court are stratospherically better than they are, countless stock market punters reckon that they're in with a chance to emulate Simons or Buffett when it comes to investing. Too many people simply *assume* that they have the skill that it takes to be a successful investor. In fact, it's a worldwide delusion on a mass scale.

Even bad investment decisions fail to quell this delusion. Much of the problem has to do with performance feedback. Each time you play a dud tennis shot it's immediately and embarrassingly obvious that you're no good. But, when you make a dud investment, the outcome is typically disconnected (by time) from when you first made it. From the day you first invest it can be months or even years before your investment is in the sewer. By then your recollection about how things transpired can be more than a little foggy.

Add in the fact there is no definitive end point in the game of investing. With tennis, a bad shot is obvious at the time and you lose the point. Not so with investing. A stock might be down but hopeful investors continue to believe that it will come good one day. Hence, our minds can tolerate a significant disconnect between perceived and actual investing ability.

How do investors gain an edge?

So, how do great investors and traders gain an edge? The answer can largely be distilled down to a single word: *information.*

What's more, this word has always answered this question. Since stock markets (as we know them today) kicked off four centuries ago, investors' hunger for superior information has been ever-present. Let me give you a couple of early examples to demonstrate my point.

In 1688 Joseph de la Vega wrote of events on the Amsterdam Exchange. Here's what he said:

> 'When the merchants come to know about an event which certainly will bring about a change of price, they turn to the brokers in order to derive benefit from this change. But they give their orders only to those who will not divulge their names before the order is carried out, for it seems to them that the financial standing of the principal [giving the order] might be doubted [or] that the price might be changed before its execution.'

He is describing the advantage bestowed by trading on price sensitive information before it becomes widely known. Today we refer to it as trading on inside information and it is illegal.

The author of a 1725 English investing pamphlet describes the competition for news among traders as 'the general industry of great numbers to be first acquainted with every material occurrence to the public, and to be earliest in the improvement of their information in adventures of this nature'.

So, if insider trading is illegal, are there other ways that information can provide an edge? Fortunately, yes, in two broad ways:

1. **Speed:** The use of some form of technological advantage in order to obtain and act on information before other investors can. A brief window of time is provided that delivers financial advantage. Today we see this in the form of high-frequency trading (HFT). While not illegal, many make the case that HFT is morally questionable.

2. **Process:** An ability to sift through publicly available information and identify pricing inefficiencies that others haven't yet found or are incapable of finding; in other words, possessing enough insight to recognise that the market price is likely wrong and then to act on this inconsistency before it corrects.

Note the two names that I've given to the two points: speed and process. I know that so far this all sounds a bit vague, but don't worry, I drill down in more detail in the chapters that follow. I devote the next chapter to speed and the three that follow to process.

You don't have to win every point to be declared the winner

Famous US investor James R Keene said of investing, 'The man who is right six times out of ten will make his fortune'. I want you to fully appreciate this point because it's essential to understanding how great investors succeed. They don't win with every investment that they make. They make bad investments as well as good ones.

Again, I'll use a tennis analogy to strengthen this truism. Let's crunch some actual numbers. Tennis great Novak Djokovic kicked off his professional career in 2004. When he first turned pro, he was ranked 680th in the world. It wasn't until the end of his third professional year that he had elevated his ranking to number three in the world.

The following table shows the relationship between the average number of points that he won and his world ranking.

Novak Djokovic's points won versus world ranking

Period	Ranking	Matches won	Points won
2004–2005	100+	49%	49%
2006–2010	3	79%	52%
2011–2016	1	90%	55%

Take a look at the seismic shift in his world ranking that was delivered by a marginal improvement in points won (from 49 percent of points won to 55 percent of points won).

This improvement in points won might seem small but it took a gargantuan effort from Djokovic for him to achieve it. It took him endless hours of intense practice and training. The same applies to investing. Success comes to those who possess character traits that are conducive to becoming a great investor (more on that later). But they must also be prepared to put in a supreme amount of effort over many years.

Even then, great investors, like great sportspeople, know that they won't win every time they act. They accept the investment or trading losses. But, through their hard work and insight, they aim to win more than they lose. They know that's all they can ever expect.

It's important that you recognise this point. Not even the best win every time.

Investing can also be likened to the game of poker

A few years ago, I was flicking through my email inbox when I spotted an invitation to come and present to a large investor group. The topic that they wanted me to discuss was, 'What can we learn from Warren Buffett?'

Now, that's a tough one. The reality is that we can't learn much from Warren Buffett, except that investing is a really tough gig, and most people would be better off placing their money in a low-cost index fund and finding something else to do with their time. Indeed, that's what Warren Buffett suggests most people do with their money anyway.

But, hey, it would have been a very unhappy audience if that was the only message that I delivered to them. So, I decided instead to pose the following question to the investment group: Why has Buffett been able to invest successfully when, for nearly everyone else, it's nothing more than a game of chance?

In order to answer that question, I posed another. This is the actual question that I asked my audience: 'What do card counters, Norwegian lab rats and Warren Buffett all have in common?'

A weird question? Maybe, but over the next few pages I'll share with you how I answered it.

First up, I explained that what determines outcomes in life is rarely as obvious as we believe. We largely view outcomes to be either wholly due to skill or wholly due to luck. But, in reality, most outcomes are a product of both.

It's better to consider life's outcomes as being on a luck–skill continuum with varying degrees of either luck or skill influencing the outcome (depending on the activity being undertaken). That continuum runs from pure luck at one end (such as the outcome of a coin toss) to predominantly skill at the other end (think of a world-champion chess player or record-breaking athlete). Most outcomes sit somewhere between the two extremes. Think this way and you'll better understand the discussion that follows.

Investment outcomes, for those investors who lack an edge, are sitting hard up against the luck end of the spectrum. That rare breed who have developed an investing edge through insight and hard work have nudged themselves away from the pure luck end and a little way towards the skill end. I say towards the skill end, rather than hard up against it, because skill never becomes the sole determinant of investment outcomes.

Now, what about gamblers? Most people would say that they're sitting right down at the luck end. Don't be so hasty. There are gamblers out there who bring a degree of skill to the table. You won't find them at the roulette wheel or the slot machines, but you will find them at the poker table.

Skilled poker players bring a wide variety of skills to the game. A couple of big ones are the two 'm's: maths and memory. Skilled poker players remember which cards have or haven't yet appeared during the course of play. They use this information to calculate the odds of key cards appearing in future hands.

Theirs isn't a world of certainty, but it is a world of advantage. They have tipped the odds away from pure chance and added a modicum of skill. If their opponents are less skilled, then they are ducks waiting to be plucked. Skilled players calculate the odds of key cards appearing and this influences the size of their bets. And, while individual hands can be lost, if the games are played for long enough, then usually more is won than is lost.

Now, if you doubt what I'm saying, then I challenge you to sit down and shuffle the deck with a poker champion. And, after playing for a while, I hope that you are left with the shirt on your back.

Professional poker player Annie Duke penned a bestselling book about this very topic entitled *Thinking in Bets*, in which she explained that truly great poker players typically lose 40 percent of their hands. That's a lot of being wrong! But, clearly, it also means that skilled players win around 60 percent of hands. Play one or two games and they might be a loser. Play long enough and they'll likely walk away from the table with more chips than they brought to the game.

As Duke argues, 'Improving decision quality is about increasing our chances of good outcomes, not guaranteeing them.'

With that background, I now want to reinforce in your mind an extremely important point. Given 30 minutes and a few deals of the deck a pure novice can learn the basic rules of poker. They can then partake in a game with a skilled poker player. But, since they bring no real skill to the table, for them it's only ever going to be a game of pure chance.

For me, the analogy of the novice card player describes perfectly how most investors approach investing (and that includes many professional fund managers). They know the rules, so they believe that they're playing effectively. But the reality is that they don't have what it takes to win. That winning edge is a difficult thing to obtain. It takes the right character traits to start with and a commitment to undertake enormous amounts of hard work beyond that.

Now let's move on to why I asked my audience that day what Norwegian lab rats have in common with Warren Buffett and poker players.

Do rats have what it takes to become great investors?

Philip Tetlock, a professor at the University of Pennsylvania, describes in his book *Expert Political Judgment* a neat demonstration that he observed 30 years earlier. It was a game of wits between a Norwegian lab rat and a group of university undergrads. It was intended to determine which could better recognise a random binomial process – the rat or the students.

Now don't be put off by the fancy name. The concept of a random binomial process is quite easy to get your head around. Imagine that you have a biased coin which, over the long run, lands 60 percent of the time on heads and 40 percent of the time on tails. (Of course, no such coin exists; I'm simply asking you to imagine that it does.) Even though this coin lands on heads more often than it does tails, you don't know before any single toss whether it's going to land on heads or tails. That's the concept of a random binomial process: random but with a bias. (It reminds me of those annoying weather forecasts that say there is a 60 percent chance of rain tomorrow. Come tomorrow you'll be no more surprised if it is dry than if it is raining.)

It was easy to explain the test to the students. Not so easy with the rat. So, the test was delivered to the rat in a novel way. A maze was constructed with two pathways. Each pathway had its own entry and endpoint. At just one of the two endpoints was placed a single piece of cheese. The rat then navigated its way through the maze. If it took the correct path, then it got the cheese. If it took the wrong one, it got nothing.

The experiment was repeated a number of times, with the cheese placement changing between the two points. But the reward was placed with a bias. While on superficial inspection it appeared to be random, the cheese was placed consistently more often on one side compared to the other.

In other words, the cheese was positioned according to a random binomial process. Let the games begin.

The rat worked out the trick. If it varied its path, then it was exposing itself to the full impact of randomness. But, if it only went to the outcome-weighted side, then it would get the cheese more often than not. So, it started going only to the favoured side. Like a professional card counter, the rat had tipped the odds in its favour. It didn't take long before rodent brain power had worked it out. Score one – rat!

So, how did the students go? Not so well. They didn't have to trek down mazes, but they were presented with random binomial problems to solve. The students huddled in groups and searched for complex sequences that simply weren't there.

You know what I mean – they believed that the solution must be complex, so they engaged in codebreaker-type stuff. But there was no hidden or complex solution. The students didn't recognise the simplicity of what was being presented to them – that is, it was random but with a bias.

Why couldn't they identify its simplicity? It's because humans seek definitive answers, the key that explains every outcome – a 'formula' or 'code', if you like. We want everything to be black or white. So, for these students, there wasn't that shade of grey that the rat seemed prepared to accept. The students were searching for one neat single, watertight rule that explained every single outcome. Every. Single. Time!

They made no allowance for chance as a partial determinant of outcomes. But the rat accepted the situation for what it was.

That's card counters and rats covered. Both are capable of operating effectively in a grey world. Let's now move on to Warren Buffett. What common quality does he share with professional gamblers and rodents?

Most investors are like the novice poker player and the graduate students in the stories just provided. That is, they believe that their actions are making a difference. But the reality is that they're operating in an environment that – for them at least – is entirely random.

Buffett knows all of this. He accepts the fact that financial markets are largely random in nature. For him it's a given, and nothing he can do will change that. But, equally, Buffett is like the Norwegian lab rat and the skilled poker player. He's developed a method of investing that provides him with a slight but measurable edge over all the average punters. His method delivers him a modicum of consistency among all that randomness. He has moved himself away from the pure-chance end of the spectrum. He doesn't always get it right, but he's been playing for a long time now, and over that time his edge has delivered him a meaningful reward.

I talk more about Buffett's edge in chapter 15.

A final word about poker

Before I leave the subject of poker, I want to mention Alex O'Brien, who is a UK science writer and amateur poker player. She has seen benefit in teaching her five-year-old to play poker. O'Brien says that there is a long list of skills to be gained from studying the game, including:

- risk assessment
- probabilistic thinking
- emotional resilience
- discipline and patience.

Says O'Brien, 'It's a highly complex and strategic and cerebral game'. She says a good poker player leans on skills in maths, psychology, endurance and even philosophy.

O'Brien adds that playing poker helps to improve understanding of 'not just your own emotions but those of your opponents, or of somebody else that you interact with'. In order to play your best game of poker you need to strip away the emotion and focus on the facts you have, and work with those. She adds, 'You cannot think critically, if your emotions are clouding your thinking, because then you're not led by logic'.

I just want to say that no greater truth than all these words can be said of investing. In fact, if you removed the word 'poker' and replaced it with the word 'investing' in the sentences just quoted, then they would not lose any of their meaning.

With all this background, let's move on and further explore what an investing edge looks like. I have to warn you that it's not obvious. Investment skill is sort of like the stealth bomber of the investing world. Adding to the mystique is the fact that what constitutes an edge for one investor is often quite different for another.

Strategic mediocrity

Skilled bond investor Ben Trotsky described the investing edge that he employs as 'strategic mediocrity'.

Respected investor Howard Marks had years earlier described the same investment process (although not using the same term) in a letter he distributed to his clients. The letter, distributed in October 1990, was titled 'The Route to Performance'. Marks told his clients of a portfolio manager who had developed the same investing edge as Trotsky later did (although he didn't refer to Trotsky specifically).

To the casual observer this manager's short-term results were unimpressive. Over a 14-year period the fund manager had never delivered a single year in which his performance was above the 27th percentile. That means he had never come in the top quarter of fund manager performance in any one of those 14 years. It also means that he would never have been noticed by those who use league tables to select a fund manager. But, equally, he had never had a year below the 47th percentile. In other words, his performance had almost always been in the top half.

For 14 years his annual performance essentially flew under the radar. No one would have perceived him as having skill. Yet, when all of those individual years were considered together, his 14-year performance placed him in the fourth percentile of all fund managers. And that meant he was close to being the best!

Bond investor Ben Trotsky did even better than this manager. His aim was to consistently be in the top third in any single year. Trotsky's bond fund was never number one in any single year that he managed it; yet, after ten years of managing his fund, Trotsky was ranked the best 10-year performer in the Lipper survey of mutual funds.

Trotsky tipped the odds in his favour through a process of intense analysis. He sought out imbalances between moderate degrees of investment risk and favourable levels of return. But he never went out on a limb. He never tried to hit a home run. He let the other managers take the big swings and miss. And that's why he wasn't noticed by anyone scouring the list of top funds in any given year. Trotsky's race was steady. He won. They lost.

The fund manager who practises strategic mediocrity doesn't aim to win big every time. Big calls are risky. Big calls can also lead to big losses. Strategic mediocrity is a percentage game. To the casual observer it all seems to be very ordinary. But those who play it well know exactly what they are doing. Skilled investors have identified their edge before they bring it to the game.

Most investors can't play this game for the following reasons:

- They lack patience. They want a big win right now!
- They don't possess an edge in the first place. And neither hope nor hubris (common emotions in the world of investing) deliver an edge.
- They behave inconsistently. Strategic mediocrity requires a consistent game plan. Most people change their investment strategy in response to the ever-changing mood of financial markets.

Summarising what an edge looks like

I want to stress that if you can't clearly articulate your edge, then you don't have one. And if you are trying to find someone who does have one, then I wish you the best of luck. Because until the game has been played, and won, winners are far from obvious. (Remember also that it needs to be a long-fought and convincing victory before you can place any credence in the result.)

So, how might you identify future winners at an early stage in their career? Well, you could sit down with them early on and let them explain to you what their edge happens to be – that is, to judge the efficacy of their winning process. But are you really in a position to judge whether their edge is valid or not? If you are that clever, then why not undertake the process yourself?

No doubt some of you are getting angry with me by now, asking why I'm not providing you with a clearly defined investment framework so you can go forth, employ your newly won edge and trounce the market.

If this describes the way that you are feeling right now, then you have totally missed the point, because:

- an edge cannot be obvious
- an edge is personal – it must suit your temperament
- an edge cannot be easy to perform, even once it has been identified
- an edge isn't something that is commonly found in investment books
- an edge ultimately becomes redundant over time, so it requires modification or a new one needs to be devised
- if someone claims to have an edge, then why would they choose to broadcast it? There is no better way to destroy an edge than to share it widely with others.

So, if I'm not delivering you an actual edge, then why am I telling you all of this? Because I want you to appreciate how difficult it is to develop one. But if you still want to chase the dream, then you will need to find your own edge.

As the great Roy Neuberger said:

> 'My advice is to learn from the great investors – not follow them. You can benefit from their mistakes and successes, and you can adapt what fits your temperament and circumstances. Your resources and your needs are bound to be different from anyone you may want to emulate.'

Similar sentiments were delivered more than 90 years ago by Fred Kelly in his book *Why You Win or Lose*: 'Your only chance to take money from Wall Street is to be somewhat unusual.' Just remember to temper that 'somewhat unusual' that Kelly is talking about. Too much swinging from the trees can easily find you on the forest floor.

I hate to sound like a defeatist but, even without knowing you, statistics tell me that it's extremely unlikely that you've got what it takes. But I'm certainly not going to stop you if you really want to try.

The great news is that Part IV of this book shows you how to become a sound investor without developing an edge of your own. You see, you don't have to become a world champion in order to play well.

Chapter 14
Speed

'Knowledge is power.'
– Attributed to many

I have explained that investors can legally gain an information edge in two main ways:

- by moving information around more quickly than their competitors (speed)
- by using information that is already in the public domain more insightfully (process).

I want to devote this chapter to speed. What I'm essentially talking about here is the legal application of information before your competitors get hold of it.

At first brush it sounds very much like insider trading, which is illegal. I'll leave the determination of what is legal and what isn't to the appropriate regulatory authorities. But the legal employment of 'speed', as I refer to it in this chapter, has typically involved some form of superior technology in order to relay the information.

Today we see this in the form of high-frequency trading, where milliseconds matter. But the need for speed is nothing new; it has always been important. Let's take a step back in time and I'll show you what I mean.

For the first couple of centuries that the stock market operated, information transfer was extremely slow by today's standards. For example, the transfer of information across water relied on sailing ships. The London-based journal *Tatler* observed in 1725 that a news blackout between England and the Continent could result 'when a West wind blows for a fortnight, keeping news on the other side of the channel'. Equally, news moved at a snail's pace over land. Over medium to long distances it relied on carrier pigeons, the horse and semaphore signalling (a system of flag-waving between people on hilltops). Over shorter distances it relied on human legs.

It wasn't until the 1840s that things really got moving. You could say that this period marked the birth of the information 'space race'. And it's still going on today. Let's take a look.

The telegraph (1830s)

Samuel Morse built on the ideas of others in order to develop his superior version of the telegraph in the 1830s. It worked by an electric signal travelling down a copper wire at previously unimaginable speed. The electric impulse activated a telegraph sounder at its destination, producing click-like sounds. These were decoded by telegraph clerks into short messages. By the 1840s it was becoming more widely adopted.

The transatlantic cable (1866)

Intercontinental communication was boosted when the first successful transatlantic cable was laid in 1866. It reduced communication time between New York and London from weeks to minutes.

Think about that for a moment. There are over 10,000 minutes in a week. So, immediately, the transatlantic cable had improved the transfer of information between these two major financial centres by a factor of 10,000!

The stock ticker (1867)

Edward Calahan invented the stock ticker in 1863 and it was implemented commercially in 1867. The ticker was an instrument that automatically converted telegraph signals into letters and numbers printed onto paper tape. It revolutionised the way stock market prices were transmitted between the stock market floor and broking and investing houses both within a financial district and beyond.

Let me share with you a story that shows how quickly the new technology displaced the old. Before the stock ticker was developed, fast, young, athletic messengers (referred to as 'pad shovers') moved information around the financial district. One of Wall Street's most celebrated pad shovers was a man called William Heath, better known as the 'American Deer'. Six foot six inches tall, gaunt and angular with a prodigious drooping moustache, he cut a conspicuous figure on Broad Street and Wall Street as he raced between the Exchange floor and the broking houses. According to an article in *The New York Times*, Heath was 'as quick in his locomotion as in his operation'.

In late 1867 broker David Groesbeck & Co installed a Calahan stock ticker in their offices. The Groesbeck brokers were gathered around their new stock ticker as Wall Street's fastest pad shover burst into their office. In his panting voice Heath reeled off the prices of recent trades on the stock market floor. But he was too late – ticker tape bearing the same information had already spewed from the stock ticker onto the office floor.

Overnight Heath's speed was rendered redundant. A new era of speed had dawned.

The telephone (1876)

On 7 March 1876 Alexander Graham Bell was granted the patent for his new invention – the telephone. Investors could now place orders with broking houses almost immediately from anywhere in the country that had a phone connection.

As I said in chapter 10, British journalist Francis Wrigley Hirst was moved by the development of all this new technology to write in 1911, 'It is difficult to see, now that the tape machine and the telephone have been perfected, how the invention of aids and facilities to speculation can go much further'. Clearly, Hirst was wrong. Things have advanced significantly since he wrote those words.

Modern technology (the 20th and 21st centuries)

The developments in communication that I described in the previous sections were certainly earth-shattering in their day. But much, much more was yet to come.

Over the past 100 years the speed and sophistication of communication has been further enhanced by the development of fibre optics, space satellites, the worldwide internet and microwave transmission. Today, an advantage in transmission speed is no longer measured in terms of weeks, days or minutes; today it is measured in terms of thousandths of a second. But this need for speed has become ever more costly to satisfy. High-frequency traders pay millions of dollars for preferential data feeds supplied by high-volume stockbrokers. They then pay many millions more to buy room on fibre-optic transmission lines in order to carry that data.

So, where do you, as a humble investor, sit among all of this expensive trading technology?

There is no way that a simple punter like yourself, sitting in a home office, can play in this stadium. So, none of it will supply you a competitive advantage. Case in point, when countless young Americans got caught up in the trading of meme stocks during the COVID pandemic of 2020 and 2021, they were like lambs to the slaughter. Their trading information was derived largely through social media. No doubt many believed that a trading edge was delivered through reading those posts, which were, in truth, being written by equally uninformed punters.

All these punters were prey. Their trades provided a rich source of trade-flow information that was being sold to professional traders who, in turn, were profiting from it. As Warren Buffett said of poker in his 1987 letter to Berkshire Hathaway shareholders, 'If you've been in the game for 30 minutes and you don't know who the patsy is, you're the patsy'. The big traders, through the use of cutting-edge technology, were frontrunning the hapless day-trading minnows.

So, before you plan to trade on your own account, you need to ask whether you are the hunter or the hunted. Without the multimillion-dollar budgets required to mix it with the big players, I can assure you that you will be the hunted. And, since you can never hope to compete in this game of speed, you can appreciate why this chapter is so short.

Chapter 15

The Graham/Buffett Era

'Your only chance to take money from Wall Street is to be somewhat unusual.'
– Fred Kelly

So far, I have employed broad terms to explain what an investing or trading edge looks like. You could say that my description so far has been a bit vague. So, I thought it would be helpful to drill down into how two highly successful investors, Warren Buffett and Jim Simons, have each gone about carving out their own particular edge. That way, I can provide you with some specifics. In this chapter I'll talk about Buffett; in the next, Simons.

Both Buffett and Simons have employed publicly available information to develop their edge. But, each sought different types of information and used it in their own unique way.

Before we get going, let me again stress two essential points:

1. What I will be describing are but two examples of the many, many ways that an edge has been or could be developed.
2. Learn from what others have done but don't automatically assume that you can emulate their success. Skilled investors typically bring something unique to the table.

Warren Buffett

Most people have a vision of how successful investors operate. They perceive them as perpetually glued to a computer or a trading screen performing complex financial calculations and constantly buying and selling stocks.

But what if I told you that Warren Buffett, one of the greatest stock pickers of all time, doesn't have a computer on his office desk? What if I told you that he doesn't use a calculator to perform his financial calculations? He deems one to be unnecessary because the calculations he performs are so simple that he can do them in his head or by using a pen and paper.

What if I told you that he doesn't perform any stock trades himself? It's a role he delegates to someone else in the office acting under his direction.

What if I told you that he doesn't possess a secret stock valuation formula that everyone is aching to know about?

Because all of these things are true.

So, if Buffett doesn't do any of the stereotypical things that people would expect a great investor to do, then what is his edge? And how does he spend his day?

He spends his day reading. Yep, that's it – he just sits at his desk and… reads. It's not what most people expect a billionaire investor to be doing. Yet, through a lifetime spent reading, he has generated spectacular investment returns.

Let's now take a look at the quantum of his outperformance. To do that I'm going to quote figures from the 2021 annual report of the investment company that he heads: Berkshire Hathaway.

Since taking the helm of Berkshire in 1965 Buffett has generated an astounding annual compound investment return of 20.1 percent. It's almost double the annual return delivered by the broad-based US benchmark the S&P 500 (with dividends reinvested). The S&P 500 has delivered an average annual return of 10.5 percent over the same period.

At first glance these figures tend to understate the degree of Buffett's outperformance. So, let me present them to you in a different way. If you had invested $1000 in the broader US stock market back in 1965 and reinvested all dividends then you would now have $198,800. But $1000 invested in Buffett's Berkshire Hathaway would now be worth $27.4 million. That's 140 times as much money. Such is the power of compounding at double the annual rate!

So, was Buffett extremely lucky or was his outperformance due to skill? It's easy to assume skill. But it's wrong to assume anything.

Buffett's outperformance is a question that I've spent years looking at. As I stated in the preface of this book, I've travelled to Omaha on five occasions to listen to Warren Buffett and Charlie Munger speak at the Berkshire Hathaway AGM. On two occasions I listened to an analyst who had worked with Buffett at Berkshire's head office at Kiewit Plaza talk at length about Buffett's methodology. Over the years I've read everything that I could find about Buffett. As well, I've listened to a good number of CEOs of Berkshire subsidiaries speak about him.

This 'under the bonnet' experience certainly delivered me great insights into Buffett's modus operandi. What's more, I've considered all of this information from my own perspective as a financial analyst. It's a perspective that has certainly provided me with a deep appreciation of what he has achieved. And outperformance of the magnitude that he has delivered over such an extended period of time is highly indicative of – and, in fact, almost certainly due to – the application of skill.

Let's track Buffett's pathway to success

Buffett started investing at a young age: when he was 11!

The young Buffett devoured every book on investing that he could get his hands on, but the book that had the most profound impact on him was Benjamin Graham's *The Intelligent Investor*. Buffett first read it in early 1950 as a 19-year-old. Benjamin Graham was well known to the investing public. He was well entrenched in a successful Wall Street career and lectured finance at Columbia University. *Security Analysis*, an earlier book of Graham's, was highly regarded by financiers, academics and investors worldwide.

Graham died in 1976, 26 years after writing *The Intelligent Investor*. But, for the last two decades of Graham's life, he and Buffett formed a strong bond. Buffett first met Graham when he was a student in Graham's finance class at Columbia University. Buffett briefly worked for Graham and regularly sought his counsel.

Graham taught Buffett how to identify stocks that were trading at a cheap price. Buffett successfully applied this method of stock selection (termed 'value investing') for decades. His profound success eventually brought him into the public consciousness and ultimately earned him the tag 'the most successful investor of all time'.

Buffett's best years were his early ones. Between 1956 and 1969 he operated an investment partnership that delivered an average annual return of close to 30 percent. That equates to an average doubling of member's funds every two-and-a-bit years.

In 1965 Buffett took over as the head of listed investment company Berkshire Hathaway, a company that he still heads at the time of writing. As I mentioned earlier, Buffett's stewardship over this 57-year period has delivered a return 140 times greater than that of the general stock market. That's an edge if ever I've seen one.

But is Buffett's edge still as effective today as it once was? Probably not. You see, over the past 15 years, Buffett's performance has dropped off. In fact, for the past decade-and-a-half it's been lineball with the returns delivered by the general stock market. So, what has changed between his stellar 13-year period from 1956 to 1969 and more recent times?

Many factors could be impacting his performance. No doubt a big one is Berkshire Hathaway's sheer size. It has grown into a near-$700-billion company. Due to its size, it has become increasingly difficult for Buffett to find investment opportunities. He necessarily ignores small investments. They don't move the dial. As Berkshire has grown in size its potential investment universe has shrunk dramatically.

Of course, you will never face this issue as a small investor. So, the question remains: is it possible for you to effectively employ the methods that Buffett did when he was managing much smaller sums of money?

Maybe. Let's explore how Buffett generated his edge.

Value investing, the investment technique that Buffett employs, relies on a constant search for fairly priced and underpriced securities. An essential part of this process is for an investor to determine their own (independent) value for a security (termed its 'intrinsic value'). The investor then compares this price to the price that the security is trading for in the market. If the investor believes that the market is offering it at a fair or cheap price, then he or she might buy it.

I won't delve deeply into the technique of value investing here but I do want to focus on why Buffett has been able to execute the technique so effectively.

Buffett is an exceptional individual

In all walks of life there are traits that bestow an advantage to one person over others. Investing is no exception.

In November 2012 long-time *Fortune* magazine editor Carol Loomis was interviewed on *Charlie Rose*. Sitting next to her during the interview was an 82-year-old Warren Buffett with a slightly embarrassed look on his face.

Interviewer Charlie Rose was peppering Buffett's long-time friend Loomis for the reasons behind Buffett's investment success.

Here are the seven principal reasons that Loomis put forward during the course of the interview:

1. Buffett understands accounting statements. He places particular significance on reading the footnotes because this is where the bad news is often buried.
2. He has an extensive knowledge of business, so that when a potential investment opportunity arises, he has a frame of reference within which to place it.

3. He is rational. When prices fall, he doesn't get emotional.
4. He is disciplined.
5. Buffett 'only gets into situations where he knows the value'. In other words, he develops a deep appreciation of the future prospects for the business he's looking at.
6. He wants to invest in companies that possess an 'enduring competitive advantage five to ten years out'.
7. Commonly he is familiar with the company before an opportunity to invest in it arises.

Now these seven points can be distilled down to three essential ingredients:

1. Buffett is first and foremost a businessman.
2. He possesses certain character traits that aren't handed out freely at birth.
3. He works very, very hard.

Let me now expand further on the insights delivered by Carol Loomis in that interview.

Buffett is first and foremost a businessman

People are born to do different things. Buffett was born a businessman. Let me explain why I can so confidently say that.

While visiting Omaha I met with and listened to journalist Steve Jordon speak about Buffett on three separate occasions. Jordon had worked at the *Omaha World-Herald* for five decades, including 35 years as a business reporter. He was their 'Buffett expert'.

Jordon had just published a pictorial biography about Buffett (and he kindly gifted and signed a copy for me, which now sits on my bookshelf). On page three of his book is a full-page photo of the three Buffett siblings: Warren and his two sisters, Doris and Bertie. The Buffett siblings are standing outside their family home on Christmas Day, 1937. The young Warren is clutching his new nickel-plated coin changer, which he came to use in one of his early business ventures: selling Coca-Cola and chewing gum. The photo demonstrated that the seven-year-old Warren already had thoughts of business.

In a mid-1980s interview Buffett delivered further insight into how important a business-orientated approach was to his style of investing. In response to a question about why he felt that he was different to 90 percent of investment managers Buffett replied, 'Most of the professional investors focus on what the stock is likely to do in the next year or two… They do not really think of themselves as owning a piece of a business'.

Buffett doesn't use charts, technical analysis, momentum trading, hot tips or trading forums. Rather, he identifies solid and profitable businesses operating in sectors that he understands. He forms a view on what he is prepared to pay for them and, if they aren't trading at an attractive price, then he won't buy them. Instead, he waits. If it never trades at an attractive price then he never buys it. (Robert P Miles, author of *The Warren Buffett CEO*, told me on one of my trips to Omaha that Buffett wants his initial purchase price to be returned to him within the first ten years of ownership through profits and dividends.)

This businesslike behaviour was drilled home to Buffett by his teacher and mentor Benjamin Graham, who stated, 'The true investor will do better if he forgets about the stock market and pays attention to his dividend returns and to the operation results of his companies'. To quote Graham again: 'Investment is most intelligent when it is most businesslike.'

Remember that Buffett first read those words as a young adult. They resonated strongly with the young man who already had a business-orientated character. To this day, every time Buffett sizes up a stock investment, he approaches the decision as if he were buying the entire business.

During my time in Omaha, I listened to a number of CEOs of Berkshire subsidiaries talk about their interactions with Buffett. They all told of Buffett's intimate understanding of the business that they were in charge of. Buffett knew what their production revenue and profit figures were. He knew the same for their main rivals. He understood the markets that they operated in. He knew where their customer base lay. He knew what their potential threats were.

So confident were the Berkshire subsidiary CEOs of Buffett's knowledge of their operations that they often referred to Buffett for advice. Each CEO expressed a supreme confidence that Buffett could step into their shoes at short notice. In fact, this actually happened back in 1991. Investment bank Salomon Brothers was embroiled in the 1990s treasury bond scandal. Buffett came in as interim chairman of the board to clean up the mess.

Ask yourself when you next invest in a listed company: would you be capable of managing the business that you've bought shares in?

I now want to go back even further to demonstrate Buffett's business acumen and his deep appreciation of the inner workings of the companies that he invests in. Here is a simple test. Google 'The Security I like Best'. It is the title of an article written by Warren Buffett and published in the 6 December 1951 edition of *The Commercial and Financial Chronicle*. It's a short article: just one page. Here's your challenge:

- Read every word of the article.
- Try not to be impressed that this was written by a 21-year-old. Buffett's deep appreciation of the insurance sector and of the company in the article (GEICO) is profound.

Remember that this article contains but a sample of what the 21-year-old Buffett would have understood about this subject. Now ask yourself:

- Do I understand the companies that I own and the sectors they operate within to this degree?
- If not, then would I be prepared to put in the work necessary to understand them to this degree?
- What was I doing at age 21?

Now consider how many 21-year-old 'investors' go about the process of investing today. Today, social media chat rooms are regularly viewed as appropriate sources of information from which to make investment decisions, but these forums are little more than a soft substitute for what is really required. As Buffett has demonstrated, what is required is hard work and profound knowledge.

Buffett possesses certain character traits that aren't handed out freely at birth

In a 1980 interview Buffett stated that it is more important for an investment manager to possess the correct temperament than superior intelligence. He said:

> 'You don't need tons of IQ in this business… You need a stable personality. You need a temperament that neither derives great pleasure from being with the crowd or against the crowd because this is not a business where you take polls, it's a business where you think.'

But that's not to say that intelligence is redundant. Far from it. Buffett was merely stressing the point that an abundance of intelligence is not a passport to success. How you handle yourself is essential.

So, let's explore Buffett's temperament a bit more. I want to explore five of his distinct personal traits: patience, rationality, discipline, focus and ability to delay gratification.

1. Patience

Value investing, the investment technique that Buffett employs, is an opportunistic technique. It relies on its user remaining supremely patient while waiting for the right opportunity to come along. This human characteristic is rare. However, Buffett has it in abundance.

On three of my five visits to Buffett's hometown of Omaha, I was treated to the opportunity of hearing Buffett's oldest child, Susie Buffett, talk about her father. What interested me most was when she described his character. When Susie was asked what qualities best described her father, she didn't hesitate; she responded with the words 'integrity' and 'patience.'

So integral to Buffett's success is his supreme patience that I have devoted an entire chapter to the subject later in this book. I've done so because it's not just Buffett who has achieved success through exercising patience; it's an essential characteristic for any investor to possess.

2. Rational behaviour

Back in chapter 4 I explained how easily and unconsciously we can be influenced by the crowd. Of course, the problem is that the crowd can often be wrong. Therefore, when investing, it's better to apply sound logic to arrive at independent conclusions.

Benjamin Graham stressed the importance of Socratic thinking when he wrote, 'You are neither right nor wrong because the crowd disagrees with you. You are right because your data and reasoning are right'.

For Buffett this has come easily. His psychological make-up was tailor-made for him to function as an independent thinker.

We all like to believe that we make our own choices in life. The reality is that we are more likely to be unconscious slaves to groupthink.

3. Discipline

A disciplined person displays a near unfaltering obedience to rules or to a code of behaviour. And, as I've already discussed, it's essential for an investor to behave this way in order to successfully execute their investment edge.

Skilful investors have identified an edge. To execute it requires discipline. To deviate from that execution means that they are no longer employing their winning formula.

Buffett is supremely disciplined when employing his. Let me give you an example.

In the late 1990s Dot.com mania was in full swing. Any ill-considered, capital-destroying start-up company with the letters '.com' pinned to its tail was hot property on the stock market. A worldwide army of investors lost their collective minds and shunned quality stocks in favour of loss-making corporate dross.

In June 1998 the stock price of Berkshire Hathaway, the company that Warren Buffett had successfully led for 33 years, hit $84,000. Just 20 months later its stock price had halved to $41,300. Clearly this rejection of Berkshire by investors was in stark contrast to the Dot.com fervour of the time. Buffett had long spoken out against the crazy prices being attributed to what he viewed as worthless Dot.com start-ups. So, while the rest of the market was making whoopee, Buffett stayed the course. He shunned Dot.com companies altogether. His investment game plan remained unchanged.

As Berkshire's share price sank further the press turned against him. *Barron's* magazine carried a headline that asked, 'What's Wrong, Warren?' Other headlines read 'Disgraced with Poor Rankings' and 'Fallen Angel'. Australia's *Financial Review* newspaper carried an article on 30 December 1999 that bore the headline 'Buffetted by the Winds of Change'. Buffett was copping a barrage of very pointed and very personal criticism. But he refused to deviate from his predetermined and deeply entrenched investment strategy.

Within weeks of the *Financial Review* article the whole Dot.com con imploded. The Nasdaq index, which included many of these companies, peaked in March 2000 but was down 78 percent two-and-a-half years later.

Buffett was vindicated. Over the course of the decade following the Dot.com crash, Berkshire's share price outshone even the US blue-chip-oriented S&P 500. With dividends included, the S&P 500 index fell by 9 percent. Berkshire's share price climbed a staggering 77 percent over the same period.

Buffett's game plan never skipped a beat over the entire period.

4. Focus

Buffett possesses a capacity to focus that is almost unworldly. He sits in his office, alone, reading for hours on end without a break.

Buffett's daughter, Susie, described this trait. She said that, when she was young, her father was often socially disengaged. He was in another world, thinking about other things. Susie and her two siblings had to tell their father things in 'sound bites'. She added that even now ten minutes is a long time to ask for.

Buffett's ability to maintain an intense focus for a sustained period has endowed him with a prodigious reading ability.

On my second trip to Omaha, I met Robert P Miles, author of *The Warren Buffett CEO*. I got to know Bob quite well, also meeting up with him on a couple of subsequent trips, and on one of those visits Bob shared the story of how he came to write the book. Bob had been discussing with Buffett the idea of writing another Buffett-centric book, but Buffett suggested to Bob that the real heroes at Berkshire were the CEOs of the many subsidiaries that operated under the Berkshire umbrella. Buffett suggested that the book should be all about them. What's more, Buffett offered to tee up interviews with a number of the CEOs so that Bob could compile plenty of notes for his book.

Bob wrote the book and, when he had the manuscript pretty much done, he met with Buffett over lunch to discuss the outcome of the project. Bob handed Buffett a copy of the manuscript to read, seeking Buffett's blessing before it went to print.

Now, here's the amazing part of the story. The two men went their separate ways after lunch. Buffett returned to his office in Kiewit Plaza and later that day went home for dinner. Bob suspects that Buffett probably didn't miss his usual game of bridge after dinner. Yet, despite the short period of time, Buffett called Bob early the following morning to outline his views on the manuscript. At first Bob thought that Buffett must have skimmed through its pages, picking out sections here and there to read. But then Buffett said, 'I read the whole 400 pages and there's only six mistakes. I'll run you through them'. Buffett directed Bob to specific pages, highlighting specific corrections that he felt were necessary.

So, how did Buffett read Bob's manuscript in the brief time available to him? Well, during the 45-minute telephone conversation with Buffett, Bob asked him 'Warren, how fast can you read?'

Buffett replied, 'At my peak I could read five books a day'.

Even now, on a normal working day Buffett spends six hours reading.

Focus is a character trait that both Buffett and long-time Berkshire vice-chairman Charlie Munger looked for when seeking their eventual replacements at Berkshire Hathaway. Two men, Todd Combs and Ted Weschler, were employed a decade ago to manage a segment of Berkshire's investment portfolio as part of the Buffett/Munger succession plan.

Combs first set eyes on Buffett while still a student at Columbia University years before he came to work at Berkshire. Buffett was presenting to his finance class. At the time another student in the class asked Buffett how one could best prepare for a career in investing. Buffett told the class to read 500 pages every day because knowledge builds up over time – it was like compound interest. He added that few people could do it.

When the young Todd Combs heard Buffett say this, he took it on board. He started reading prolifically. By the time he kicked off his investing career, he was reading 500 to 1000 pages a day.

But, as Buffett told the class, few people can do this. The problem is that few people:

- possess the necessary focus
- would devote the time necessary to do it even if they did possess the focus
- would accept this methodology as a pathway to successful investment outcomes
- are capable of actually retaining the dry facts and figures that the pages contain.

This reminds me of another story told by Steve Jordon, the journalist I met who worked for the *Omaha World-Herald*. On one of my visits to Omaha, Jordon had just written a newspaper article that embodied both the focus and discipline demanded of value investors, centred on an interview that he conducted with Todd Combs. Combs explained that he, Buffett and Weschler often spent hundreds and hundreds of hours investigating a single investment opportunity. And, after all of that effort, if they found a solid reason for not investing in it, then they'd walk away. Few people can do that. After investing so many hours to a cause, most would feel committed to buy the stock or company. They'd dismiss their negative findings, focus on the positive ones and invest anyway.

5. Ability to delay gratification

I admit that it's a bit misleading to describe what Buffett does as 'delaying gratification'. It's more that he doesn't have high material needs in the first place.

At the 2019 Berkshire Hathaway AGM Charlie Munger was asked by a shareholder how to help kids develop the skill of delayed gratification. The saving process that delayed gratification facilitates is an essential element of successful investing. Munger's response was short and clear: 'You come out of the womb. So, you identify it, not develop it'.

Buffett, who was sitting next to him, added to Munger's response that delayed gratification wasn't an appropriate (or possible) behaviour for everyone, and that it was easy for him (Buffett) because he had never wanted for material objects. He always felt that he had enough.

If, like Buffett, you are essentially a non-materialistic person, then you have a head start as an investor. If not, then you are going to have to work on things – if, in fact, you are bothered to. And if you aren't prepared to curb your spending and boost your efforts at saving and investing, then that's OK. I've heard that some people can exist just fine on social security.

Buffett works very, very hard

Listening to what Buffett's daughter Susie has said about him, it's clear that she deeply loved and admired her father. But, equally, she described his powerful work ethic as something that often kept him apart from his family. Each evening, following the family dinner, Buffett would go upstairs to read. Annual reports were often on the reading list. His driving force was a love of his work. Indeed, even now, at age 92, he still describes himself as 'tap-dancing to work'. And he does the dance six days a week.

Ask yourself, would you – or do you – feel the same way about sitting at a desk hour after hour reading dry annual reports and trade journals at the age of 92?

In life, I find that people prefer to do things that are easy. It's why charting, technical analysis, investing chat sites, 'hot tips' and gut feel are the way that most people choose to invest. These techniques appeal to the more typical human traits of pattern-seeking, ease and social confirmation.

Buffett had the right skills for his time. Born later, his investing style might well have been less successful.

There is no formula for value investing

So, what's with all this reading Buffett does? It all seems so passive. What's more, isn't investing all about numbers, calculations, markets and graphs?

Not necessarily. Buffett's style of investing requires plenty of non-numerical legwork. He is building on his already massive body of knowledge. It's like a bank that he draws from when making investment decisions. Other investors, even those who pretend to emulate Buffett, don't fully appreciate how important this is to Buffett, and how insignificant mathematical calculation and the application of valuation formulae are.

There exists a worldwide army of value investors who falsely believe that the key to value investing is the application of an appropriate formula. Punters new to the game hold these valuation formulae in awe. It's as if their first exposure to these simplistic algebraic relationships has delivered them the key to unlocking the secrets of the stock market. Not true.

The concept of discounted cash flow (DCF), from which these formulae are derived, has been understood for at least eight centuries, and most likely longer. Our earliest written record of DCF dates back to the book *Liber Abaci*, written in 1202 by Leonardo Pisano.

No edge can be delivered by simply getting your head around a basic 800-year-old concept.

It's interesting to note that, in a presentation delivered by Buffett author Alice Schroeder at a 2008 value investing conference, she said she saw no evidence of his using DCF. I've also heard Charlie Munger, his close friend and business associate of six decades, state that he has never seen Buffett use a DCF formula to derive the intrinsic value of a share.

At Berkshire Hathaway's AGM in 1995 Buffett was asked, 'When you discount back the future earnings, how many years out do you go?' His response goes a long way to explaining why he doesn't bother using a calculator:

> 'Despite the fact that we can define that in a very simple and direct equation we've never actually sat down and written out a set of numbers that relate to that equation. We do in our head, in a way… we really like the decision to be obvious enough to us that it doesn't require making a detailed calculation.'

Despite this stated fact I have seen countless books and read several that claim to have unlocked the secret to Buffett's success. Most have at their core a lengthy discussion regarding a formula based on the concept of discounted cash flow.

I will complete the discussion about Buffett's edge emanating from the employment of an intrinsic value formula with just two words: red herring.

Does value investing still deliver an edge?

Value investing is based on a rational argument. It acknowledges that markets are fickle – that, in the short to medium term, stock prices are driven in large part by social influences. These influences can cause prices to deviate significantly from their intrinsic value (however you might choose to determine that!). An edge is delivered to those who can independently derive intrinsic values that are, if not absolutely correct, at least closer to correct than the masses are capable of determining.

In theory these investment principles should stand the test of time. The problem, however, is that, if enough investors possess and practise this skill effectively, then the advantage is lost.

I question whether a reading of Graham's *Security Analysis* or Buffett's chairman's letters from Berkshire Hathaway's past annual reports still deliver the edge that they once did. Today there are many more analysts who employ Graham's principles than there once were. That, in itself, has probably killed the edge.

But don't just take my word on it. Both Graham and Buffett have expressed their opinions on this matter.

Benjamin Graham died in 1976, but in his final year the man dubbed the 'father of value investing' said this of the craft he spent a lifetime promoting:

> 'I am no longer an advocate of elaborate techniques of security analysis in order to find superior value opportunities. This was a rewarding activity, say, 40 years ago, when our textbook "Graham and Dodd" was first published; but the situation has changed a great deal since then.'

Graham said these words several decades ago. Since then, the changes that he talks about have only been magnified, which means that his comments are truer today than they were back in 1976.

Let's now hear from Buffett on the same matter. At the 2019 Berkshire Hathaway AGM Buffett remarked of stock picking, 'Early in my career it was a bit more like treasure hunting. There wasn't a lot of competition'.

The fact is value investing was born in another era. (It actually long predates Graham; it's just that his name is often linked with it.) By way of example, when the New York Society of Security Analysts was founded in 1937 (by Benjamin Graham, among others), it had 20 members. Today's iteration, the CFA Society of New York, operates worldwide and has more than 178,000 active charter holders. There is now a worldwide army of highly qualified analysts who are all employing the same techniques in a competition for the same prize.

Greenwich Associates founder Charles Ellis recently stated, 'Over the last 50 years, we've gone from roughly 5000 people engaged in active investing to comfortably over 1 million people engaged in active investing'.

The final word on Buffett

If you think that you can make a study of Buffett and emulate his success, then you are on a fool's errand. Not only is it unlikely that you possess his innate skills, but I also question whether his skills are as relevant as they once were.

That's not to say that exploring his methodology is a waste of time. His personal traits of patience, rationality, discipline, focus and ability to delay gratification are still relevant to investing. Whether they will deliver the outsized returns that they once did is an entirely different matter. However, what the adoption of these principles will do is enhance the chance of you becoming a safe, rational and capable investor.

Chapter 16

Quants

'Never send a human to do a machine's job.'
– Agent Smith in *The Matrix*

In the previous chapter I described seven-year-old Warren Buffett clutching his new nickel-plated coin changer on Christmas Day, 1937, and that it demonstrated how the young Warren already had thoughts of business at a young age.

Similarly, fellow American Jim Simons, founder of the hedge fund Renaissance Technologies, knew by the age of eight that he wanted to become a mathematician. His aptitude for maths had been on prominent display since he was just three years old.

So, it was no surprise to anyone who knew the young Simons that he did ultimately forge a career as a highly respected mathematician. At age 23, Simons gained his PhD at Berkeley University. He then worked with the National Security Agency as a code breaker during the Cold War. In 1976 he received the Oswald Veblen Prize in Geometry. He also lectured in mathematics at both MIT and Harvard University.

Simons was clearly a member of an elite group. He rubbed shoulders with some of the most respected mathematicians in the USA. Yet, at age 40 he gave it all away. Instead, he wanted to make his fortune trading the financial markets. Despite the late start to his new career Simons went on to become the most successful trader yet known.

Let's quantify his success. During the three-decade period from 1988 to 2018 Renaissance Technologies delivered an average annual return of 66.1 percent before fees (39.1 percent after fees). That's three times the annual return that Warren Buffett has achieved at the helm of Berkshire Hathaway and almost seven times that delivered by the US stock market. It's massive. It allowed Renaissance to earn $104.53 billion in outright trading profits over the 30-year period!

As much as Jim Simons and Warren Buffett have played in the same arena, each has followed an entirely different game plan. Buffett has been known to go an entire year making just a couple of trades. Jim Simons' computer-driven Medallion fund can make hundreds of thousands of trades in a single day.

Buffett is on the constant lookout for quality businesses selling at a fair or cheap price. Once purchased, he then holds onto them for the long haul. As I have already stated, Buffett's investing style has been heavily influenced by Benjamin Graham's advice to view every share as an ownership interest. And that makes good sense; if you plan to hold onto a slice of any business – which is what shares are – then it is wise to ensure that the business is a sound and profitable one.

In stark contrast, mathematician Jim Simons never felt the need to study business fundamentals. In fact, Simons has never taken a single class in business. His approach to the markets has always been first and foremost as a mathematician. Simons and his vast team feed code into computers in an effort to identify tradeable pricing irregularities. Their efforts span a broad range of different financial markets. What causes these pricing irregularities to occur is of little importance to Simons. He merely seeks to identify them. One of Simons' highly successful traders, Elwyn Berlekamp, stated that he barely knew how companies earned their profits and had no interest in finding out.

Simons wasn't the first to adopt this computer-based mathematical approach, in the same way that Buffett wasn't the first to adopt value investing. That both men have achieved significant success isn't because they were groundbreakers in their respective fields. Rather, it was due to their profound skill in executing their chosen method.

Another stark contrast between Buffett and Simons is their reliance on computers. While Buffett doesn't have even the most basic of computers sitting on his office desk, Simons couldn't operate without his vast computing power.

Simons is a member of a breed of traders called 'quantitative analysts' (or 'quants' for short). In order to explain how Simons has developed his edge, it's necessary to first describe how quants go about their business.

Algorithms

Let's start with algorithms. An algorithm is a strict list of instructions that, when followed, is used to perform calculations and solve a problem.

Today our entire world runs on algorithms. But that doesn't mean that algorithms are a new thing. In fact, algorithms have been around for thousands of years. They were the plaything of Babylonian and Egyptian mathematicians long before Christ was born. Even the word 'algorithm' is an old one; it was derived from the name of the 9th-century Persian mathematician Muhammad ibn Mūsā al-Khwārizmī ('al-Khwārizmī' was transliterated into Latin as 'Algoritmi').

Like bacon and eggs, algorithms and computers were always going to be a match made in heaven. It's as if algorithms were waiting patiently in the wings for thousands of years for computers to be invented. Today, algorithms are fed into computers in the form of computer code.

The beauty about algorithms is their mechanical approach to problem-solving. And that's a very attractive thing in the world of investing. You will remember back in Part I that I explained how human decision-making has many faults. Conclusions are compromised by the corrosive forces of bias, social influence and groundless fear and emotion. Well, computers don't experience any of these things. Their mechanically derived answers aren't influenced by irrational noise. Their trading decisions aren't muddied by human emotion.

Now, you can't create your own computer-enhanced investing edge simply by purchasing a desktop computer and loading it with proprietary software. So, stay well clear of spivs flogging options-trading packages. The people who succeed – like Jim Simons – are smart; they unearth market irregularities for themselves. They write their own computer code. And, most importantly, once they develop a trading edge, they don't share their secrets with others. If they did, then their advantage would be lost.

Let me explore emotion in a little more detail.

In 1954 Paul Meehl, a professor of psychology at the University of Minnesota, published a book called *Clinical Versus Statistical Prediction: A Theoretical Analysis and a Review of the Evidence*. It compares the accuracy of human judgment versus that derived through the simple application of predetermined rules. This is effectively the same thing that we have been discussing: human judgment versus rule-tracking algorithms. Meehl reviewed 20 studies on the subject and concluded that following simple mechanical rules typically delivered superior answers than human judgment alone.

For example, consider a rule-based model that requires ten inputs to forecast a possible future outcome. A weighting is applied to each input based on how much each is likely to influence the outcome (referred to as a 'correlation'). The rule-based system is then applied in an unerring manner and an answer is delivered.

Consider now that human judgment alone is applied to the same problem – no rules, just human judgment. Bias and inconsistency now influence the determination. It means that important factors fail to be considered and insignificant factors are given unnecessary relevance. The answer is now far less reliable.

Credence given to the irrelevant is why employment studies have found that physically attractive people are more likely to be hired and also to be offered higher salaries than those who are less attractive. It's also why judges in the talent show *The Voice* have their backs to competitors when initially selecting their teams.

It's also why panicked investors shy away from stock markets in the wake of significant market corrections despite it offering the best value in years.

Several decades ago, US researcher Lewis Goldberg undertook a study in which he pitted the gut feel of individuals against rule-based models of themselves. It sounds crazy given that the models could only ever be simplified versions of the people's far more complex and sophisticated selves. Yet, the models outperformed the originals in the decision-making stakes. How is this possible?

I could run through Goldberg's findings in detail, but essentially what he found is that seat-of-the-pants judgments (made by the human) are too easily swayed by a myriad of irrational and inconsistent influences, whereas the rule-based judgments were not.

It seems that the jury has decided. Rules and algorithms outperform humans.

Another reason quants use computers

There are two main reasons that quants use computers. The first I've just explained: computers don't get emotional.

The second reason is the massive volume of data that computers are capable of processing and the speed at which they can do it. Put simply, loaded with the right algorithms, computers are like heat-seeking missiles firing through terabytes of historical data in the search for present and future trading opportunities that are both incomprehensible and unidentifiable to our reptilian brains.

Adding power to their search, computers learn from and correct prior mistakes. They can improve on their performance without any adjustment to their code by humans.

So, what sort of information are quants seeking?

Quantitative analysts feed code into their computers to scour historical data for tradeable patterns, relationships and correlations. They hope those past correlations will persist into the future so that they can profit from them. Here are some simple examples just to give you a feel for what I'm talking about:

- Do stock prices tend to trade higher on Monday mornings than they do on Friday afternoons (all else being considered)?
- Do currency prices reflect initial overreaction and later recovery following central bank interest rate announcements? And, if so, then by how much on average?
- Is there a tradeable relationship between past weather patterns and current wheat futures prices?
- Does chatter on social media assist in forecasting short-term share price movements?
- Does tracking oil tanker movements around the world provide useful information? For example, does the number of tankers bear a relationship to the price of oil or future economic activity?
- Does counting the number of cars parked in Walmart (from satellite images) deliver some insight about the retailing giant's next profit result?

You get the idea. All manner of information is explored. Only when tradeable correlations are demonstrated is the information used. Often the relevance isn't clear, but that isn't an issue for a quant. They seek profitable trades, not to explore cause and effect.

Additionally, quants are indifferent to the markets that they trade. They delve into currency markets, commodities and bond markets, options, futures and physical markets. If they can turn a buck, then they're there. But for the big quant firms, there needs to be sufficient depth in the chosen market in order to facilitate the size of their trades.

What skills do quants bring to the table?

As I've discussed, the quants hired to work at Jim Simons' Renaissance Technologies had to be super smart. A head count in 2010 showed that of 250 staff, 60 had PhDs.

A background in finance was considered to be irrelevant. In the minds of those at Renaissance, Wall Street types didn't have the skills that they were looking for. They saw the finance part as something that could easily be taught later on and only if it was necessary. Instead, new hires were poached from areas such as quantum physics, artificial intelligence research, statistics, computational linguistics, number theory and astronomy.

For example, two of Renaissance's heavy hitters, Robert Mercer and Peter Brown, had worked together at IBM researching and developing computer-based language recognition systems. It became clear to Mercer that trading stocks bore similarities to speech recognition. Renaissance went on to poach the best talent from IBM's computational linguistics team. A huge salary can be quite a temptation for a career move, even for a passionate research scientist!

Now, you might have spotted that Jim Simons employed some astronomers. While astronomy might appear to be an odd skill to bring to financial trading, the relevance is in the way that astronomers approach problem-solving; astronomers are used to sifting through huge data sets in a search for meaning among apparent chaos. And this is exactly the task that Simons wanted undertaken at Renaissance.

Tradeable effects

Finance types have long sought tradeable effects, and certainly long before quants were a thing.

The 16th-century Antwerp commodity trader Christopher Kurz believed that future prices could be forecast through astrological observation. And, no, Kurz wasn't anticipating the employment of astronomers in 21st-century quant funds. He was seeking a link between the movement of celestial bodies and market prices.

Henry Hall described a rule-based investing system more than a century ago in his book *How Money is Made in Security Investments*. Hall described a relationship between stock market price patterns and the Gregorian calendar. He wrote, 'In 27 years since 1890 inclusive,

January prices have been higher than in the preceding month, 17 times. They have been top of the year, 6 times'.

Hall described how one might expect prices to behave in each of the 12 months of the year. His method was crude, observational and simplistic. One could question the statistical significance of his small sample size. But it is the sort of thing that quants search for today, just on a much larger and more intense scale.

This 'January effect' described by Hall has been attributed, perhaps a little unfairly, to others. *The Journal of Financial Economics* published a study in late 1976 that carried the Hall-like title 'Capital market seasonality: The case of stock returns'. Its authors, M Rozeff and W Kinney, found that January was an unusual month for stock markets around the world in that the returns of equally weighted stock indices were remarkably high.

Another simple trading rule that Henry Hall described in 1916 was the five-year trading rule. Advocated by others at the time, it said, 'A stock is to be bought when it has fallen to, or below, its average price for the past five years'. Again, this is a trading rule that, today, computing power could validate (or not) as delivering a trading advantage. Hall didn't have the benefit of a computer to test the system, but he dismissed it as useless anyway, after manually back-testing its efficacy over prior years.

Reversal patterns in stock prices are commonly proposed as the basis for trading rules. For example, if a stock has done well in recent years, then will it show a tendency to do less well in the future?

In his 1997 bestselling book *What Works on Wall Street*, author and financier James O'Shaughnessy promoted the use of some easy-to-understand trading rules. His rules were based primarily on buying stocks with attractive value metrics. These metrics included low price earnings (PE) ratios, low price-to-book ratios, low price to cash flow ratio, low price-to-sales ratio and high dividend yields, just to name a few.

But you won't find quants reading books like O'Shaughnessy's. No quant would expect to outperform by employing simple methods from a bestselling book. Quite the opposite. For example, Jim Simons has long made new Renaissance employees sign ironclad non-disclosure agreements as a condition of their employment.

The list of tradeable effects that I've described so far is by no means complete. Far from it. All I've attempted to do is to provide a flavour for the types of inefficiencies and opportunities that quants search for.

Another huge area for quants is arbitrage. In its purest form arbitrage is where the price of something is different in two different markets at exactly the same time. This delivers the opportunity to buy it cheaply in one market and immediately sell it in the other for a risk-free profit. But the term 'arbitrage' can also be applied in a much broader sense. For example, when an identifiable relationship exists between the movement in price of two financial instruments or securities, then this can deliver a rich source of arbitrage.

Despite academics preaching their sermons that financial markets are always efficiently priced, the fact is that they aren't. The reality is that markets are riddled with price inefficiencies and inconsistencies. The only concession that I would give the academics is that these inconsistencies are rarely obvious. Most people are incapable of either identifying them or acting on them.

Before I leave this subject, I just have to share with you something that Renaissance Technologies heavy hitter Robert Mercer once told a friend; it adds power to my earlier comments about what an edge looks like. Mercer said of Renaissance, 'We're right 50.75 percent of the time, but we're 100 percent right 50.75 percent of the time. We can make billions that way'.

The problem with being wrong 49.25 percent of the time is that it comes with its own set of difficulties. Over the course of one week during the GFC, Renaissance's Medallion fund lost more than $1 billion. And, due to the accepted near 50 percent loss rate, it wasn't clear to them at the time why it was happening. Could it have been due to a fault in their code? Or were they just experiencing a losing streak that was soon to turn around? Renaissance had the choice of either pulling the plug out of the wall or double-checking their code and letting it remain running.

If the code appeared to be sound, then all they could do was hope that the tide would turn!

How would you go investing or trading under such conditions? Could you maintain faith in your system – if, in fact, you had a system – in the wake of a $1 billion loss?

On the other side of the quants' winning trades are losers

I explained earlier that the financial markets represent a finite pool of money, and that if some are taking more than their share out of the market, then others must be losing.

Henry Laufer, Vice President of Research at Renaissance, once offered a potential source of the massive excesses that Renaissance was extracting from the market, identifying the losers in a comment to a colleague: 'It's a lot of dentists'.

Laufer's words describe the principal similarity between all forms of successful trading and investing. In this respect, Renaissance Technologies has done the same as what Buffett has done. Both have pitted their skills against the frailties and inadequacies that are rife among the market's masses. Each could identify their edge.

What's your edge?

Chapter 17

Artificial Intelligence

'It seems probable that once the machine thinking method had started, it would not take long to outstrip our feeble powers.'

– Alan Turing

Alan Turing was a brilliant mathematician, computer scientist and code breaker who lived during the first half of the 20th century. He was fascinated with artificial intelligence (AI). In a 1950 paper titled 'Computing Machinery and Intelligence', Turing proposed a test to assist in judging when a computer was adequately mimicking human intelligence. It later became known as the Turing test. Under the Turing test, a computer is considered intelligent if a human interrogator can't tell the difference between it and a human.

So, have we yet produced a machine that meets Turing's benchmark? For example, does Apple's Siri fit Turing's definition? 'She' certainly appears to answer questions in an intelligent way. So, why not ask Siri how to beat the market?

Unfortunately, Siri isn't our girl. She won't make us rich. What's more, an interrogator could easily trip her up.

Based on Turing's definition, machines have yet to develop human-like intelligence. Computers have a powerful ability to store and regurgitate facts. They can even be designed to mimic human behaviour. But neither of these things represents true intelligence.

What about machine learning? That's where computers learn from past mistakes and modify the way that they process information so as to enhance their future performance. Machine learning has been with us for a while. Quants have already successfully harnessed this technology, building machine learning into their computer-based trading systems. In fact, computer-based trading has developed to the point where human traders have been made redundant. The hand-drawn charts and the visual interpretation of historical price graphs that human traders undertook in the past are as relevant today as the Ford Model T is to motoring.

The ascendency of machine-based trading over human trading might be likened to the ascendency of planes over birds. The aluminium fuselage of a 747 jet might be less sophisticated than the bone, feathers and flesh of birds, but I know which I'd back in a race between London and Sydney.

So, where is it all heading? Where does this computer-driven financial 'space race' end? Because it's far from finished yet.

Computers already dominate short-term trading (high-frequency and Simons-style trading). Will Buffett-style investing ultimately be the domain of the smartest AI?

And what about artificial general intelligence (AGI)? AGI is where machines can learn any intellectual task that a human can. Will it be necessary for AGI to develop adequately before stock picking can be dominated by machines? Will AGI deliver the ultimate form of traditional buy-and-hold investing? Will machines not only match our present intellectual capabilities but ultimately also leave us far in their wake? And will computers ultimately become so capable at seeking out pricing inefficiencies that inefficiencies cease to exist? The stock market would then be rendered an equal playing field that is fair to all.

And that wouldn't be such a bad thing. Then active fund managers (even the good ones) would be as relevant to investing as buggy whip manufacturers are now to transport.

What will it take for computers to become great investors (Buffett-style)?

Humans process information in a linear fashion. We can get our mind around simple relationships like how 'A' impacts 'B' and 'C' impacts 'D'. We keep things simple because we have to. It's about all that our brain can handle. Things become more difficult when we attempt to consider numerous interdependent inputs to a problem – for example, those of 'X', 'Y' and 'Z'. And that, while 'Y' influences 'X', 'B' sometimes influences 'Z', but only if 'K' is influencing 'Y' but not 'P'. This sets up complex interactive loops.

The human brain is poor at processing information in an interactive manner. But this is exactly what good financial analysis requires. Smart computers of the future will likely leave us in the dust with respect to interactive thinking.

Professor Paul Slovic, the founder and president of Decision Research, studied the extent to which professional stock market analysts utilise interactive reasoning and linear thinking when making stock recommendations. His generous assessment was that 4 percent of the analysts' decisions could be ascribed to an interactive process. This means that, in many situations, the greater overwhelms the lesser. Placing your trust in human-derived research findings can, at times, be likened to drinking from a water supply that contains 96 percent raw sewerage.

Even if our capacity to invest is ultimately surpassed by computers, there are likely to be people who continue to rely on the old grey matter. There will remain devotees who genuinely enjoy the process of searching for good investment opportunities, just as humans are likely to continue driving cars on closed tracks long after they are banned from driving them on public roads. Cases in point:

- drummers have kept drumming despite the invention of electronic drums
- synthesisers didn't stop people from playing pianos
- motor cars didn't stop people riding horses
- powered boats didn't stop people sailing.

So, it's possible that the development of more advanced computers and investing software won't stop some people from putting their minds to investing.

But all of this carries one giant proviso: much of the pleasure of investing comes from the attainment of financial reward. If that reward is quashed, then so too is one of the main reasons for investing. Would people still go fishing if they knew that there was no chance they'd ever catch a fish? Will investors still research stocks by using human brainpower if they know that there will be no financial reward?

I know that I wouldn't bother. So, maybe people will leave investment analysis solely to computers. Only time will tell.

PART III

THE MAST

Chapter 18

Be Realistic

'Losing an Illusion makes you wiser than finding a truth.'
– Karl Ludwig Börne

I now want to shift direction. The tone of the book so far has been fairly negative.

I have shone a light on the likely limitations of your investing ability. I have described things that don't work in the world of investing despite the oft-widespread belief that they do. I have warned you of the traps and snares in which you can become caught – of the siren songs that will seduce you away from sound investment principles and behaviour, and that might even lure you onto the rocks of financial destruction.

Negative it might have been, but I see it all as essential knowledge. In fact, an appreciation of these pitfalls acknowledges the best investment advice that I've ever read. Ironically, the advice wasn't delivered by an investment professional, nor did he mean it as investment advice. Yet, it is resoundingly relevant to the process of investing. It's the advice at the top of this page, delivered two centuries ago by German political writer and satirist Karl Ludwig Börne.

Börne's advice is powerful because we unconsciously adopt untruths as truths, fantasy as fact. We place our faith in fictions despite there being no evidence to support that faith. We then use those fictions to make bad decisions. It's rife in the investment world.

It's Börne's advice that has driven the structure of this book. It's why I have gone to great lengths in attempting to destroy any untruths that you may be harbouring. Untruths about your investing skills. Untruths regarding the returns that you are capable of achieving. Untruths regarding the claims that other, ill-informed people make about what they can achieve. Börne's advice is exactly the reason I have devoted so much effort to telling you what doesn't work.

But it's now time for me to start talking about what does work. I want to empower you to make sound positive decisions. So, let's talk about what is real in the world of investing.

And that's what the rest of the book is about.

Fractured finance

A good friend of mine works in the media. He reckons that the mantra of TV and newspaper editors is, 'If it bleeds, it leads'. Hence the success of radio shock jocks.

Let's face it, the media is a business. The aim of the media has always been to attract as many eyeballs to its content as is possible – or, in modern parlance, to get as many 'clicks' as is achievable. This sees finance commentators describe the stock market not as 'correcting' but as 'plunging'. Equally, the stock market is often described not as merely 'rising' but as 'soaring'.

These descriptions play with our emotions. Case in point: I have a friend who feels richer when the stock market rises on any day and poorer when it falls on any day. He feels it no matter how small the move.

But, for the long-term investor, it's long-term returns that are meaningful, not inter-day oscillations. So, let's take a look.

Long-term Australian stock market returns

The following figure shows how the Australian stock market has performed over the past 120 years (in price terms). It even includes an event that is still pretty fresh in our minds: the 2020 COVID-19-induced stock market fall.

And I think you'll agree the Australian stock market has performed very well indeed over the past century and a bit.

The Australian stock market over the past 120 years

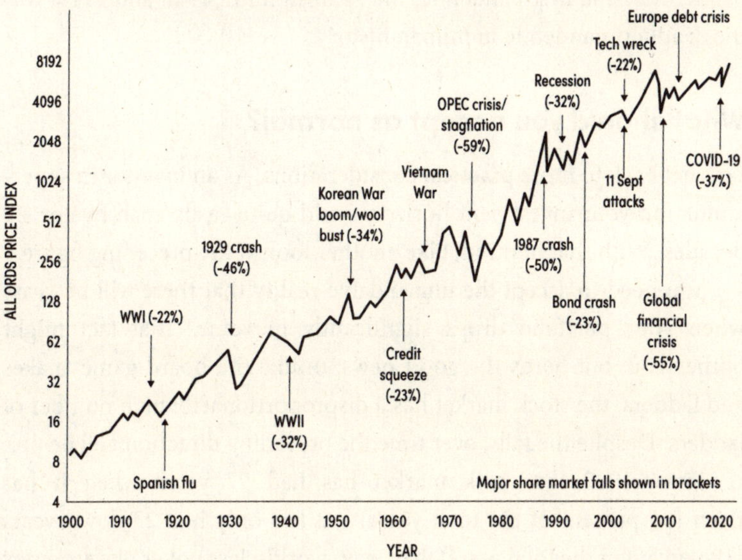

SOURCE: ASX, AMP CAPITAL

There are a couple of important points to note that add further power to the stock market's performance:

1. Take a look at the numbers to the left of the Y-axis (the rise in the index). A logarithmic scale has been employed. If a linear scale had been used, then the graph would be ten people high.
2. The graph only reflects the rise in stock market prices. If the graph included reinvested dividends, then the line would be challenging domestic airspace.

Just to pin some numbers on the impact of the 'reinvestment' of dividends, $10 invested back in the year 1900 would now be worth

$7.5 million (not adjusted for inflation). And that result would have been achieved without adding one single cent to the initial $10 investment.

Now I'm well aware that no one has an investment horizon that spans 120 years. I just wanted to make the point that the stock market has recovered strongly from every crisis that's ever been thrown at it. And that list includes recessions, fuel crises, two world wars and two pandemics. The first pandemic, the Spanish flu in 1918 and 1919, was the deadliest pandemic in human history.

What should you accept as normal?

Let's get back to more practical considerations. As an investor in superannuation your investment horizon could quite easily span five or six decades. With that in mind, take another look at the preceding figure.

You need to accept the unavoidable reality that there will be years when your portfolio drops significantly in value. That fact might bother you, but here's the good news: unlike the board game snakes and ladders, the stock market has a disproportionately high number of ladders. Despite the falls, over time the prevailing direction will be up.

Since 1900 the stock market has had 97 years when it has risen (81 percent of the total years) but has only had 23 down years (19 percent of the total years). Not even world-class poker players enjoy such attractive odds! It means that, the longer you play, the more likely you are to succeed.

Let's now consider what are realistic returns when investing in shares. Since 1900 the Australian stock market has delivered an annual average return of 13.2 percent before inflation and around 7 to 8 percent after inflation. Let that be your benchmark return against which to judge all claims, hopes, dreams… and lies.

My experience

I'm entering my 35th unbroken year of investing in the stock market. So, my portfolio has been variously hit by three monster financial events: the October 1987 Crash (stock market down 25 percent in a single day), the GFC (down 55 percent overall) and the 2020 COVID-19-induced calamity (down 37 percent in a period of weeks). After those three onslaughts I have now come to view stock market corrections to be as significant to my welfare as a Leopard tank driver would consider a bug hitting his windscreen: I don't care!

I started investing in early 1987, just months before the biggest one-day percentage collapse that the stock market has ever suffered. Now, you'd think that, after an early knock like that, I'd simply pick up my bat and ball and go home. But I didn't. My investment view was a long-term one.

So, let's now pin some numbers on how the stock market has performed since then, and why my decision to keep playing was the right one. I'm now going to talk about a very important investing time period: mine!

The All Ordinaries Accumulation Index (now called the Total Return Index) kicked off 1987 at 3991 points. This index takes into account the reinvestment of all dividends. As I write, the same index is at 86,509 points. I'll save you reaching for your calculator: it's a 21-fold increase. Let me remind you, that return has been delivered despite the stock market experiencing:

- its biggest one-day collapse in history
- the world's worst financial crisis for 80 years
- the most profound pandemic in a century from which no part of the globe was spared.

If you ever suffer from a dose of the 'stock market wobbles' then take a big step back, a big deep breath and get some perspective. Because this is the reality of investing in the stock market. There will be ups. There will be downs. Keep the faith. Over time the rewards will be profound.

Chapter 19

Diversify

'Diversify. In stocks and bonds, as in much else, there is safety in numbers.'
– Sir John Templeton

When a stock investment turns sour, most of those who have invested in it feel pain. Research tells us that investors feel double the pain when they lose money compared to the pleasure they experience from a gain of the same magnitude.

It's even worse when a company goes bust. Then, unlike a share price drop due to poor corporate performance (with the chance of a subsequent recovery), it's a finite loss. There is no hope of making that money back. The company, and your money, has goneski.

So, what can you do in order to minimise this potential for pain? You can diversify your investments. Spread them around. As they say in the classics, don't put all your eggs in one basket. That way any single loss is obscured by the performance of the rest of your portfolio.

Now, I have to warn you that diversifying your investments across a wide range of investment classes (such as shares, bonds and real estate), or across a wide range of different shares, is not met with universal enthusiasm. While diversification can limit the downside damage, it can equally limit the upside gain. If a winning stock represents a small proportion of your portfolio, then you will likely kick yourself that you didn't buy more of it.

At the 2019 Berkshire Hathaway AGM, Charlie Munger referred to this event as 'diworsification' (not his term but he acknowledged that he was happy to borrow it). Munger felt that investors had a better chance of doing well if they invested in a select group of well-researched stocks. Diversification defeats the purpose of undertaking skilled and informed research.

Warren Buffett has his own take on diversification. He famously described the strategy of diversifying one's assets among a very large number of companies as the 'Noah's ark' technique of investing: 'One buys two of everything and in the end owns a zoo'.

If Munger and Buffett both feel this way, then why did Buffett write in Berkshire's 2013 annual letter to shareholders, 'My advice to the trustee couldn't be simpler. Put 10 percent of the cash in short-term government bonds and 90 percent in a very low-cost S&P index fund'. That's a lot of diversification Buffett is adopting there, investing in 500 different companies.

Buffett's conflicting advice can be easily reconciled. First up, I get what Munger and Buffett are saying about the downside of diversification. You can't hope to outperform a benchmark by essentially investing in the benchmark or close to it. Diversification might be safe but it pretty much locks in average (or close to average) returns. But Buffett and Munger can make comments like these because they are both great investors. And, if Buffett had practised diversification over the course of his career, then he would not be worth what he is today. Buffett's request that his family's money be diversified by investing in a broad-based index fund is equally sound. He knows that his family doesn't possess his investing acumen. He wants his family's money to be safe after he's gone.

Buffett's advice to diversify applies equally well to every average Joe and Janice investor out there. And by that, I mean almost everyone. And it should include plenty of professional fund managers as well!

Having said that, I am amused when I hear the derogatory term 'diworsification' being parroted by others who don't possess any investing smarts. It's particularly loud from those with a vested interest in actively managing other people's money. Rather than recommending diversification, they mock it – primarily because they want their clients to pay them high fees for managing their money.

I'd ask you to check the investment record of those with the loudest voices. I have and it's rarely a performance worth bragging about. It astounds me that many have the temerity to make these claims when their underperformance is on public record for all to see.

I would suggest that, for you, diversification is like Ulysses' mast. So, bind yourself to it. It will protect you against those seductive claims from imposters claiming to be market-beaters.

Chapter 20

Reversion to the Mean

'Reversion to the mean is the iron rule of the financial markets.'
– John Bogle

As vague and imprecise as the world of finance can often be, there are a handful of truisms. One of them is that the predictions made by so-called experts – whether they be about the future state of the economy or where the financial markets are heading – will more likely be wrong than right. Few people realise that the bulk of the commentary from economists on TV, the talking heads on CNN or even the heads of central banks is worthless noise. And that makes things difficult. After all, people place their trust in these 'experts'.

So, what can you do about it? I learnt years ago that the best way to judge the state of the market is to embrace a concept called 'mean reversion'. It's not applicable all the time but occasionally it comes in very handy.

Now, unless you have a leaning towards mathematics, you probably aren't aware of mean reversion. So, let's explore the concept. To assist in the explanation, I want you to visualise the movement of the pendulum in an old grandfather clock. Once in motion, watch as the pendulum swings from one side to the other. However far it swings in its arc, it eventually stops momentarily and then swings back in the opposite direction. It's as if the central vertical position is where it wants to be. The centre marks the 'average' of all the positions that the pendulum is ever in.

Now, the mathematical term for an average is the 'mean'. So, by always reverting back towards the midline, we can think of the pendulum as 'mean-reverting'.

This is the concept that I apply to the financial markets when I'm judging where things might be heading. Let's use interest rates as an example.

Now, I don't hold strong views about where interest rates are heading in the short term. But, when interest rates are at extremely low levels or extremely high levels, then I'm willing to take a long-term view regarding their future direction.

I remember back in 1990 when I was working in the financial markets. The overnight cash rate was at the astronomical level of 17.5 percent. I was chatting to a bond dealer at the time. I suggested to him that, because interest rates were so high (by historical standards), the odds were that they'd fall and, over time, significantly. He told me I was on drugs.

It seemed that this guy was suffering from some form of inertia. He believed that the future was going to be little different to the present. This type of thinking is quite common. People's future view is often overly influenced by what is happening right now. That interest rates might fall from their lofty 1990 heights was simply beyond this guy's comprehension.

Well, interest rates did fall. In fact, they fell virtually from that point on. Four years later the overnight cash rate had essentially normalised to around 5 percent. It stayed around that level for close to 12 years. For that entire 12-year period I didn't hold a view as to where interest rates were heading because they were no longer at an extreme level.

Interest rates eventually started to fall again. By late 2020 the overnight cash rate had reached an all-time historical low of 0.1 percent. In my mind the pendulum was now at the other extreme of its arc.

I then saw interest rates as being excessively low. Unsurprisingly, they moved up rapidly over the course of 2022.

Did I have insight? Not really. I just know that extremes are unsustainable.

How did I identify when the most extreme level had been reached and that things were about to turn? I didn't know. But I could identify when things were way, way out of whack with historical norms. My timing was never going to be so precise that I would pick the turn. Only plain dumb luck will deliver that sort of precision.

So, what do you do when markets, commodities, currencies or interest rates aren't at an extreme level – that is, when they aren't far removed from their long-term average? Things are difficult to call then. They could go either way. It means that, most of the time, the concept of mean reversion can't be applied.

The problem with extremes is that, while they present opportunity, few people have the patience to wait for them to come along. Even fewer people have the confidence to act on them when they do.

Even market professionals have difficulty identifying these times of extreme opportunity. I remember during the depths of the GFC, after the stock market had collapsed by more than 50 percent and buying opportunities were everywhere, a well-known market commentator appeared on television and told viewers that it was far too dangerous to enter the stock market – that investors would be best to remain in cash.

His comments almost perfectly marked the turn. Share prices rocketed from there. A year later the market was 40 percent higher. The irony is that this bloke claims to be a capable market timer!

While financial markets don't swing with predictable precision like the pendulum of a grandfather clock, consider mean reversion as a guide to facilitate judgment. It can be used as your normaliser of behaviour when others are losing their heads. Consider it as another financial equivalent of Ulysses' mast. I'd recommend that you tie yourself to the concept of mean reversion when the financial world is going crazy.

Exploring those means or averages

The following table shows a few long-term averages and ranges that relate to Australian financial markets. They will help you to place prevailing economic and stock market conditions in perspective.

Remember that mean reversion is not an accurate tool and should not be your sole reference when making decisions about the status of the financial markets. But it does act as a 'grounder' at times of extreme market conditions. As prevailing conditions approach the mean, mean reversion carries less value in making judgments regarding the future.

Some long-term averages and ranges relating to Australian financial markets

Category	Average/range	Time period
RBA overnight cash rate range	From 0.1% to 17.5%	Past 32 years
Average inflation rate	4.9%	Past 55 years
Average PE ratio	16 times	Past 42 years
Average dividend yield	4.1%	Past 42 years
Average annual stock market return	13.2% before inflation and including dividends	Past 122 years

More on the price earnings ratio

The price earnings (PE) ratio is a financial ratio commonly used by share investors to assist in judging relative value. Typically, it is applied to individual companies and is calculated by dividing the company's current share price by the most recently reported earnings per share.

But the concept of the PE ratio can also be applied to the stock market as a whole. General stock prices are considered to be high (by historical standards) when the average market PE ratio exceeds 20 times and to be low when it reaches single digits. The long-term average market PE ratio is around the mid-teens. Some people like to use this market PE in their efforts to market-time (to time their entry into or exit from the share market).

Finance professors Jack Wilson and Charles Jones of North Carolina State University studied PE ratios associated with the US stock market back to 1871. The next table summarises their findings, which indicate that higher-than-average annual returns are typically delivered in the wake of low market PE ratios. But the converse is less clear-cut; that is, lower-than-average annual returns aren't necessarily delivered in the wake of high PE ratios, depending on the period being considered.

US stock market returns since 1871 following high and low PE levels

Period	After years when market PE <10	After years when market PE >20	All years
1 year	16.2%	11.6%	10.2%
3 years	14.8%	9.6%	9.4%
5 years	15.1%	10.3%	9.3%
10 years	14.2%	8.2%	9.1%

Chapter 21

History

'I have no way of judging the future but by the past.'
– Patrick Henry

We are searching for constants – proverbial masts to secure ourselves to and so provide us with a modicum of certainty in a financial world that has little certainty to offer. The strongest and most secure mast for me has been history.

There are many things that history can teach us. But, for me, it's been principally about human behaviour. It's amazing how consistent our behaviour has proven to be given the same or similar circumstances. That's why, in my second book, *Uncommon Sense: Investment Wisdom Since the Stock Market's Dawn*, I devoted an entire chapter to this subject. I titled the chapter 'The Human Constant'.

So, why is it important to identify recurring patterns of human behaviour? Because people's behaviour influences market prices.

Let me now share a story with you to show you what I mean. It was 20 October 1987, the morning of Australia's biggest ever stock market collapse. I was in the lift at 367 Collins Street, Melbourne, moving skywards towards the Melbourne offices of Bankers Trust, where I was working at the time. A seasoned equity trader who was travelling in the lift with me broke the silence: 'Well, I reckon it's a good thing. I mean, it's about time that it happened. The market was way overpriced.'

He was referring to the fact that, only a couple of hours earlier, Australia woke to the news of Wall Street's breathtaking 23 percent stock market plunge. It was the biggest ever one-day collapse in stock prices in the history of the US market. That day, Australia's stock market followed Wall Street's collapse. In fact, by the end of trade it had eclipsed Wall Street's fall with a monumental 25 percent plunge.

I remember my reaction to what that equity trader said in the lift that morning. While I didn't verbalise it, I thought that he was nuts. I mean, seriously, who would think that a stock market crash was a good thing?

You have to realise that I was still in my 20s at the time, and it was the first time that I had experienced a financial panic with a reasonable amount of my own money in the market. And, while stock market crashes had been happening for centuries before then, this one was different: it was happening to me! But now I am in my 60s. And, after having experienced four significant crashes – 1987, 2000, 2008 and 2020 – I know exactly what the guy in the elevator meant.

Stock market crashes are normal. They happen. They are an unavoidable part of investing. They aren't as big a deal as people make them out to be.

The stock market has a rich and deep history. The trading of shares has been going on for over four centuries. It doesn't matter that you haven't personally experienced every single one of those crashes. All the stock market's past gyrations have been recorded by an army of historians. So, there is plenty of history and past experience that you can draw from.

When I read history, I internalise it. You should do the same. History is far from irrelevant. History is a grounder. It's an anchor. It's a mast to tie yourself to.

As philosopher George Santayana said, 'Those who do not remember the past are condemned to repeat it.' Ignoring history's lessons is why so many young and inexperienced investors get burnt.

Read history like you are living it

Because decent stock market crashes don't commonly occur, the breadth of history that you read should encompass centuries rather than months, years or decades. When reading the stories, you need to imagine how people felt as they lived through those events. It doesn't matter how long ago it was. Appreciate that people of the past felt exactly the same as people feel today.

It all reminds me of a quote that appeared in *Cato's Letters* in 1721. *Cato's Letters* were essays composed by British writers John Trenchard and Thomas Gordon, first published from 1720 to 1723. This quote is just so appropriate to what I'm talking about:

> 'There must be a vast fund of stupidity in human nature, else men would not be caught as they are, a thousand times over, by the same snare, and while they yet remember their past misfortunes, go on to court and encourage the causes to which they were owing, and which again produce them.'

Investors devoid of an appreciation of financial history are easily caught in that same snare.

Let's now take a look at a great example of what this extract from *Cato's Letters* is referring to.

In 1720 England was in the grip of a financial mania referred to as The South Sea Bubble. The principal company driving the madness was an enterprise called The South Sea Company. The South Sea Company was granted limited trading rights with the New World (and in particular with South America). Stories and rumours regarding the potential trading opportunities drove the share price of the South Sea Company skyward. It climbed tenfold in the 12 months preceding August 1720.

There is nothing like a rocketing share price to draw public interest. This interest spilled over to an appetite for stocks of all kinds. Financial opportunists dreamed up all manner of enterprises to meet the public's insatiable appetite for stocks. A wide range of weird and crazy companies was created with equally weird and crazy names. Referred to as 'bubble companies', these fictitious, vacuous shells were flogged to a gullible and greedy public. (The same thing happened during Dot.com and the crypto craze: worthless creations to satisfy the public's demand. The principal purpose was usually to enrich their creators.)

Now I won't go through the full list of bubble companies here, but if you want to get a feel for how people can lose their collective minds then have a read of Charles Mackay's classic tome *Extraordinary Popular Delusions and the Madness of Crowds*. Of all the companies that were created to dupe the 18th century investors there was one he describes that stood head and shoulders above the others. Its prospectus declared it as 'a company for carrying out an undertaking of great advantage but nobody to know what it is'.

I remember how I reacted to this story when I first read Mackay's book three decades ago. I simply couldn't believe that people could be so stupid as to invest their money into a vacuum. But they were. And they still are.

During the height of the Dot.com boom in the late 1990s – which was similar to the South Sea Bubble of 1720 in so many ways – a company called NetJ.com was created. It attracted in excess of $110 million of investor's money despite its prospectus stating, 'The company is not currently engaged in any substantial activity and has no plans to engage in such activities in the foreseeable future'. Just compare the words of the two prospectuses, written almost three centuries apart! It's why I have zero sympathy for those who lost their money by subscribing to NetJ during Dot.com.

Within months of the initial NetJ offering the share price had climbed 18-fold. No doubt early investors believed that they were very clever. But all that was driving the share price was buyers' enthusiasm. Greater fools were being minted on a daily basis. They were blindly buying the worthless stock at ever higher prices. Each bought their NetJ stock from a prior fool. Or, as Adam Anderson – a former cashier of the South Sea Company – had so aptly stated a few centuries before, owners of the shares had 'rid of them in the crowded alley to others more credulous than themselves'. Anderson's words describe well what we now refer to as the 'greater fool theory'.

OK, so not everyone in 1999 had read about the South Sea Bubble of 1720. I concede that nearly three centuries is a fair stretch of history. But I will add that Charles Mackay's book and many other books outlining the events of 1720 were available for Dot.com investors to read.

Amazingly, two decades later in 2020, it all happened again.

That year, a friend sent me a text that carried a link to a Bloomberg article titled 'No Revenue Is No Problem in the 2020 Stock Market'. Despite the world being in the midst of a devastating once-in-a-century pandemic, there were still people out there who were prepared to throw caution to the wind. The article described the new-found investor appetite for financial vehicles called SPACs (special purpose acquisition companies). SPACs were being established to raise cash from guileless and optimistic investors. Their cash was earmarked to buy yet-to-be-identified companies.

It's a form of investing not unlike those lucky dips at childhood fetes: you hand over your pocket money and then reach into the depths of a deep box to select a surprise toy. But, in the case of SPACs, the surprise toys were companies. And we aren't talking about dispensing with pocket money here either. From the start of 2020 to the middle of 2022 a total of $260 billion was raised in the USA to invest in SPACs.

Let's be clear here. People parted with hundreds of billions of dollars to buy 'companies for carrying out undertakings of great advantage but nobody to know what it is'.

These crazy times – 1720, 1999 and 2021 – were all marked by the same pendulum – each time at the extreme limit of its swing.

Chapter 22

Patience

'Great operators do nothing in a hurry; they have infinite patience.'
– Henry Hall

Ulysses was bound to the mast by his crew to prevent him from steering their boat onto the rocks. But, as an investor, it's clearly not practical to ask a friend to tie you up after you make an investment. So, I need to convince you of the virtue of patience.

The 20th century's most famous economist, John Maynard Keynes, nailed the difficulty that investors have in practising patience in *The General Theory*:

> 'Human nature desires quick results, there is a peculiar zest in making money quickly, and remoter gains are discounted by the average man at a very high rate. The game of professional investment is intolerably boring and over-exacting to anyone who is entirely exempt from the gambling instinct; whilst he who has it must pay to this propensity the appropriate toll.'

Keynes is reminding us that, rather than being patient, many investors expect large and immediate returns. The problem with this thinking is that stocks that deliver rapid returns are like shooting stars: they are rare, they appear without warning and they only burn for a short time. Profiting from owning one is largely the result of luck. For most people, by the time its flight has become obvious, climbing onboard is futile because it is close to running out of fuel.

Investing is not a game in which you repeatedly pick big winners. Think of it as more of a defensive game. It's won over a long period of time by building a large score but in small increments. And that takes mountains of patience.

But don't take my word for it. Plenty of others have delivered exactly the same message.

The two oldest books in my bookshelves are Leonardo Pisano's *Liber Abaci* (written in 1202) and Joseph de la Vega's classic *Confusion de Confusiones* (written in 1688). Obviously, neither are first editions, but they are accurate reprints of the originals. I also have many books that were written in the 19th century. There is one word that regularly appears in many of these old books. That word is 'patience'. There is no doubt that patience is a characteristic that has long been identified as facilitating investment success.

Back in the 17th century investor and author Joseph de la Vega described some essential personal traits that one should bring to investing. And yes, you guessed it, one of them was patience. He wrote, 'Whoever wishes to win in this game must have patience and money'. Even more interesting is de la Vega's explanation of why these are so important:

> 'Since the values [of shares] are so little constant and the rumours so little founded on truth. He who knows how to endure blows without being terrified by the misfortune resembles the lion who answers the thunder with a roar, and is unlike the hind who, stunned by the thunder, tries to flee. It is certain that he who does not give up hope will win, and will secure money adequate for the operations that he envisaged at the start. Owing to the vicissitudes, many people make themselves ridiculous because some speculators are guided

> by dreams, others by prophecies, these by delusions, those by moods, and innumerable men by chimeras.'

Dwell on those words for a moment. Perhaps read them again. And, as you read them, remember that they were written in 1688. Yet they are so applicable today. That's because they describe human behaviour. And, as I explained in the last chapter, that hasn't changed one bit over the centuries.

Joseph de la Vega is saying that those who effect a plan, stay the course and don't fall prey to corrosive emotions are ultimately rewarded. His description of the dreams, prophesies, delusions, moods and chimeras that investors experience must be resisted in the same way that Ulysses had to resist the siren's efforts to lure him onto the rocks. He is effectively saying that investors must tie themselves to the mast!

The recognition of patience through time

Three hundred years ago the author of *An Argument* chastised stock-holders for not being patient: 'They are all in haste to sell out, at more than half below the real Value, and will not wait with Patience and cool thoughts for the profitable Dividends'.

Author Matthew Hale Smith wrote 150 years ago, 'Men who buy long and hold what they buy, reap golden fortunes'.

Author Henry Hall wrote over 100 years ago:

> 'An investor will gain nothing by haste, by acting on impulse. Patience, the infinite patience which characterises the security transactions of dominant and successful spirits in finance, is always the most profitable of all virtues in Wall Street.'

Ninety years ago, Benjamin Graham described his classic recipe for beating the stock market in his book *Security Analysis*:

> 'Obviously, it requires strength of character in order to think and to act in opposite fashion from the crowd; and also patience to wait for opportunities which may be spaced years apart.'

For those of you who might think that patience is irrelevant to investing today, let's take a look at the behaviour practised by two contemporary investors we have already come to know well in this book: Warren Buffett and Jim Simons.

Back in chapter 15 I told you that, when Buffett's oldest child Susie was asked what qualities best described her father, she didn't hesitate; she responded with the words 'integrity' and 'patience'.

What, then, of trader Jim Simons? You might think that patience doesn't describe his trading style. Remember that his computer-driven Medallion fund might execute hundreds of thousands of trades in a single day. How could that possibly represent patience?

Remember that Simons didn't start trading in earnest until he was 40 years old. Before that he'd had a couple of false starts as an investor and trader. What's more, Simons didn't start to make decent money until he was 50 years old. It's a patient man who works that long and that hard at something before achieving success.

Also, while Simons' trading system is rapid-fire, consider the supreme amount of work required to develop that system, the countless failures that preceded the success and, dare I say it, the massive amount of patience displayed by Simons and his team before that success was achieved.

Let's be frank here – patience isn't sexy

Several years ago, I received a call from an old school buddy. I don't catch up with him that often but when I do it's always great to see him. He'd just been left a sizable sum of money from his mother's estate, and I suspect that it was the largest chunk of cash that he'd ever had in one place at one time. The problem he wanted me to help solve was what to do with it.

Now, usually I'd tell someone in this situation to go and visit their friendly financial planner. But, hell, my old school buddy was very much a do-it-yourself sort of guy. Case in point: he'd built his own house using timber that he'd felled and shaped in his own timber mill.

It's unlikely that he ever would have bothered going to see a financial planner. All he wanted to find out from me was what his options were. Nothing specific. He'd take it from there.

After chatting for a few hours – we had a lot to catch up on – we came around to the idea of investing his new-found wealth in a broad equity-based index fund that charged low fees. I told him that this type of investment had historically delivered an annual return of around 7 to 8 percent (after inflation), but not in a straight line. The strategy would be safer than choosing his own stocks but it did require patience. Given enough time, general index equity funds were great compounding machines.

What I didn't realise was that, the whole time I was talking about blue-chip investments, he was thinking about cryptocurrencies and marijuana stocks. And that's where he ultimately put his money. Apparently, they were way sexier. I have yet to catch up with him to see how things are tracking.

I guess patience, for most, is something that they are born with… or not.

Chapter 23

Compounding

'My wealth has come from a combination of living in America, some lucky genes, and compound interest.'
– Warren Buffett

I had just wrapped up my presentation to a large group of investors and was making my way towards the exit. That's when I spotted her glaring at me with a look that could kill.

As I approached the doorway, where she had propped, she let me have it.

'What use is it to give us a presentation like that?' she snarled. 'That's an hour of my life I'll never get back. Don't you realise that, for someone my age (she looked about 75-ish), the investment strategy you just outlined is absolutely useless?'

As the intensity of her berating started to ease, a man about her equal in age walked past and flashed me a big smile and a thumbs up. 'Great presentation', he said. 'I've done everything that you talked about'.

So, what had I just talked about? What is the investment strategy that drew such polarised reactions?

My presentation was about compounding, the most powerful weapon that any investor can carry in their arsenal.

The story goes that Albert Einstein, when asked what he considered to be the greatest of mankind's discoveries, answered, 'compound interest'. And, apparently, he then went on to declare it to be the eighth wonder of the world. While no evidence exists that Einstein actually said this, the sentiment remains powerful.

But it's not really like the other seven wonders, is it? You know what I'm talking about here – the Great Pyramid of Giza, the Colossus of Rhodes or the Hanging Gardens of Babylon. This wonder isn't a building, nor did it ever rate as a tourist attraction. But I agree with the sentiment that it is equally wonderful. So, let's take a look. There's no entry fee to this world wonder!

I learnt about compound interest at a very young age. My sixth grade teacher, Mr Curtis, told our class all about it. But when you're 11 years old you don't relate a lesson in mathematics to investing. So, it was a concept that didn't carry any 'eighth wonder of the world'-type magic for me until I was a lot older.

Its power is a mathematical one. Those with a mathematical bent can envision it by eyeballing the compounding formula. And here it is – drum roll please…

$$A = P\,(1 + r/n)^{(nt)}$$

Where:

A = the final amount
P = principal (the amount you start with)
r = interest rate (expressed as a decimal)
n = number of times interest is compounded per unit 't'
t = time

My guess is that the formula didn't do it for you, did it? You'd rather have gone to see the pyramids. Trust Einstein to get excited about a formula. But stay with the game here, and let me now show you why it's a lot more exciting than $E = mc^2$ for most people.

To show you how the formula works, let me use a simple example. Say you had a bank account that paid 5 percent interest at the end of each year. If you had $1000 in the account then you'd be paid $50 interest at year end. If you withdrew the interest from your account each year, then after ten years you'd still have $1000 in the account and you would have earned a total of $500 bucks in interest payments. Add the principal and interest together and that works out to be $1500 (although it's unlikely you'd have that amount after ten years because you'd have probably spent the interest in the meantime – but you get the idea).

Now consider how much you would have if you instead left the earned interest in the account and didn't withdraw it each year. Then you'd end up with $1,628.89 at the end of ten years. That's an extra $128! So, where did the extra money come from?

It was due to compounding. By leaving the first year's interest payment of $50 in the account rather than taking it out at the end of the first year, in year two not only will you again earn 5 percent on the initial $1000 (that's $50) but you'll also earn 5 percent on the first year's interest that you left in. And in year three, as well as earning 5 percent on the initial $1000, again you'll earn interest on the interest from year two and interest on the interest on the interest that you earned from year one!

Now, before we get ourselves tied up in knots here, you can see where we're heading with all of this. Let the thing run for long enough and it really starts to pick up some momentum. In fact, there are three things that determine how big the final pot of loot ends up being:

1. the amount of money you feed into the compounding machine in the first place – the more you feed in, the more you end up with
2. the rate of interest that you earn in each period – the higher that is, the more you end up with
3. how long you let it run for – the longer that is, the more you end up with.

And if you want to check that what I've just told you is correct, then simply revisit the formula that I used to kick off this whole discussion. There they are in the formula: principal, interest rate and time.

Now that's how compounding works, but I don't reckon I've got you as excited as Albert Einstein was supposed to have been just yet. So, let's push on.

I now want to share an age-old example of the power of compounding. Lots of people have used it to demonstrate the impact of time on the compounding process. In fact, I used it in my first book, *Creating Real Wealth*. So, in an act of self-plagiarism, allow me to repeat what I wrote back then.

It's the story of how New York's famous Manhattan Island was acquired from the longstanding residents of Mannahatta, the Lenape. In 1626 Peter Minuit, the colonial governor of New Amsterdam (as today's New York was then referred to by the Dutch colonists), 'bought' the entire island of Manhattan from the locals for 60 Dutch guilders' worth of trinkets. Now, 1626 was long before US dollars were issued, but in 1846 historian John Romeyn Brodhead equated 60 Dutch guilders to about $24.

It is reported that the Lenape had no concept of land ownership and consequently no understanding of what they were agreeing to. Nevertheless, they accepted the beads and ribbons from the Dutch. The concept of purchasing 23 square miles of what was to become one of the world's most significant real estate holdings for a mere $24 might seem ridiculous until you calculate what $24 would be worth today had it been invested and the returns allowed to compound. Had the Lenape not accepted the trinkets but rather placed the $24 in a Dutch bank at a modest 6.5 percent rate of interest, then the $24, with no addition to the initial principal amount, would have compounded to $763 billion by 2010. By 2020 the capital would have surpassed $1.4 trillion and would have been growing by $255 million per day.

Now I just want to check that we're all still on the same tram here: a trillion dollars is a million, million, dollars. And that near incomprehensible amount of money was generated solely from a hypothetical one-off investment of 24 bucks that was compounded at a lousy 6.5 percent per year.

Now we can start to see why Albert was getting so excited.

The reason the final amount is so mind-blowingly large is because we really dialled up the time component of the formula. After all, 394 is a decent number of cycles around the sun to wait before making a withdrawal from the account!

So, what about the other two inputs into the compounding formula? They were the amount of money initially plugged in and the interest or investment rate at which the compounding occurs. Well, the first – the amount initially invested – is intuitively obvious. If the Lenape had asked Peter Minuit to cough up an extra $24 for Manhattan back in 1626 then they'd have ended up with $2.8 trillion today instead of a piddly $1.4 trillion. Double the money at the start equals double the amount at the end.

But the interest rate behind the compounding, like the time involved, can potentially have an even bigger impact on the final result. And this is where investors chasing high returns really need to sit up and take notice. So, it's now time to plagiarise another example from my first book. What would you prefer: to receive $1 million today or 1 cent today which will then be doubled every day for 30 days? The counter-intuitive but correct answer is the latter, since 1 cent doubled every day compounds to over $10 million by the thirtieth day. Even starting with 1 cent and doubling it at the end of each month yields $687 million after three years.

The reason the amounts are so large in this example has less to do with time than does the Lenape example. Three years is a pretty short time for any investor and 30 days is just a blink. The turbo-boost here comes from the high rate of return – or, referring back to our compounding formula, the high rate of interest (r).

But the fact is that no one can double their money every month, let alone every day. Doubling represents a 100 percent return! The only reason I used these extreme examples is because you're more likely to remember that the power of compounding depends upon three things:

1. plugging in as big a chunk of money as you can afford and continuing to add as much as you can over time

2. getting the best rate of interest or investment return that you can achieve (keeping in mind that you don't want to be lending it to Dodgy Dave in order to get that return)
3. starting to invest early (that is, when you're young) in order to let the compounding machine run for as long as you possibly can.

Let's be clear, a long period of compounding is the engine that sees real investors reach their final destination.

So, now that the lesson on how compounding works is over, let's get cracking and plug some realistic numbers into our formula. Because that's the bit that you are likely to find really exciting.

I'm going to give you some homework here. Since it's all about you and your financial future I reckon that you'll enjoy it. I want you to visit the compound interest calculator at moneysmart.gov.au/budgeting/compound-interest-calculator. Plug the appropriate figures into the following fields to reflect:

1. how much money you are starting your compounding journey with (initial deposit)
2. how much you can realistically save each month (regular addition to the initial amount)
3. the compounding rate that you expect to receive
4. the number of years that you expect to invest for.

A lovely graph and a final dollar figure will appear.

Let me plug in some figures for a hypothetical you. I'm going to use superannuation as the investment vehicle. Let's say:

- you already have $50,000 in your superannuation fund
- your employer is obliged to contribute to your fund, and you can realistically top up the contributions with a similar dollar amount ($850 per month in total after contributions tax)
- your fund is heavily weighted towards share investments so you expect to receive an annual return of 7.5% after tax (compounding rate)
- you are presently 30 years old and plan to retire when you hit 65.

Let's feed that all in... and out pops $2.2 million. That's a lot of moolah.

And, given that we have used a post-inflation compounding rate of 7.5 percent, the $2.2 million final figure is a fair reflection of what your future spending power will be in today's dollars. The final figure in nominal (or non-inflation-adjusted) terms will likely be a lot more.

Old Albert was bang on about compounding!

Chapter 24

Great Investors Don't Need to Be Champions

'To invest successfully over a lifetime does not require a stratospheric IQ, unusual business insights, or inside information.'
– Warren Buffett

Let me pose a question. If you were the parent of a ten-year-old, then would you enter them into the Wimbledon tennis tournament or the US Open golf championship? Or, for that matter, any type of sports championship or event where only the world's elite athletes typically compete?

Sounds like a crazy question, doesn't it? What if I now told you that your ten-year-old has a fair chance of beating most of the other competitors in the tennis or golf tournament?

Let's now dial up the craziness a few more notches. What if I told you that the result could be delivered with just ten minutes of instruction before your child prodigy stepped onto the tennis court or golf course?

Yes, it's all totally ridiculous. But in the world of investing, posing such questions isn't ridiculous at all. Not one word of it. That's because any ten-year-old could, with ten minutes of instruction, outperform most professional fund managers both reliably and consistently.

Remember back in chapter 9 when I talked about SPIVA (S&P Indices Versus Active [managers])? The SPIVA results demonstrate that, over a five-year period, around 80 percent of active funds underperform their respective broad-based stock index. Results are similar worldwide. So, if there was a way of simply investing in the index, then you could instruct your child to outperform most professional fund managers.

The good news is that there is a way to do exactly that! There are no-brainer index funds out there that are easy to invest in. These funds will allocate your money to exactly the same companies, and in the same proportions, as the index itself. By replicating the index, these funds make no attempt to outperform the index, only to match it. And that means index returns are delivered by these funds.

Well, almost. You see, even the index funds charge a fee for managing your money. But it's typically a fraction of what the active managers charge. And it's these low fees that provide index funds with their biggest edge over the active managers.

The thing is that you don't have to train like Warren Buffett, Jim Simons or any of the other world's elite investors in order to win. It's possible to outperform most professional fund managers simply by investing in broad-based index funds that charge ultra-low fees.

Remember what Warren Buffett advised his trustee to do with his family money after he's gone? It was to invest it in a very low-cost S&P index fund. Buffett's mentor, Benjamin Graham, held the same belief. In a speech delivered to a group of pension executives two years before he died, Graham said:

> 'More and more institutions are likely to realize that they cannot expect better than market-average results from their equity portfolios… this should move some of the institutions toward accepting the S&P 500 results as the norm for expectable performance.'

Don't get Graham wrong. He's not saying that it's impossible to outperform the market benchmark indices. He's simply acknowledging that for most it isn't possible. Which means that investing in the stock market through a low-fee index fund is a supremely rational alternative to active investment.

Exchange traded funds (ETFs) have made this process even easier. ETFs are bought and sold in the same way that the shares of individual companies are. With a single purchase through your stockbroker, you are investing in the entire index.

And that winning move took less than ten minutes to explain!

Chapter 25

Passive Management

'Buy index funds. It might not seem like much action, but it's the smartest thing to do.'
– Charles Schwab

I want to talk more regarding the benefits of index funds. Maybe you are yet to be convinced.

Despite the stock market being around for centuries and the first stock index having been created way back in 1884, it's only more recently that people have cottoned onto the idea of index investing. Things started to stir after the January 1960 edition of the *Financial Analysts Journal* included an article by Edward Renshaw and Paul Feldstein titled 'The Case for an Unmanaged Investment Company'. Their paper proposed:

> 'A case can be made for creating a new investment institution, what we have chosen to call an "unmanaged investment company" – in other words a company dedicated to the task of following a representative average.'

The article posed a perplexing question: why has the unmanaged investment company not come into being?

The widespread development of the passive fund management industry is commonly linked to one man: John Bogle. While Bogle was neither the first to come up with the idea of an index fund nor the first to create one, he did more to promote and develop the concept than anyone else.

In April 1951, Bogle, then a 21-year-old Princeton University student, submitted a hard-researched thesis for assessment. It was titled 'The Economic Role of the Investment Company'. One sentence, which appears early in his thesis, describes well what underpinned Bogle's lifelong obsession with the benefits of index investing: 'Funds can make no claim to superiority over the market averages'.

In 1975 Bogle founded The Vanguard Group. The next year he opened the Vanguard 500 Index Fund. It was the first passive investment fund open to retail investors (mum-and-dad investors).

The indexing story was now starting to gain some momentum. Also in 1975 Charles Ellis, managing partner of Greenwich Associates, wrote an article that appeared in the July/August edition of the *Financial Analysts Journal*. Titled 'The Loser's Game', it was another early nail hammered into the active managers' coffin. Ellis proposed that active managers were wasting their time attempting to outperform the broader index. This wasn't an entirely original idea. But, to have it printed in a journal with a readership base comprising almost exclusively active fund managers, it was quite a controversial statement.

Ellis was suggesting that the returns achieved by active managers were largely due to the outcome of random events. Outperformers were lucky. Underperformers were unlucky. His actual words in the article were, 'The investment management business is built upon a simple and basic belief: professional managers can beat the market. That premise appears to be false'.

It was lucky for Ellis that financial analysts are a pretty law-abiding bunch. No hitman was contracted and he is still with us at the time of writing, 47 years after he wrote the article.

And it wasn't just Charles Ellis and John Bogle who were rocking the boat. There was a tidal wave of academic research coming out in the

1960s and 1970s that backed up their claims. Academic heavyweights Eugene Fama and Paul Samuelson were among those who added their voices; their research findings found that most stock pickers engaged in little more than a spin of a roulette wheel.

John Bogle's legacy

Bogle died in 2019 but he has left a lasting legacy. Unlike many fund managers, who are in the game for self-enrichment, Bogle did more to benefit the investing public than anyone else in the history of funds management.

Bogle established Vanguard as a mutual. That means its investors are its owners. With no profit-hungry owners skimming off the top, Vanguard has been able to keep its management fees ultra-low.

Tracking an index also means less is spent paying the armies of large salaried investment analysts that active managers typically employ. Lower fees means more money in investors' pockets.

Not surprisingly, Vanguard has since grown to become the largest provider of mutual funds in the world and, at the time of writing, has over $7.5 trillion in assets under management.

My initial reaction to index funds

Now, I must admit, when I first heard about index funds my reaction was similar to when I first heard about bottled water. I mean, you can get water simply by placing a glass under a tap, so why pay for the stuff?

Equally, I questioned why people would accept index (read average) returns when outperformance was in the offing.

I now realise that my reaction was due to ignorance. Yep, I didn't have all the facts on board. As psychologist Daniel Kahneman likes to say, I was suffering from a classic case of WYSIATI: what you see is all there is.

So, learn from my ignorance. Accept the research, not the self-interested counterclaims from the active fund managers.

Buffett's bet

Now let me tell you a story that carries a pretty powerful punch. It's how the world's greatest stock picker beat a hand-picked bunch of active managers by using – yes, you guessed it – an index fund!

In January 2008 Warren Buffett did something that he ordinarily wouldn't contemplate. He placed a bet.

Now I'm not talking about a bet on the gee-gees, the doggies or the pokies; nor was it anything as trivial as buying a couple of scratchies. Buffett bet that no investment pro could select a group of at least five hedge funds (high-fee active funds) that would beat the 10-year performance of a passive index fund (Vanguard 500 Index Fund).

Buffett bet the lot on the index fund coming out on top. And he threw out the challenge to anyone that was prepared to take him on. The combined stake money of $1 million ($500,000 each from Buffett and his opponent) would be invested for the ten-year duration.

When Buffett threw out the challenge, he suggested that there should be no shortage of pros to take him on. After all, they had their reputations to defend. And, as Buffett stated, 'These fund managers urged others to bet billions on their abilities. Why should they fear putting a little of their own money on the line?'

Well, they did fear putting their own money on the line. The active managers were silent. Clearly silence was the safest way to keep their reputations intact!

And then… one manager took the bait. Ted Seides – a co-manager of Protégé Partners – was the only manager to take up the challenge.

Seides selected five 'funds-of-funds' to mount his challenge. And those five funds-of-funds in turn invested in over 100 other professional fund managers. (Under the terms of the bet the names of the funds-of-funds have never been disclosed.) It was a David and Goliath battle with an army of pinstripe-suited egos pitted against a simple passive index fund.

But Buffett was quietly confident. He knew the odds were tilted in his favour. That's because Buffett's chosen fund charged ultra-low fees. His profit-centric opponents charged significantly higher fees.

So, what was the final ten-year result? Not only did Buffett win the bet but the result was an absolute shellacking. So resounding was Buffett's victory that Protégé threw in the towel before the ten-year finishing post was even reached.

In the end Buffett doubled his money. Protégé's strategy delivered a 24 percent return over the entire period. That's a puny 2.2 percent annualised average return. (The answer is not derived by dividing 24 percent by ten years. Rather, it is correctly calculated on a compounded or geometric basis.)

Dissecting the result even further, not one of the five hedge funds that Protégé selected managed to outperform the index fund that Buffett had put his faith in.

Once the ten years were up, Buffett handed over the sizable winner's cheque to a local Omaha charity.

One bet that Buffett did lose

Warren Buffett doesn't always win bets.

In 2001 Buffett was caddying for Tiger Woods at a charity golf game in Florida. On the 18th hole Woods threw out a challenge to Buffett. Woods claimed that he could beat Buffett in a one-hole challenge despite him playing the entire hole on his knees.

Buffett agreed, borrowed a club and then used it to play a mediocre shot off the tee. Woods fell to his knees and drove his ball 250 yards down the fairway. Buffett's second shot went into the water. Wood's second shot, again played on his knees, landed on the putting green.

On the plane trip home, Buffett's mate, Charlie Munger, asked Buffett how he had gone against Tiger Woods.

Buffett responded, 'On the 18th, I brought him to his knees'.

In the face of evidence, why do fund managers keep managing?

I have a favourite saying. In fact, I've been using it for years to help explain things when the reason isn't initially obvious. A number of years ago I shared it with a friend who says it's helped him understand many things since. When it's unclear why people are behaving in a certain way, it helps to identify where the money is flowing. Often things then become supremely obvious. I refer to it as the 'Big M Principle'.

So, let's apply it to the question that I've posed in the heading of this section: in the face of the evidence, why do fund managers keep managing? Well, it's because they're making lots of money by ignoring the evidence.

Active fund managers are quick to declare that the evidence in favour of passive investing is wrong. I cannot help but think of French philosopher René Descartes who stated four centuries ago, 'A man is incapable of comprehending any argument that interferes with his revenue'.

Let's now make one last dissection into this very cold cadaver. Consider a starry-eyed and freshly minted finance graduate who lands a job in funds management. Being smart, he or she might even be aware of the research showing that the chance of their fund outperforming is extremely slim. What might be going through their mind?

Just two things: blind optimism and the size of their first pay cheque.

Chapter 26

Low Fees

'Great rewards grow from small differences in cost.'
John Bogle

I have a mate who I regularly chat with about finance-type stuff. He's worked in the industry, which means that we can intersperse our chats with lashings of finance jargon. We know that each gets what the other is talking about.

I remember a phone call that I received from him several years ago. He was very excited about an article that he'd just read in *The Wall Street Journal*. It was all about a fund manager called Steve Edmundson. Edmundson works as the investment chief for the US-based Public Employees' Retirement System of Nevada. At the time of the article the fund had $35 billion under management.

Now, you'd reckon that Steve would need plenty of hands on deck to help him manage that much cha-ching. Case in point: an Aussie industry fund I know about has a similar quantum of funds under management and employs in excess of 250 bodies. It's worth noting that the industry funds constantly tell us how they work to keep costs low for the benefit of all their members, and a low head count should equate with low costs in any organisation. So, using that reckoning, 250 employees might be a bare minimum that Steve Edmundson requires in order to manage his US fund.

Or maybe not. According to the article, Steve has no co-workers on the investment side. He rarely takes meetings. And he often eats leftovers at his desk for lunch.

Let me repeat that: Steve has no co-workers. His is an investment team of one! And that means there is no one to engage with in time-wasting meetings, no economic and investment analysts to supervise, no unnecessary business trips (junkets) to go on and no internally generated, meaningless reports to plough through.

Steve doesn't even have a stock price terminal on his desk. And he doesn't waste his time watching CNBC either. In fact, he ignores the economic news altogether, perceiving it as little more than worthless noise. Yet the performance of his fund has been outstanding. Case in point: his one-, three-, five- and ten-year returns have whipped the largest public pension fund in the USA, the California Public Employees' Retirement System.

So, why doesn't Steve see an army of employees as necessary? It has much to do with his investment strategy. Basically, it's a strategy of doing as little as possible, which usually means… doing nothing at all.

The truth of this was put to the test when my Aussie friend contacted Steve in order to tee up an interview and asked when he might be available via a phone call or on Zoom.

Steve emailed straight back, 'Happy to chat. My diary is free this week and next'.

Now all of this inactivity begs the question, why is Steve's performance so good compared to other fund managers – that is, the ones who employ hundreds of analysts, economists and paper pushers? It's because it costs so little to run his fund. Low costs translate to low fees for its members. And lower fees lead to bigger investment returns, all else being equal.

Steve rides solo in the office because he knows that the vast majority of financial analysts are simply spinning their wheels in their attempts to outperform the market. He knows that they would be equally effective if they were split into two groups and then allocated one of two jobs: the first half could dig holes and the other half could fill them in again.

Steve has studied all the academic research and discovered that the best way to deliver attractive returns to his members is to:

- not even attempt to outperform the market
- keep management costs ultra, ultra low.

It's a deeply ingrained mindset for Steve. He even trims costs in his personal life. At the time of the article, he was driving an 11-year-old Honda with over 175,000 miles on the clock. And the reason he eats leftovers at his desk rather than buying his lunch is that he sees it as a personal annual saving of thousands of dollars.

OK, enough with the cost-cutting. What does Steve actually invest in? He invests it all in low-cost funds that mimic stock indices. And, as far as fiddling with the cooking, he might make one change to the portfolio in a year.

And, as I keep telling you, you can do the same thing yourself by investing in low-cost index funds or ETFs that are based on a broad market index.

Management costs matter

I now want to hang some numbers on the impact of management fees.

Let's say that you start saving money via superannuation at 25. Let's also assume that you contribute $27,500 per year (pre-tax) right up to retirement (at 65). I appreciate that the allowable contribution amount will lift over the years but let's keep the example simple. Assuming a pre-fee return of 7.5 percent after inflation (the typical historical long-term return for the stock market), let's now do our comparison regarding how much you could potentially have when you retire.

If you invested in a low-fee fund (say, a 0.1 percent annual management fee) then, based on these assumptions, you'll end up with $5.18 million when you hit 65 years old (inflation adjusted in today's money).

Now consider how much you would end up with if you had instead invested with a fund that delivered the same pre-fee investment performance but charged a 1.5 percent management fee (and plenty of funds charge more than this). You would expect to have $3.62 million when you hit 65.

Note that there is only one difference between the two scenarios, and that's the fees charged by the two funds. Yet, by investing in the high-fee fund, you have foregone a massive $1.56 million that you otherwise would have had. It's theft by stealth. I say stealth because you never saw the money flows, which meant you were never aware that it was happening to you.

I just want to finish up with a fact that I read recently in a respected Australian investment report: out of the 5494 Australian funds researched with a ten-year track record, 81 percent underperform the industry standard benchmarks by an average of 2.21 percent with average fees of 1.79 percent.

This is a great demonstration of what you get when you deduct big fees from average performance: substandard performance.

Let me repeat myself here. Investors have no reliable method for selecting capable or skilled fund managers at the start of their investment journey. But they do have discretion about keeping management fees low. This is their most powerful weapon in achieving acceptable returns.

Let's now summarise what we have found regarding active versus passive management:

- Active management (undertaken by professional fund managers) aims to deliver above-market investment returns.
- Passive management aims simply to track market returns (less a modest fee).
- Considered as a group, active fund managers have failed to outperform market returns.
- The returns delivered by active managers vary on a case-by-case basis, but there is no method for determining which active managers will outperform before the fact.

- League tables displaying past investment performance are worthless indicators of future performance.
- The rational investment choice, should you wish to have your investments professionally managed, is not one of active versus passive management, but rather to select low management fees over high management fees.
- SPIVA research has shown that your chances of receiving acceptable returns are increased by investing in ultra-low-cost, index-tracking funds, and your chances of receiving unacceptable returns are increased by investing in high-cost, actively managed funds.

Chapter 27

Investing Is about Farms, not Casinos

'Their [the "princes of business"] interest lies not in the sale of the stock but in the revenues secured through the dividends.'

– Joseph de la Vega

Over 20 years ago I was asked by a couple to help them set up their own portfolio of stocks. They had reached retirement age and wanted their investment portfolio to deliver them a source of ongoing income during their golden years. It was sound thinking. After much discussion, they settled on a portfolio of quality, high-yielding listed real estate investment trusts (REITs). REITs are managed trust structures that contain a portfolio of commercial properties.

An investment in quality REITs means you are a part owner in properties that will deliver you a reliable, long-term rental stream. What's more, the properties are professionally managed, which means you'll have nothing to do except sit back and watch the rent money periodically hit your bank account.

My assistance of this couple came with a strong provision: because these REITs were listed on the stock exchange, I knew that their prices were subject to similar price volatility (ups and downs) that other entities listed on the stock market were. Forget the fact that these are investments in property; if stock prices got the jitters, so too would the market prices of their REITs. I advised the couple that it was important to ignore all the short-term price fluctuations and to instead focus on the quality of the properties, the tenants and the regular and reliable distributions that would be delivered. I implored them to remember that it was the rental stream, not the shifting share prices, that would service their future income needs. I even extracted a promise from them that they would refrain from regularly checking the fluctuating market prices of their investments.

So, what happened? After they bought them, they regularly checked the REIT prices, sometimes several times a day. I started receiving phone calls about how the prices of their REITs were tracking.

Then the GFC hit. The prices of all stocks were body slammed. REITs weren't immune. The phone calls became more regular. Eventually the decision was made (not by me) to convert the entire REIT portfolio back into cash. The proceeds were then held in a bank account.

Needless to say, the prices of their REITs recovered strongly after they had sold them. What's more, the interest paid on their bank deposit was significantly less than the distributions that the REITs were paying.

This is a sad story of misperception. And maybe much of the fault lay with me; it was wrong of me to assume that a simple request that they ignore price volatility would have been enough to quell their concerns.

Maybe, given similar circumstances, you would be equally nervous and react the same way. But I hope not.

I'll now explain how I learnt to ignore stock price volatility.

Shares deliver an income stream

I view my share portfolio as a permanent pool of capital. I add to it now and again, but I rarely sell. I view that pool of capital as a source of income – a source that I don't have to work for (referred to as 'passive investment income').

I look past the stock codes and fluctuating share prices to instead imagine all the people working at the companies that I own. I visualise them commuting to and from work, putting in a solid day digging, driving, selling, typing, restocking or designing. Then I imagine them clocking off and going home to their families.

I am their boss. And they are working for me. That's what shares represent to me. When I started to think this way, I began to care more about the long-term productive performance of my companies and less about their fluctuating share prices.

Let me make the point as strongly as I possibly can: think about income distribution, not share price fluctuation, and you'll sleep easier at night.

Now, all this talk has made me think of something else, so allow me a brief diversion. I pay a hefty wallop of tax each year. I don't resent it. I live in a great country. But I do occasionally joke to my family that I pay enough tax to support a good number of other families as well – those who are receiving pensions and social welfare. Then I quip that not one of those families bothered to send me a card last Christmas.

Well, I don't want to commit the same crime when the shoe is on the other foot. So, if you work for an Australian listed company, then I want to thank you right now. No, I mean it. Thanks for all your hard work that contributes to my welfare and that of my family.

Investing should never be a trip to the casino

This morning (at the time of writing) I read an annoying comment in the newspaper. It was written in a column that was masquerading as investment advice. Here it is: 'The ever-relevant adage of investing is not to put in anything you couldn't afford to lose'.

I could attack the comment from so many angles but I want to focus on just one. This newspaper advice is better applied to gambling and not to investing. Too often investing is confused with gambling. And it shouldn't be. The implication embodied in the advice is that investors are setting themselves up to potentially lose all their money. If your investing protocol is so loose that this could happen, then I'd suggest that you aren't investing at all.

Investing should never be likened to a visit to the casino. Rather, it should be viewed as a process of building a financial farm (portfolio) that will ultimately deliver you a bountiful financial harvest.

And don't take that as an original idea of mine. Here are some words written in 1688 by Dutch stock investor Joseph de la Vega:

> 'Every year the financial lords and the big capitalists enjoy the dividends from the shares that they have inherited or have bought with money of their own. They do not care about movements in the price of the stock. Since their interest lies not in the sale of the stock but in the revenues secured through the dividends.'

Joseph de la Vega's financial lords are treating their portfolios as farmers treat their farms. And farmers rarely sell their farms or buy new ones. Nor do they base a decision on whether to buy a farm, or sell one that they already own, on next week's weather outlook.

Can you imagine Farmer McDonald turning his eyes to the sky and thinking, *Hmmm, it looks like it won't rain this week, so I'd better sell up quick before the market for farms takes a hit*. Nor would Farmer McDonald check the grain or livestock prices several times a day. Yet this is what people do with respect to the stock market. They are swayed by the changing economic news and the fluctuating prices of their stocks.

Farms, property, companies – they're all long-term assets that deliver income. So, they need to all be viewed the same way.

Building my financial farm

I have built my own financial farm over a long working career. Over a 35-year period I consistently spent less than I earned and diverted what was left over each month into investments. Over time those investments grew into a sizable portfolio, and as the portfolio grew it generated an ever-increasing amount of passive income (dividends and rent). I used that income to make further investments. The combined sources of income meant that my financial farm was growing ever faster as the years progressed.

Let's draw an analogy here with Farmer McDonald again. While I was working, I was buying my financial farm, acre by acre. Eventually, I had a big farm covering many acres. And, now that I've stopped working, my farm is big enough to support all my and my family's needs. Every year my financial farm delivers a harvest (in the form of dividends) that I can spend. And all that I will ever spend going forward is each year's harvest. The farm will remain intact. However, the reality is, because I managed to build such a large farm, I'm still saving. So, despite no longer working, I'm in the fortunate position that my farm is still growing!

What about stock market crashes?

Farmers have to deal with drought, bushfire, floods and insect plagues. Years can swing from bumper harvests to lean pickings. What's more, the prices that farmers sell their produce for varies from year to year.

Even so, the farm endures. And so should your stock portfolio.

I acknowledge that, if a portfolio never reaches the size that enables a person to live on the dividends alone, then a portion of the portfolio will need to be sold each year in order to put food on the table. I also acknowledge that a bad time to sell shares is in the wake of a stock market crash. But this is exactly the reason people in this position should maintain at least one year's living expenses in the form of cash at all times.

People overplay the significance of stock market crashes. In the wake of a crash, dividends never take as big a hit as share prices do.

Bottom line is, when it comes to your stock portfolio, I want you to think like Rip Van Winkle and spend your time sleeping – not checking stock prices.

How big does the farm need to be?

There's an important question that few people ask: what is it that I am trying to achieve as an investor? Your stated goal might be to make lots of money. But, trust me here, investing is not solely about making lots of money. Investing can facilitate other forms of success.

So, I urge you to view success in broader terms than purely financial ones. I like to describe investing as much in emotional terms as I do numerical ones.

German polymath Albert Schweitzer was one of many who got to the bottom of things when he said that success is not the key to happiness; rather happiness is the key to success. Extending this thinking to investing means that investment success should not be defined as the accumulation of an unlimited amount of money. Rather, it should be viewed as the accumulation of *enough* money. Your financial farm should be big *enough*.

Enough to do what? Enough to do the things that actually matter. Enough to give you time to spend with friends and family. Enough for you to be free of the bonds of financial stress. Enough for you to stop being a slave to activities that you'd rather not be doing.

I have always felt that straight thinking around money needs to first and foremost be deeply rooted in philosophical, emotional and social issues. They are important. Very, very important.

Appropriate to this discussion are the words of Scottish economist and philosopher Adam Smith, who asks in *The Theory of Moral Sentiments* almost three centuries ago, 'To what purpose is all the toil and bustle of this world? What is the end of avarice and ambition, of the pursuit of wealth, of power, and pre-eminence?'

A succinct answer, and certainly one that applies to the investment process, was proposed by investment advisor Linhart Stearns, who suggested, 'The end of investment ought to be serenity'.

Serenity? Yes, I get it. Serenity. Peace. Happiness. Contentment.

What about value?

Before we leave Part III, I need to admit something: I have deliberately ignored a subject that I could have legitimately included. In fact, it's a subject that most serious investors would say is *the* most obvious topic to include in a discussion about masts (and tying yourself to such).

It's the subject of value – or, more precisely, intrinsic value.

Intrinsic value is considered by many experienced investors to represent an important foundation or anchor against which shifting market prices can be judged. I say that because an ability to confidently nail an intrinsic value on a stock (as opposed to the market price) allows skilled investors to ignore all the market noise, price gyrations and ill-considered commentary so prevalent on the stock market. To the skilled investor, intrinsic value is their rock in an otherwise chaotic world.

Yet I've left it out of Part III entirely! Why?

For all the reasons that I delivered back in chapter 8 ('The Siren Song of Stock Picking').

You see, the supreme skill and effort involved in deriving a meaningful intrinsic value is way beyond the pay grade of most investors. I left it out because I wanted to provide you with masts that you could practicably apply. And calculating intrinsic values is, for most, not one of them.

Now, let's move on to the most important part of the book.

PART IV

THE ULYSSES CONTRACT

Chapter 28

Investing Is about a Ulysses Contract

'Investing is an operation that distributes assets to people who have a strategy and can execute it from those who either don't or can't.'
– William Bernstein

I have saved the best for last. This is not only the final chapter but also the most important chapter. In fact, it's the main reason that I wrote this book. At its heart, this chapter describes a financial epiphany that, for me, was four decades in the making.

Call me a slow learner but I only recently worked out how this investing game works. I have come to realise that, for anybody who chooses for it to be, successful investing can be a supremely simple process.

I don't feel embarrassed that it took me so long to come to this conclusion – first, because many things don't become obvious until you work them out for yourself; and second, because I'm in esteemed company in taking so long to realise it. The late, great investor Benjamin Graham stated before he died:

'In my nearly fifty years of experience in Wall Street I've found that I know less and less about what the stock market is going to do but I know more and more about what investors ought to do; and that is a pretty vital change in attitude.'

Peter Di Teresa of Morningstar Research Services stated, 'It usually takes a long time for investors to become sophisticated enough to realise how simple investing can be'. So, is there some special secret that underlies this simplicity?

John Bogle, the powerhouse investor and founder of fund management group Vanguard, answered this question succinctly when he wrote, 'The secret of investing is, finally, that there is no secret'.

There's nothing cryptic about all this advice. The plain fact is that, the sooner you stop searching for pots of gold at the end of fictitious rainbows, the better.

Most people assume that to become successful at investing requires a special skill. But that assumption is misguided. You see, despite all the noise, the jargon, the supposed difficulty, the worthless commentary and the unfounded prognostications delivered by phoney experts, investing should be, and can be, amazingly simple. You just need to apply, and then stick to, a few basic principles.

The first thing to understand is that the *most important* inputs to becoming a successful investor aren't intellectual ones. They are ones of personal character. They are the personal traits of discipline, consistency and patience.

Tattoo those onto your brain. Discipline. Consistency. Patience.

Let's face it, most of us stumble at the starting line with respect to at least one of these traits. The good news is that there needn't be a problem if that describes you. With the right plan you can overcome each of these human frailties. That plan is one built on an unrelenting commitment to a soundly executed financial Ulysses contract – to let it do all the heavy lifting.

Setting one up is easy to do in today's digital world where finances can run on autopilot. The saving. The investing. The compounding. It requires minimal intervention. It's as if an army of invisible workers is building your financial farm for you. The more that you can put your investment plan on autopilot, the easier it will be to ignore the corrosive, irrelevant and seductive temptations that the financial markets will be throwing at you.

The plan itself can be exquisitely simple. You will be well served by following the advice delivered by Charlie Munger, the vice-president of US company Berkshire Hathaway:

> 'All kinds of people ask me for some foolproof system for achieving financial security or saving for their retirement... Spend less than you make; always be saving something. Put it into a tax-deferred account. Over time it will begin to amount to something. THIS IS SUCH A NO-BRAINER.'

Let's summarise Munger's simple plan:

1. Spend less than you make.
2. Always be saving something.
3. Put it into a tax-deferred account.

Point three acknowledges that your investments will compound at a greater rate when placed in the lowest tax environment possible. For the typical working Australian this is superannuation.

For you, and nearly everyone else, this plan is as good as it gets. I know it isn't sexy, but investing was never meant to be sexy. You just need to commit and then stay the course. The destination will be reached. And trust me, for most people, that destination is one of the few things about investing that can legitimately be considered as sexy.

To me, ironically, the seduction for most people ultimately lies in the avoidance of seduction.

So, what does the destination look like?

Now all this talk about saving and investing is all well and good, but you need to have a plan. As American baseballer Yogi Berra famously said, 'You've got to be very careful if you don't know where you are going, because you might not get there'.

The bottom line is that investing only makes sense if you know why you are doing it in the first place, what your destination looks like and how you are going to get there.

So, for the purpose of this discussion, let's assume that you are doing it in order to establish some form of future financial security. How much do you need to accumulate in order to deliver that financial security? And within what time frame does it need to be accumulated?

Let's firstly address how much is required. The Association of Superannuation Funds of Australia (ASFA) regularly delivers updated figures regarding this. As of June 2022 ASFA considered that a retired couple who own their own home (mortgage free) requires an annual income of $66,725 in order to live a comfortable lifestyle. Super Consumers Australia have come up with a higher figure; they feel that around $73,000 per year is required.

Your own target might be different. Maybe you require a much larger amount. Maybe you want to holiday for six weeks in Europe every year and buy a new car every three. Or maybe you can get by quite comfortably on less than the ASFA figure. You don't like travelling, you keep chooks and you grow all your own veggies in the back garden. If that's the case then the age pension might be just fine.

Case in point, let me tell you about my grandfather, Ralph. Ralph died when I was in my early 20s. Even so, he taught me some great things about life. He didn't lecture me, but rather I learnt by observing how he conducted his own life.

Ralph appeared to be a very happy person. What intrigued me the most was the source of his happiness. It was all about human relationships. People loved him. He lit up a room when he walked into it.

He never really owned much. He never owned a house or a car. He got around on public transport. He and my grandmother lived in the same rented flat for all of their married life. He wasn't interested in buying the shiny trinkets that most people seem to crave.

Clearly, his financial needs were two tenths of close to nothing. Ralph never built a financial farm. But nor did he need one. Clearly Ralph didn't suffer. His life is well described by the words of Henry

David Thoreau that I delivered back in chapter 1: 'That man is richest whose pleasures are the cheapest'.

On face value some people might consider Ralph to have been poor. But, knowing him, I consider him to have been rich. And that goes to show the diverse range of financial requirements within our society.

So, how much income do you think that you need? Only you can answer that question. Once answered, it defines the size of the farm that you need to build in order to deliver it. The larger the harvest that you demand each year, the larger the farm that you will require in order to deliver it.

A mandated Ulysses contract

Through the introduction of compulsory employer-funded superannuation the Australian government has helped set up and kick off millions of financial Ulysses contracts for millions of working Australians. Superannuation is a saving and investment plan that operates on autopilot as far as workers are concerned.

But it's far from a panacea. There are plenty of potential cracks in the superannuation system for people to fall through. For example:

- Superannuation isn't mandated for those who are self-employed.
- Low-income or part-time workers are less likely to end up with a sufficiently large sum.
- Significant periods of time out of the workforce mean that, for many people, employer-funded payments are small.
- During times of financial hardship, the government bends the rules and lets people dip their hands into the superannuation cookie jar. By taking money out before retirement age is reached, the final balance can be significantly reduced.

So, it's important that every Australian takes an active interest in how their superannuation is set up and how it is performing.

Read the statements of performance that your superannuation fund sends you. Read the fund's product disclosure statement (PDS). It will outline both how your money is being invested and the fees that you are being charged. And, if you can't make sense of things, then don't be afraid to ask someone who can explain it all to you.

By selecting a fund that charges low fees and delivers strong long-term returns (through a heavy weighting towards shares) you will typically be delivered the best long-term result.

How big does your financial farm need to be?

There are five questions that you need to answer in order to get things started:

1. How many working years are there between now and the time when you want your portfolio to start supporting you?
2. How many non-working years might you reasonably expect there to be beyond that time?
3. How much annual income will you need when you stop working?
4. How much can you comfortably save each year while you are still working?
5. Do you want to live solely on the annual harvest from your financial farm when you retire? Or, are you prepared to progressively sell off the farm during your period of retirement in order to fund your financial needs?

Obviously, it's difficult to provide precise answers to all these questions. But, if you don't attempt to come up with answers, then you won't be able to generate a plan.

To help things along let's run through an example for a hypothetical worker called John.

1. How many working years are there between now and the time when you want your portfolio to start supporting you?

John is 35 years old and expects to work for another 30 years. So, he has 30 years ahead of him to build his farm.

2. How many non-working years might you reasonably expect there to be beyond that time?

Clearly, John doesn't know the precise answer to question two. But he is an optimist, so he reckons another 35 years beyond his retirement age would be great. That is, he's hoping to hit the ton.

3. How much annual income will you need when you stop working?

To John, $80,000 per year sounds like a nice round number. After all, he wants to go on a decent holiday each year for as long as his health holds out.

4. How much can you comfortably save each year while you are still working?

John's personal bank account is currently empty and his superannuation balance is close to zero. (The government let him withdraw $20,000 during COVID-19, which he used to buy a car.) He has saved pretty much nothing. But he knows that his new employer is paying into a super fund on his behalf. And, at a rate of 12 percent of his annual salary, that now equates to $10,800 per year. (John just landed a job earning $90,000 per year.) After paying the 15 percent contributions tax it means he's actually saving $9180 per year. But is that enough? He plugs the figures into the compound interest calculator at moneysmart.gov.au/budgeting/compound-interest-calculator, using a compounding rate of 7 percent (after tax), and comes up with a final figure of just over $867,000.

John knows that an $867,000 farm won't be big enough. So, he has to be more proactive. He now works out a budget. He looks at all his expenditures in a typical year and calculates how much of his present income he could save by making a few cuts in his spending. He figures that he could comfortably save $10,000 from his pre-tax income. John now tells his boss to add the $10,000 that he's foregoing to his super contributions (called 'salary sacrificing').

In essence, John has committed further to a financial Ulysses contract. The first part was already in place in the form of his government-mandated superannuation plan, but he has beefed it up by a further $10,000 per year. And, with the extra money being automatically removed by his employer (meaning John can't get his hands on it), the temptation of spending it is removed. John has truly committed to a binding Ulysses contract!

John is now contributing $20,800 per year ($17,680 after contributions tax) to his superannuation. To get an idea where the renewed Ulysses contract will take him, he plugs $17,680 into moneysmart.gov.au/budgeting/compound-interest-calculator and out comes the answer: $1.67 million.

John takes a deep breath and checks the numbers. Yep, he's going to be a millionaire. But will that be enough money to support him in 30 years' time?

The answer is yes. In fact, it is virtually certain that the final figure will be much higher than that. That's because the 7 percent compounding figure that he's used is a typical *post-inflation* compounding rate; so, it allows for rising prices. In other words, using a post-inflation compounding rate means that the $1.67 million final figure is indicative of future spending power expressed in today's dollars.

5. Do you want to live solely on the annual harvest from your financial farm when you retire?

Will John's $1.67 million farm provide a sufficient harvest each year to deliver the $80,000 annual income that he's looking for?

Let's assume that John's portfolio is heavily weighted towards dividend-paying shares. While dividend yields vary from year to year, they are typically in the order of 4 percent after tax and a little under 6 percent for tax-exempt individuals. The good news is that, failing a change in tax policy, when John reaches 65 years old and he kicks his superannuation into pension phase then his investment income will be tax-exempt.

John plans to hold a moderately higher proportion of cash when he retires than he does now. That will lower the overall return of his portfolio a bit. So, he uses a more conservative 5.5 percent annual return in order to calculate what his income might be during the future pension phase. John now estimates his annual income during retirement as follows:

$1.67 million × 0.055 = $91,850

John pops the champagne. If he sticks to the plan, then he won't run out of money even if he hits the age of 110. And there will be plenty left over for presents for the grandkids!

But what if John fails to commit to salary sacrificing during his working years? What if he instead relies solely on his employer to contribute to his superannuation fund? Again, using his compounding calculator John comes up with a final figure of $867,000. So, he calculates his estimated annual retirement income as follows:

$867,000 × 0.055 = $47,685

Clearly, that's a lot less than the $80,000 John was hoping for. He has two options in order to achieve the $80,000 target: either he must try harder to fulfill the plan of salary-sacrificing $10,000 per year or, after he retires, he must sell off some of the farm each year to meet the income shortfall.

So, let's take a look at that second option. Assume now that John has retired at age 65 with $867,000 from employer-funded super contributions. John plugs $867,000 into an account-based pension calculator (drawing out $80,000 per year). Oh no! His pension fund is drained dry in 15 years. And, while that's a long way in the future, he can already feel the pangs of financial hardship. John must either stick to option one (salary sacrifice) or plan to live a more austere retirement.

OK, example over. I'll let you play around with your own numbers.

Now, it's important for me to tell you about what I haven't included in the preceding example, and that is Centrelink payments. At the time of writing, the government will supplement low income streams emanating from low superannuation balances. It does that through the age pension. And, while that might always prove to be the case, if John is anything like I was when I was 35 years old then he fears how government policy might change in the decades ahead. He feels safer relying on his own resources.

The role of financial planners

I need to talk about financial planners. They are the people trained to assist in developing personalised investment plans. I ask that you seek their input to develop a plan if you don't feel confident enough to develop one yourself.

But, a word of warning here: some financial planners charge high fees. The fee might come solely in the form of a fee for service (like you would pay a doctor or lawyer), but you could potentially also be charged a fee based on the amount of funds that you have under management (sometimes as high as 1 percent of funds being managed). So, I recommend that you request a full and complete run-down on all the fees that you could be charged before you commit to the service.

Also ask about the management fees charged by the funds that the planner is recommending you invest in. The planner's fee and the funds management fee represent two separate costs that you need to add together in order to work out the total fees that you would be charged to have your portfolio managed.

Remember, if total fees are in the order of 1.5 percent and your fund is only delivering a return of 5 percent pre-fees, then you are paying away 30 percent of your potential earnings (because 1.5 divided by 5 equals 0.3)! That's massive.

The plan that I followed

Let me now share with you my own investment journey.

I can picture the evening when it all began. It was about three decades ago. I was sitting in my study plugging figures into an Excel spreadsheet that I had open on my computer. Sounds a bit maths geeky, doesn't it? While it certainly doesn't sound like a typical fun night in, the spreadsheet was certainly holding my attention.

I had recently finished reading Jeremy Siegel's new book *Stocks for the Long Run*. It had delivered answers to some essential questions that I'd long been seeking. It had informed me that the US stock market had delivered investors a long-term average annual compounded return of 10 percent (7 percent after allowing for inflation). You can conservatively work with similar long-term returns for the Australian market. Using this post-inflation average return was important because it gave me the missing input for the compounding formula on my spreadsheet. I could now get an idea of where my financial future was heading.

Nothing was certain but I could now calculate a potential 10-, 20-, 30- and 40-year future value of my stock portfolio.

I had always spent less than I earned, so I calculated how much I could save each month and dedicate towards long-term share investments. My plan involved paying the maximum amount possible into superannuation. The balance of my savings would be invested back into my investment company.

In went the figures to the spreadsheet… and out came the answer.

Nope. That couldn't be right. Something was wrong. There was one zero too many there.

So, I checked all my numbers again. And I got the same answer.

My holy Ulysses. Old Albert was right – compounding really is the eighth wonder of the world.

Now, I won't share my figures with you; they're a bit personal. But what I need to stress is that it was discipline, more so than Buffett-style investing acumen, that allowed me to reach my destination. Remember that: it's discipline that will deliver the investing result that you're looking for. There is absolutely no need to get fancy when investing.

Where am I now?

It's now three decades on from that night. I have spent the entire 30 years adhering to my Ulysses contract. It wasn't difficult. In fact, it was quite easy. And I made no financial sacrifices along the way.

Every month I saved a set amount. Every month I invested it in stocks. I ignored all the ups and downs of the stock market over that 30-year period. I didn't waver from my plan.

And the final result was that I beat my anticipated target – that is, the figure my Excel spreadsheet spat out on that night in my study almost 30 years earlier was significantly smaller than it ended up being.

So, what now? How do I manage the farm now that I'm 65 years old? It's all pretty much on autopilot.

Slightly more than half my family's non-residential wealth is tied up in managed investments, most of which are low-cost, broad-based ETFs. I know how much effort is involved in picking individual stocks so my career commitment to stock picking has now expired.

Just under 20 percent remains in singularly listed quality companies that I bought years ago. They are gems that have delivered me way more in dividends than I paid for them in the first place. I'll likely pass them on to my kids.

A further 20 percent of my family's non-residential wealth is tied up in physical real estate in the form of tenanted commercial offices. My daughter manages these now. And, while they have been a great investment, if I had my time again I wouldn't have bought them. Instead, I would have limited my real estate investments to REITs.

And 10 percent remains in cash. After all, I want to be prepared the next time the stock market takes a sizable stumble.

And life in general? Well, I'm doing stuff I really enjoy… like writing this book!

Let me finish off with a ten-point summary that I hope distils the message this book aims to deliver:

1. Define where you are now, where you want to get to and how much you regularly need to save and invest in order to get there.
2. Establish a system of regular automatic cash transfers that will add new savings to an established and growing investment pool.
3. Unless you are a stock picking genius, invest in low-cost, broad-based index funds (provided your investment horizon is long).

4. Ignore investment tips from family and friends. Your neighbour, brother-in-law or best friend has no idea what's going on.
5. Shut down the internal voices of fear and greed.
6. Ignore all economic and financial predictions.
7. Don't attempt to market-time.
8. Don't be tempted by the latest investment craze.
9. Don't trade.
10. Be patient.

And, finally, sign that Ulysses contract with indelible ink.

OK, now you're ready. I wish you a safe and successful investment voyage!

Appendix 1

Index Funds

There are many index funds based on Aussie stocks. The most popular ones track two of our broad-based stock indices – namely, the S&P/ASX 200 and the S&P/ASX 300. The ASX 200 index covers roughly the 200 largest companies on the Aussie stock market (as measured by market capitalisation). The ASX 300 covers roughly the 300 largest.

When index funds were first made available investors handed their money over directly to an index fund provider, who then issued the investor units in their fund. You can still invest this way but there is now a simpler and cheaper option in the form of ETFs.

ETFs are bought and sold on the share market in exactly the same way that you would trade any individual listed company (such as BHP or Woolworths).

Which index fund to invest in?

There are thousands of ETFs available worldwide with a couple of hundred different ETFs traded on our own Australian Securities Exchange (ASX). Not all ETFs are based on the index investing principle, but the most popular ETFs mimic the broad stock indices.

In deciding which of these ETFs to buy, you need to think about their size and the fees that they charge. Larger funds are more likely to remain in business, which means that your money will continue to be invested with them (rather than returned to you if a fund ceases to operate). Larger funds are also more likely to charge lower management fees.

For a complete list of ETFs by category, take a look at the ASX website: asx.com.au/products/etf/managed-funds-etp-product-list.htm.

Appendix 2

Listed Investment Companies

To help understand what listed investment companies (LICs) are, let's break down the term 'listed investment company' into its two component parts.

First off, 'listed' simply means that they are quoted and traded on the stock market. So, they are shares, just like the shares of all the other 2700-odd listed companies that are traded on the Aussie stock market.

Secondly, they are called 'investment companies' because they are corporate vehicles created to make investments on behalf of their shareholders.

So, what do LICs invest in? They invest in other companies that trade on the share market (such Woolworths, Telstra and BHP, for example).

LICs are effectively managed funds. The term 'managed' means that those who run the fund aim to outperform the market benchmark (such as the All Ordinaries index or the ASX/200 index). So, they attempt to deliver better returns than index funds (which deliver index returns).

I say 'attempt' because outperformance isn't always the case. For example, the biggest, oldest and best known LIC – Australian Foundation Investment Company (AFIC) – has only marginally outperformed the All Ordinaries index over the past three and ten years and has actually marginally underperformed it over the past one and five years.

Whether choosing an ETF or LIC, management fees are a key consideration. You want them to be low. All else being equal, low fees deliver better investment outcomes. That's because less money in the manager's pocket means more money in yours. Low fees are particularly important when considering long investment periods due to the magnifying power of compounded returns.

Strong demand for an LIC can see their shares trade for a higher price than the value of the assets that they hold in their portfolio. This often results in a price premium (described as a 'premium to net tangible assets' or 'premium to NTA').

Low demand can see LICs trade at a discount to the value of the assets that they hold. This is referred to as a 'discount to NTA.' Such times provide an opportunity for investors to buy cheaply. You could say that buying shares in an LIC that is trading at a 5 percent discount to NTA is like purchasing a dollar for 95 cents.

So, how do you determine whether an LIC is trading at a premium or at a discount to its NTA? LICs regularly calculate and publish this information. It can be accessed through their website or by checking their ASX announcements. The discount or premium is reported on both a pre-tax and a post-tax basis. The pre-tax NTA is the more relevant figure because the post-tax figure assumes that the fund's shareholdings are all liquidated and converted to cash (which is extremely unlikely to occur).

Accessing further information about LICs

As a rule, it's best to limit your search to the big LICs. They tend to have lower management fees and they are more likely to be around for years to come. (AFIC has been managing funds since 1928.)

Each LIC provides plenty of useful information on their website. So, access these sites and learn how your money would be invested. Also read their respective product disclosure statements (again, obtainable online). And, if you have any questions, seek professional advice.

Appendix 3

Real Estate Investment Trusts

Real estate investment trusts (REITs) are trust structures that pool money from lots of investors and then use it to buy big-ticket real estate. As one of many unit holders, you own a small slice of the entire property portfolio. Units in listed REITs are bought and sold through the stock exchange.

There are around 50 different REITs trading on the Aussie stock market. If you want to view the full list then get onto the ASX website. More specifically, you can google 'ASX REIT list'.

Most REITs deal in commercial property but some offer investments in residential property. Typically, they offer subclasses of real estate. So, there are REITs with large portfolios of offices or shopping centres or industrial estates. Some hold portfolios of pubs or farms. And some diversify across a few or several different classes of real estate.

Advantages of REITs over direct property ownership

Here are six things that I like about REITs:

1. They are easy to buy and sell. It only takes a few minutes at your computer, rather than weeks or months in the case of direct property transactions (and no real estate agents are required). If the stock market is open, then there are plenty of willing buyers and sellers on the other side of the deal.
2. The properties are fully managed. So, no annoying phone calls about that leaking roof or faulty hot water system.

3. Because your investment is spread across a large number of properties, the risk of suffering a bad tenant is minimised (and you won't have to deal with them anyway).
4. Rental income from your investment is paid directly into your bank account.
5. REITs typically own better-quality properties than you could own if you were investing directly.
6. Leases tend to be longer term.

That all sounds great, but you can't escape the fact that you still need to do your homework.

What to look out for

Here are three things to look out for when investing in REITs:

1. Check the quality of the properties that the REIT owns and the tenants that they are leased to. You can source this information from the most recent annual report. Government departments and solid blue-chip companies are ideal tenants.
2. Check out the weighted average lease expiry (WALE). The longer the WALE, the better. (They usually compare favourably to the short-term leases typically associated with direct residential property ownership.)
3. Check that the REIT you're looking at isn't financing its property portfolio with high levels of debt. For financial safety make sure that there is a large buffer between the rent received and the interest being paid.

Because your investment is spread across a large number of properties, the risk of suffering a bad tenant is minimised (and you won't have to deal with them anyway).
4. Rental income from your investment is paid directly into your bank account.
5. REITs typically own better quality properties than you could own if you were investing directly.
6. Leases tend to be longer term.

That all sounds great, but you can't escape the fact that you still need to do your homework.

What to look out for

Here are three things to look out for when investing in REITs:

1. Check the quality of the properties that the REIT owns and the tenants that they are leased to. You can source this information from the most recent annual report. Government departments and solid blue-chip companies are ideal tenants.
2. Check out the weighted average lease expiry (WALE). The longer the WALE, the better. (This usually compares favourably to the short-term leases typically associated with direct residential property investment.)
3. Check that the REIT you're looking at isn't operating its property portfolio with high levels of debt. Our financial advice: make sure that there is a large buffer between the rent received and the interest being paid.

References

Bogle, JC, *Bogle on Mutual Funds: New perspectives for the intelligent investor*, Dell Publishing, New York, 1994.

id., *Enough: True measures of money, business, and life*, John Wiley & Sons, Hoboken (NJ), 2009.

id., 'The economic role of the investment company', Princeton University Senior Theses, 1951.

Buffett, W, 'Chairman's Letter', *Berkshire Hathaway Inc.'s 1997 Annual Report*, 27 February 1998, berkshirehathaway.com/letters/1997.html.

id., 'Chairman's Letter', *Berkshire Hathaway Inc.'s 2000 Annual Report*, 28 February 2001, berkshirehathaway.com/2000ar/2000letter.html.

Clews, H, *Fifty Years in Wall Street*, Irving Publishing Company, New York, 1908.

Cooper, AC, Woo, CY & Dunkelberg, WC, 'Entrepreneurs' perceived chances for success', *Journal of Business Venturing*, vol. 3, no. 2, 1988, pp. 97–108.

Cutler, DM, Poterba, JM & Summers, LH, *What Moves Stock Prices?*, National Bureau of Economic Research, Cambridge, MA, 1988.

Duke, A, *Thinking in Bets: Making smarter decisions when you don't have all the facts*, Portfolio, New York, 2018.

Ellis, CD, 'The loser's game', *Financial Analysts Journal*, vol. 31, no. 4, 1975, pp. 19–26.

Fama, EF & French, KR, 'Luck versus skill in the cross-section of mutual fund returns', *The Journal of Finance*, vol. 65, no. 5, 2010, pp. 1915–1947.

Fridson, MS (ed.), *Extraordinary Popular Delusions and the Madness of Crowds, by Charles Mackay & Confusion de Confusiones, by Joseph de la Vega*, John Wiley & Sons, New York, 1995.

Galbraith, JK, *A Short History of Financial Euphoria*, Penguin Books, New York, 1994.

id., *The Great Crash*, 1929, Houghton Mifflin, Boston, 1955.

Gardner, D, *Future Babble: Why expert predictions fail – and why we believe them anyway*, Scribe Publications, Melbourne, 2011.

Goldberg, LR, 'Man versus model of man: a rationale, plus some evidence, for a method of improving on clinical inferences', *Psychological Bulletin*, vol. 73, no. 6, 1970, pp. 422–432.

Graham, B, *The Intelligent Investor*, 4th edn, Harper & Row, New York, 1973.

Graham, B & Dodd, DL, *Security Analysis*, Whittlesey House, McGraw-Hill Book Co., New York, 1934.

Hall, H, *How Money is Made in Security Investments*, 6th ed., The De Vinne Press, New York, 1916.

Hillstrom, K & Hillstrom, LC, *The Industrial Revolution in America: Automobiles*, ABC-CLIO, 2006.

Hirst, FW, *The Stock Exchange: A short study of investment and speculation*, H. Holt & Co., New York, 1911.

Homer, *The Odyssey*, trans. EV Rieu, Penguin Books, Baltimore, 1970.

Hughes, R, *The Fatal Shore*, Knopf, New York, 1986.

Jordon, S, *The Oracle & Omaha: How Warren Buffett and his hometown shaped each other*, Omaha World-Herald Company, Omaha (NE), 2013.

Kahneman, D, *Thinking, Fast and Slow*, Farrar, Straus & Giroux, New York, 2011.

Kahneman, D & Tversky, A, 'On the psychology of prediction', *Psychological Review*, vol. 80, no. 4, 1973, pp. 237–251.

Kelly, FC, *Why You Win or Lose: The psychology of speculation*, Houghton Mifflin, Boston & New York, 1930.

Kemp, M, *Creating Real Wealth: The four dimensions of wealth creation*, IQ Investing, Melbourne, 2010.

Keynes, JM, *The General Theory of Employment, Interest and Money*, Macmillan, London, 1936.

Marks, H, 'The route to performance', letter, 12 October 1990, oaktreecapital.com/docs/default-source/memos/1990-10-12-the-route-to-performance.pdf.

Meehl, PE, *Clinical Versus Statistical Prediction: A theoretical analysis and a review of the evidence*, University of Minnesota Press, Minneapolis, 1954.

Mischel, W & Ebbesen, EB, 'Attention in delay of gratification', *Journal of Personality and Social Psychology*, vol. 16, no. 2, 1970, pp. 329–337.

Mischel, W, Ebbesen, EB & Raskoff Zeiss, A, 'Cognitive and attentional mechanisms in delay of gratification', *Journal of Personality and Social Psychology*, vol. 21, no. 2, 1972, pp. 204–218.

Moggridge, D (ed.), *The Collected Writings of John Maynard Keynes*, vol. 12, Macmillan, London, 1971.

Plato, *Phaedrus*, trans. A Nehamas & P Woodruff, Hackett, Indianapolis, 1995.

Plato, *Republic*, trans. A Bloom, Basic Books, New York, 1968.

Prelec, D & Loewenstein, G, 'The red and the black: mental accounting of savings and debt', *Marketing Science*, vol. 17, no. 1, 1998, pp. 4–28.

Renshaw, EF & Feldstein, PJ, 'The case for an unmanaged investment company', *Financial Analysts Journal*, vol. 16, no. 1, 1960, pp. 43–46.

Roberts, HV, 'Stock-market "patterns" and financial analysis: methodological suggestions', *The Journal of Finance*, vol. 14, no. 1, 1959, pp. 1–10.

Rozeff, MS & Kinney, W, 'Capital market seasonality: the case of stock returns', *Journal of Financial Economics*, vol. 3, no. 4, 1976, pp. 379–402.

S&P Global, 'SPIVA | S&P Dow Jones Indices', accessed 25 November 2022, spglobal.com/spdji/en/research-insights/spiva/.

Selden, GC, *Psychology of the Stock Market*, Ticker, New York, 1912.

Shiller, RJ, 'Investor behaviour in the October 1987 stock market crash: survey evidence', National Bureau of Economic Research working paper series, no. 2466, 1987, pp. 32–33.

Smith, A (pseud. of G Goodman), *The Money Game*, Random House, 1968.

Smith, A, *The Theory of Moral Sentiments*, printed for A. Millar, and A. Kincaid and J. Bell, Edinburgh, 1968.

Smith, EL, *Common Stocks as Long Term Investments*, Macmillan, New York, 1924.

Smith, MH, *Twenty Years Among the Bulls and Bears of Wall Street*, J. B. Burr & Company, Hartford (CT), 1870.

Taleb, NN, *Fooled by Randomness: The hidden role of chance in life and in the markets*, Random House, New York, 2005.

Tetlock, P, *Expert Political Judgment: How good is it? How can we know?*, Princeton University Press, Princeton (NJ), 2005.

Wilson, JW & Jones, CP, 'An analysis of the S&P 500 Index and Cowles's Extensions: price indexes and stock returns, 1870–1999', *The Journal of Business*, vol. 75, no. 3, 2002, pp. 505–533.

Working, H, 'A random-difference series for use in the analysis of time series', *Journal of the American Statistical Association*, vol. 29, no. 185, 1934, pp. 11–24.

Young, A, *A Six Months Tour Through the North of England: Containing, an account of the present state of agriculture, manufactures and population, in several counties of this kingdom*, W. Strahan, 1770.

Index